WELCOME TO THE REAL WORLD

WELCOME TO THE REAL WORLD

You've Got an Education, Now Get a Life!

Stacy Kravetz

W. W. NORTON & COMPANY

NEW YORK · LONDON

Copyright © 2004 by Stacy Kravetz

For information about permission to reproduce selections from this book, write to Permissions, W. W. Norton & Company, Inc., 500 Fifth Avenue, New York, NY 10110

Manufacturing by the Haddon Craftsmen, Inc.
Book design by Chris Welch
Production manager: Anna Oler

Library of Congress Cataloging-in-Publication Data
Kravetz, Stacy.
Welcome to the real world : you've got an education, now get a life! / Stacy Kravetz.
p. cm.
Includes index.
ISBN 0-393-32480-x
1. Job hunting. 2. Vocational guidance. 3. Finance, Personal. I. Title.
HF5382.K734 1997
650.14—dc20 96-43602
CIP

W. W. Norton & Company, Inc., 500 Fifth Avenue, New York, N.Y. 10110
www.wwnorton.com

W. W. Norton & Company Ltd., Castle House, 75/76 Wells Street, London W1T 3QT

1 2 3 4 5 6 7 8 9 0

CONTENTS

and Your Roommates · Covering Yourself · When You're Ready to
Move Out—Breaking a Lease

ACKNOWLEDGMENTS

My sincere thanks to the following people, who provided feedback, information, time, and energy, all of which were necessary in large amounts to get this book finished on schedule: Geoffrey Baum, Debbie Braun, Glen Cooper, Sheryl Craig Cooper, Seth Epstein, Liz Fogel, Jeff Goldsmith, Amy Johnson, Dana Kravetz, Howard Kreshek, Rich Lester, Paulette Light, Jake Matthews, Ken Ramberg, Nick Rothenberg, Kathy Sims, Jeff Sinaiko, Robert Smith, Meredith Stiehm, Bruce Tulgan, Gary Weisberg, and Scott Yara. I'd also like to thank several people who gave me vital pep talks and offered to stand in line at the first book signing: Amy Clark, Vandy Howell, Matt Richtel, and Matt Tarses.

A special thank you to Gail Brooks, who has been using this book in her curriculum at FIDM for years and who has always welcomed me into her classroom.

Thanks to my agent, Angela Rinaldi, who had faith in this project and encouraged me when I wasn't sure I wanted to write another draft of the proposal. And thank you to Kerry Samovar for putting us in touch. A big thanks as well to Patricia Chui and Nomi Victor, two top-notch editors who took this book from page one through second edition with very little sweat.

A debt of gratitude to my parents, Bryan and Joanne, my biggest fans and the ones who taught me everything I needed to survive up until college and more than a few things I've relied on since. A huge load of love and thanks to Jay Goldberg, voice of reason, my own personal cheering section, and my best friend. And a final thanks to Jesse, just for being you.

WELCOME
TO THE
REAL
WORLD

INTRODUCTION

It's a Big, Big World Out There and Someone's Got to Clip the Hedges

Why do you need a survival guide? Are your chances of survival so slim that you need a book to tell you what to do? Isn't life after college kind of like life in college only without books and with someone giving you a paycheck every month? Sort of.

You wouldn't take a trip to Bhutan or the Andes with just a knapsack on your shoulder and a couple of bills in your wallet. You'd bring a travel guide. A book to help you figure out where to stay and where to hike and how much to spend on a llama. So why should graduating from college be any different? No one should expect you to slap on the gown and mortarboard and be instantly transformed into the graduate with a clue. That's a bit much to ask, don't you think?

I remember saying many times that I couldn't wait to get out of college and get into the real world. I wanted to be paid real money and I wanted the Ikea chairs and the Bose stereo system with surround sound. The only problem was that the job market was tight, the Bose stereo was expensive, and my parents weren't the roommates I had in mind.

I needed a survival guide so I wouldn't make mistakes like declaring two exemptions on my W-2 form and end up owing a wad of taxes. I needed someone who knew better to stop me before I sent out twenty-five unsolicited resumes to advertising agencies and got twenty-five rejection letters back. In order to really survive on my own, there were a few other little things I'd needed to do. And no one had ever explained that not everything has to be done the hard way.

I needed to buy a car without getting taken for the ride of a lifetime. I needed to open a checking account without being charged $8.50 a month for the privilege. I needed to figure out some innovative ways to look for work. And most of all, I needed to get an apartment, a roommate who didn't refer to herself as her cat's "mommy," and something other than Bud Light posters for decor. I needed to get a life.

If you like doing things the hard way, you probably don't need this book. Masochists should read no further. But if you'd rather not reinvent the wheel, if you'd like to learn from those who've been there before you, if you don't want to make a career of finding a career, read on. Doing things the hard way is overrated.

Welcome . . .

So you're in your early twenties, you have a college diploma in your hand, and you've sought inspiration from the classics, watching *The Graduate* for ideas about what to do next. Clearly, "Plastics" isn't going to cut it anymore when it comes to advice. But what is? In four years of undergraduate education, has anyone taken the time to tell you?

When I first visited the megalopolis that passes for my corner bookstore, I browsed the huge section of career books and was immediately stricken with the urge to throw up. Overwhelmed and anxious were the operative words here. More surprising than my physical response, I found that none of the existing books even had what I was looking for, mainly because they didn't seem to know who I was.

To them, I was Jessica Jobsearcher, somewhere between the ages of 22 and 55, and looking for something between adventure travel and a corporate pension. In reality, I was much like the rest of my post-college contemporaries: somewhere between 21 and 25, short on cash, aggravated with the twin bed in my old-bedroom-turned-home-gym in my parents' house, and looking for an interesting job that had nothing to do with my major. Since no guide to such a life existed, I began to think that one should. At least fifty friends I surveyed agreed. The consensus: "I would have bought that book. . . . In fact, I'd still buy that book."

As I said, initially I didn't set out to write a book; I set out to buy one. I figured I'd take the easy way out and hope someone had come along before me to make sense of the post-collegiate world. No dice.

The books I found treated the job search as something that could be done in a vacuum without the worries of paying off credit cards, budgeting, dealing with housing and transportation needs, and coping with life's financial emergencies. A big reason the job search is so grueling is that Real Life responsibilities create financial stress, which definitely factors into how fast we're willing to grab a job, *any job*, just to end the nightmare.

Many books haven't caught up with new trends that are being pioneered by young entrepreneurs and forward-thinking companies. Some books are written by labor economists with in-depth knowledge of job trends or fifty-something authors who don't remember what it's like to be 20 and interior decorating with plastic milk crates. Our generation wants different things from previous ones. The object of this book is to help you deal with the issues and questions that are most challenging and important at this time of life.

What this book won't do is tell you how to deal with office politics or remind you to wear deodorant to your interview. What it *will* tell you is how much money you can make, how hard it is to get certain kinds of jobs, and how soon you'll be able to move into a cool apartment with 300 cable channels and the hope of pay-per-view.

Finally, there's the ever-present need to explain each decision, detour, and reroute to your parents, who wonder why, after four years of school, you don't know exactly what you're doing. Parents may never pipe down about not having a doctor in the family and just let you live their life (I mean yours), but they'll always be happy to brag about how well you're doing once you get a life of your own and start to thrive in the real world.

PART 1

GETTING
A JOB

THE JOB SEARCH

You're Not Supposed to Know Everything Now

Just because someone stuffed a diploma in your hand doesn't mean you have to know the direction of your life like you're holding a magic compass. The next few months or years will be a process of exploration, a chance to look at all the possibilities and find a direction you like.

There are certain realities that are going to affect your career search and you need to know what those are. It makes sense to have a realistic idea of what you'll face out there before you start sending resumes, so you can strategize. You may also find it helpful to know what fields are growing and which ones offer the most opportunities for recent graduates.

The Good News

At this time of life, you have something that older generations don't have: freedom. Right now you have the opportunity to find your direction, the freedom to change jobs, and the chance to try things out until you find something you like. So rather than viewing this time of life as a confusing trip through an adult world you'd prefer not to visit, see it as a time to take risks. Mistakes you make now are easily erased with the passage of time. And it's not like everything you do now is going to be a mistake. But no matter which direction you choose right now, you'll have time to amend it and chart a course somewhere else. Take advantage of the freedom that comes with having responsibility only to yourself.

The prospect of all this freedom can be daunting, especially when you see around you people who seem to have always known exactly what they wanted to do. Meanwhile, you're having the first of what you're certain will be many premature midlife crises before you're finished. But fear not. Freedom is a good thing.

Understanding the Job Market

Today's job market is not, I repeat NOT, the same one faced by our parents when they were our age. So don't listen when they say they had it tougher back in the days when . . . Trust me, this is one case when we're the ones hiking through the snow in mere cotton socks, while they've had the comfort of heated boots and a monorail. This is how things used to be: You'd get out of college and recruiters from the big corporations of America would be waiting to fill their entry-level slots with shining stars who'd work their way up from the bottom. Soon you'd be in middle management, all the while earning a corporate pension and setting your sights on an office with a view. Then, at retirement, there it was: the gold watch, the fully vested pension, and the end of your earning years, right on the money at 65.

That was the American dream. This is the American reality: People change jobs several times in a lifetime, often shifting into a whole new career. More people work as independent contractors, freelancers, self-employed consultants, and small business owners than ever before. Big corporations are smaller, a phenomenon known as downsizing. Their lean and mean approach has thinned out their middle management tier. Layoffs and buyouts have meant that some of these former middle managers are reentering the workforce in lower-level positions, often at reduced salaries. What does that mean for college graduates hoping to snag these lower-level positions? Competition from more experienced workers, making the job market harder to crack. So you, the newly minted graduate, need a new approach to your future career.

What's Happening?

The U.S. Bureau of Labor Statistics predicts that between 2000 and 2010, there will be more than 20.5 million new job openings in the service-producing sector. Professional specialty jobs will lead the pack in job growth and fastest rate of employment. These are jobs that generally require a college degree and pay higher-than-average wages. Some sectors, listed below, are expected to grow faster than average, but don't feel like you have to pick a job in one of these areas. There will be steady growth in many other fields as well.

Jobs Predicted to Grow Faster than Average (35 Percent or More) between Now and 2010*

- *Computer software engineers specializing in applications*
- *Computer support specialists*
- *Computer software engineers specializing in systems software*
- *Network and computer systems administrators*
- *Network systems and data communications analysts*
- *Desktop publishers*
- *Database administrators*
- *Personal and home care aides*
- *Computer systems analysts*
- *Medical assistants*

*Source: U.S. Bureau of Labor Statistics

Put on a Suit of Armor

It gets a little old—all that talk about how this is the worst job market in the history of humankind. How many times do you want to hear that unemployment for college graduates is higher than for the public at large? Is flipping burgers going to be the most viable way to utilize your physics degree and accompanying knowledge of gravitational properties? Hardly.

Here's the good news. It comes from one of the most worn-out truisms that happens actually to be true: when the going gets tough, the tough get going. It's cliché, but it will see you through the bad job markets and the good ones. A tight job market just means you're going to develop a really thick skin. You'll learn how to get by even in the worst of conditions. This will make you fireproof, quit-proof, completely impermeable to strife on the job. You'll never be afraid to leave a bad job situation, try an entrepreneurial idea, or change careers entirely, because you'll have the ingrained knowledge that you can survive anything. Don't underestimate this.

Do you see the baby boomers leaving their jobs, even though they complain endlessly that they hate them? When they entered the working world, life was simpler. Doing well when times are good isn't nearly as impressive as what you're about to do: succeed when there are more challenges. But there's no reason that you can't do exceptionally well, as long as you know what's out there and how to tackle the system. That's what the first half of this book is all about.

Be Prepared to Educate Your Boss

It may sound like a contradiction in terms, since you're not sure what you could possibly teach someone who's already been in your field for years, but the truth is that you're a different kind of worker than the ones bosses have seen in the past.

They might tell you you're overqualified to accept a certain position, but if it makes sense for your career path, explain why. Your boss might expect to watch you like a hawk and proofread every document you write, but explain why you don't need to be micromanaged in order to do the job well. Teach your boss, your parents, and anyone else who takes an interest exactly what this generation is all about. They need to know what to expect from you, so you need to teach them the tenets of your work ethic:

- Learning is more important than impressive titles on a resume, so they should hire you based on what you know and expect you to leave when you've learned all you can.
- Taking risks is the only way to achieve rewards, so you're going to try the untried while you're on the job. Then when you're ready to move on, you will, even if the move seems risky.
- Achieving success is more important to you than living up to the ubiquitous slacker label. You're going to work hard, save money, and probably change jobs on your way to career success. You won't be looking for the gold watch, but you'll have money saved for retirement, nonetheless.
- Networking is the way you'll stay informed, build a cadre of colleagues, and develop your career. You'll be asking questions

---

Keys to Success

1. *Take risks.*
2. *Be flexible.*
3. *Do what you love.*
4. *Be persistent.*
5. *Do your research.*
6. *Use technology to make life easier.*
7. *Never be afraid to leave a job you hate.*
8. *Try anything.*
9. *Always keep your goals in mind.*
10. *Fear not.*

and expressing your enthusiasm about your career plans until your plans become your career. Use the state of flux in the working world to carve out a permanent place for yourself.

Prepare Yourself for the Electronic World

There was a day when only dorky computer geniuses talked about spreadsheets and beta coefficients. That was when typewriters with self-correcting tape were cutting edge. Today, however, computers aren't an option—they're a way of life. Every business uses them and you can greatly enhance your marketability by knowing some computer basics. That may mean knowing enough to talk about spreadsheets in an interview. It may mean knowing a little about desktop publishing or movie scripting or word processing using more than one program.

Technology can either provide the means for finding out about jobs, in the form of Internet-posted resumes and online help-wanted ads, or it can be the job itself, in the form of anything from editing an online magazine to working in a lab at a biotechnology firm. Most careers today require some amount of computer literacy and many jobs are made easier through knowledge of the Internet.

Don't look at job ads that ask for computer experience in anything from HTML to Flash animation and say, "But I'm not qualified." Instead, get qualified. Most programs are not difficult to learn, especially with the wide variety of computer books "for dummies." If you know someone who uses a certain computer program, offer to bring over lunch in exchange for an hour lesson in the basics.

The Parent Thing

One unfortunate reality is that parents may never understand. Even after you explain the logic behind finding your bliss, working hard at something you like, and holding out for a rewarding career—not just one with material benefits—they may still be a bit baffled. Some parents just love to parade the slacker label around like a flag, bemoaning how such productive people (them) could have kids with such little motivation to find jobs. They just don't get it.

It's that generation gap thing again. They don't know from unpaid internships, independent contracting, and "sorry, we're just not hiring." They might as well be the Cleavers.

Maybe they're just jealous. Maybe they wish they'd held out for jobs they liked instead of following a formula that someone pawned off on their generation. Who knows? The point is, there's no point in bridging the generation gap, especially since you're not doing anything wrong if you don't know exactly what you want to do or if you want to do something your parents don't understand.

Give yourself the credit you deserve for taking your time and going after a career you like instead of just pandering to the paycheck. It will serve you well in the long run, so don't be so concerned about the short run. Just pick some things that sound interesting and start working. You'll figure it all out in due time.

2

FIND <u>YOUR</u> THING

The Myth of the Right Major

There's a lot of talk when you're in school about picking the right major. You come home for spring break and Aunt Tillie remarks, "Oh, you're majoring in English? What are you going to do with that?" There's this mistaken impression, among the less informed, that your major needs to have a purpose. This is not so.

Your major was a way to study something specific that would give you a different bed of knowledge from the person next to you. Not a better or worse bed of knowledge, just different. So allow yourself to dispel the rumor that you were supposed to be able to do something with your major. Some majors have a more traditional post-college application, like engineering or computer science, but most liberal arts majors do not translate into a job description. Don't worry about it. It doesn't matter what you majored in. In fact, if you majored in something you liked, you've already said something about what's important to you. You've also set a precedent for yourself. Now your task is to find yourself an equally likable, satisfying job.

This chapter is about figuring out what you've always liked doing, figuring out what you're good at, and deciding on a logical career direction from the information. Again, this is only a direction. It is the difference between pursuing a career in science and one based around literature. Even if your major had nothing to do with a potential career, there are ways to make your college degree have workplace applications. There's a huge difference between getting *a* job and getting *the* job.

When I say *the* job, I mean the job for right now, not the ultimate in workplace salvation. That would be a bit much to ask for your first job out of college, don't you think? When I ask the following question, it's an offer to begin thinking about what you want, not an invitation to begin torturing yourself because you don't already know. So here it is, the question everyone's been asking you lately: What do you want to do?

What Do You Want to Do Right Now?

This doesn't mean "What do you want to do with the rest of your life?"—that question is too inhumane even to contemplate asking. Not that your relatives won't try. Instead, the question is, "What do you want to do right now, for the next year or so?" Nothing? You're not alone.

If you say you want to do nothing, you probably don't mean you literally want to stare at a blank wall, doing nothing. You probably mean there's nothing that jumps out at you at the moment that you desperately want to do. That's okay. You don't have to have some kind of clairvoyant picture of the rest of your life before you get your first job. You can still do something.

Sitting on the couch drinking a Starbucks double no-foam latte isn't going to cut it as a plan, so what is? The main thing to keep in mind is that you can change jobs several times before you hit on one that's a keeper, and you probably will. The idea is to start at square one, gain some skills, and find the job you want after that. And contrary to what most boomers will tell you, you CAN afford to hold out for a job you like.

On the other hand, you may know exactly—or even approximately—what you want to do, but you might not know how to get there. Again, you'll begin a process now of starting at square one, acquiring the skills you need to move ahead, and working toward your career goals.

Don't Get Hung Up on Should Haves

You can always find people to tell you what you should have already done by now to ensure yourself a job. You'll hear that you should have visited your college career center long before you graduated. That's great advice to be getting now if you're done with school. You were supposed to begin buttering up the career counselor after freshman orientation so you'd be able to find a job now? Give me a break. Career counselors are an egalitarian bunch, and if yours takes no interest in you because you weren't the model freshman buddy, there's nothing you can do. But you can still make use of the career center, even if you're an alum.

Then you'll hear that the only way to pull your head above water in today's job market is to have begun interning sometime around your fifth birthday. And here you thought Slip 'n' Slide was a perfectly good way to spend your summer. Relax. There are still internship opportunities in nearly every field under the sun. People will never get tired of having smart, able young thinkers working for them for pennies or less.

The point is, forget about all that useless advice about what you should have done and concentrate on what you should do NOW. Getting on the career path in your twenties is not exactly late. It's right on time.

Don't Let People Assume What You Want to Do

You'll find that more than a few people want to give you their two cents about what you should do with your life. In fact, if you really had two cents for each of these opinions, you'd never have to go out and get a job. But the reality is, you do.

When I was in college, I studied political economies even though I wanted to write. I just figured that when it was time to start writing, I would. Before I knew it, though, I was graduating and people were saying, "So I assume with that kind of major, you'll be working for a think tank, going to law school, or looking into politics." Oh. Was that what I was doing? I realized the danger that loomed ahead of me if I even attempted to force more econ problem sets on my feeble brain.

Don't let anyone sway you by telling you what they always thought you'd be doing. And don't let your choice of major dictate your future either, unless that's what you want. Now is the time to throw out the advice you've gotten from your parents who want you to land on the moon, your boyfriend who wants you to be the senate minority whip, your girlfriend who thinks you should be the reptile handler at the zoo, and anyone else who butts in where they don't belong. It's your life. So pick something you like.

Setting Goals

Your goals should give you something to work toward without making you crazy. Don't make them so lofty and so specific that you're dooming yourself to failure. In other words, don't set goals like "I want to be CEO of IBM by the time I'm 25."

Some people do benefit from setting goals they can never reach because they think they'll always be able to aspire to something new. The problem with this theory is that you're constantly setting yourself up to feel inadequate because your goals are unreachable. The optimal thing is to strike a balance between setting your sights high and making your goals realistic.

Make sure to allow yourself a reasonable time frame in which to accomplish all you want. Throw out the idea that you can, and should, invent the next Apple computer by the time you're 25. This type of thinking can make for some pretty depressing birthdays. You don't need to spend your twenties lamenting all you haven't done. The point is that you have tons of time to do everything you set your sights on, so give yourself the time. Make five- and ten-year plans, not one-year plans.

Always give yourself a backup plan. For example, when I graduated, my ten-year plan was to try to make a living as a writer. I heard someone's voice saying "you should go to law school" echoing through the back of my brain, but I chose to ignore it for the time being. I told myself that if I didn't manage to write for a living by the time my ten years were up, I'd toss in the towel and go to law school. It just seemed easier to weather the early pitfalls of trying to write if I had a backup plan. Around five years into it, I think I'd gotten it into my head that writing would be my career, but there are still days when my backup plan is a comforting thought.

Clueing In

Like I said, you're not alone if you honestly have no idea what you want to do now or ever. But since that doesn't rank high on the list of great things to tell a job interviewer, you need to come up with some ideas. Take to heart the things you learn about yourself when you pose the questions below. Your ultimate career can originate from things you like or interests you want to pursue, things other people say you have aptitude for, or skills and talents you have in particular areas.

You Like to Do This

Think about what you've always enjoyed doing and make a list. This seems like either the most obvious piece of advice or the most unrealistic. It's neither. It's easy to forget that you're allowed to like

your career and that it should be based on something you enjoy.
It's also more than realistic that you can find something you like.
You just need to isolate what it is that you enjoy doing.

You don't have to sit at home in front of the mirror, watching
for the lightbulb over your head. Sometimes it helps if you enlist
the help of a friend because you might hit on something unex-
pectedly if you're having a conversation. Reminisce, have some
wine, talk about the happiest times in your life. Even if you only
hit on one career idea that you'd never considered before, it will
be well worth it.

This doesn't mean you should only talk about the jobs you've
liked doing—it means anything you've ever found fun. Pull out all
the stops. If you spent half your days at camp writing funny letters to your friends, that could actually indicate a career direction
you might pursue. Even if your favorite thing on earth is to watch
reality TV and you don't see how that could possibly correlate to
a career, put it on your list. You'd be surprised.

When you have your dialogue, use some of the following topics to generate career ideas:

1. *Sports*. Include any teams you've played on, sports you enjoy
   watching or following, outdoor activities like camping or fish-
   ing, books or magazines you've read on the subject.
2. *The arts*. Think about performances or exhibits you go to,
   publications you subscribe to, performing you've done yourself. Did your major focus on the arts? Do you practice fine
   arts, even something like working as a photographer for the
   campus paper?
3. *Publications*. What parts of the newspaper do you read? Do
   you start with the Style section or do you go to Business first?
4. *Television*. Are you a news junkie? Do you find yourself thinking about how they make documentaries instead of just
   watching them? Do you watch the commercials with as much
   interest as the programming? Do you find yourself criticizing
   and discussing what you're watching or using the TV to zone
   out and relax?

5. *Financial world*. Does it intimidate you or intrigue you? Do you study industry trends and watch the stock market?

6. *Hobbies*. You probably listed them on your college application and added a few since then. Whether you collect antique china or rebuild motorcycles, list all your extracurriculars.

7. *Leisure time*. Think about what you've always enjoyed doing, whether that's watching movies, writing in your journal, or hang gliding.

8. *Volunteer experiences*. Some of these things you probably did because you needed a few independent study units or you thought they'd look good on your college application. Others, however, you may have done because you liked them but no one would pay you to do them. Remind yourself of the things you'd do even for free.

9. *Travel*. Have you thought about working with foreign governments or in foreign countries? Do you like to read travel books or magazines? Do you speak foreign languages?

10. *Problem solving*. Think about whether you like getting concrete answers and solutions to problems. Do you like figuring things out, solving mysteries, reading spy novels, watching FBI whodunit movies?

You Should Do This

There is probably no shortage of opinion about what you should do with your life. Your parents may have taught you to say "doctor" before they taught you to say "bottle," but this doesn't mean you have to follow such subtle advice. But as long as you're considering different way to distill a career direction, it doesn't hurt to listen to the buzz for ideas.

Start by thinking about what friends and teachers have told you. Many times, what starts as

> "My job in corporate events planning essentially came from the fact that I'd always thrown great parties in college. Who'd have thought the fraternity social chairman would be planning black tie parties for corporate America?"
>
> —Phil, 26

a hobby becomes a career because someone says you should do it for a living and you realize you can.

If you want to get a reading on your personality and what it's best suited for, you can take the classic *Myers-Briggs Type Indicator* test. The career center at your alma mater can administer this test or give you a password so you can download the test from the Internet. This test is designed to tell you what types of careers your personality is suited for, based on questions that reveal whether you're outgoing or shy, sensitive or thick-skinned. It can reveal which careers suit personalities like yours, but it won't necessarily pinpoint something you'll like.

There are other tests, called the *Strong Interest Inventory* and the *Campbell Interest and Skill Survey*. These aren't so much personality tests as ways to catalog your interests and abilities and point them toward a career. You probably don't need such a formal test to figure out what interests you, but it can offer another opinion on what you should do and give you some food for thought.

You're Good at This

Make a list of things you can do, otherwise known as your skills. This can include the most common things that come up when someone asks about your skills, language and computer ability, but these are only the beginnings of a list that really includes everything you can do. Your list should include anything you do well, from making really great grilled cheese sandwiches to teaching golf. These are your specific skills.

You also have general skills, ones you can develop in your career. With each job you have, you'll add to this list. Use the following skill areas to remind yourself of things you can do:

1. *Create.* Not just the ability to draw or paint, but an eye for arranging objects, combining colors, visualizing new ways to present old things. Do you walk into a room and immediately see ways to arrange the furniture better? Do you come up with slogans for products and wonder why no one else has thought of them? Have you played in a band or written short

stories just for fun, but never considered how your talents might translate into a career?

2. *Analyze.* You could be sitting around with friends who are debating an issue in the news and realize you could make a case for either side. Your skill might be seeing all the angles and using them to make a persuasive argument. When you think back on the courses you did well in, were they more like ones where you'd analyze literature, or where you'd calculate statistics problem sets and come up with one answer?

3. *Remember details.* Some people are better at making associations and remembering broad concepts, while others have a better memory for names, dates, and other specifics. Neither is better in and of itself, but one might suit a certain career better than the other.

4. *Deal with people.* Some people have a natural rapport with strangers and can talk to anyone about anything. It's a great skill to have if you choose a career where you deal with people all day long, but there are all kinds of jobs that don't require this type of interaction. Do you like meeting and talking to new people? How do you feel about addressing a large group? Are you more comfortable one-on-one? Do you like to negotiate or argue your point in person or do you prefer to do it on paper?

5. *Handle stressful situations.* Do you work best under deadline pressure or do you accomplish better work when no one's breathing down your neck? All jobs involve some degree of stress, but while some people thrive in a high-pressure environment, it's not for everyone. Can you work with lots of noise? Do you get energy from other people who are meeting their own deadlines? Do you meet every deadline, no matter how much caffeine or how many sleepless nights it takes? Do you let stress get to you or can you leave it behind when you're away from it?

6. *Teach or explain.* You may have seen math tutoring as a way to pay for extras during college, but looking back, maybe you got a lot of satisfaction from teaching. Do you like to figure out

ways to present information? Do you get frustrated when people don't understand what you're trying to explain? Can you think of more than one way to teach or explain things? Are you good at organizing material?

7. *Supervise or manage.* Think about how you are among your friends. Are you the one who often plans the night out or gets everyone together for an event? Do people often come to you for advice or answers? Are you good at delegating responsibility rather than taking everything on yourself? Do you get stressed when everything rests on your head because you're in charge or do you like that sense of control?

8. *Motivate.* Does it take a crane to get you out of bed in the morning to go to class or do your work? Do you put things off until the last minute or can you make yourself do work without torturing yourself? Do you need external deadlines or can you set them yourself? Have you come up with entrepreneurial ideas that you want to try out? Have you done well on long projects where you didn't have daily deadlines, such as writing a thesis or running a semester-long lab experiment?

9. *Communicate.* This includes spoken and written communication. Do you dread writing anything from a business letter to a paper for school or do people come to you for help with their writing? Have you always found it easy to express yourself? Are you good at structuring and formulating ideas? Are you a good self-editor or a good editor of other people's work?

10. *Brainstorm.* Some people are building the better mousetrap, even outside the context of career. Have you started projects on your own as hobbies? Do you constantly come up with new ideas for products you wish existed? Are you good at coming up with ideas in a group brainstorming session?

Settling on a Direction

After answering these questions, you should have a pretty good idea of which ones apply to you. Some will very clearly define the

> *"I was contemplating taking a job in market research, which would have required me to conduct group discussions. I was trying to convince my potential boss that I love leading groups, when in reality I really work better on my own and the thought of speaking in front of a crowd is fairly terrifying to me. Don't lie, especially to yourself, when you're trying to get a job."*
>
> —Michael, 28

kind of work you do best, while others will not fit into a description of your skills. Some may even suggest skills you didn't realize you had.

Once you've isolated the skills you have and the things you like, you need to do a final self-assessment to determine if following certain career paths is suited to the way you like to work. For example, you may have determined that you've always loved photography and that you have a good eye for composition. Now you have to think about what the career path for a photographer is like: Do you mind working freelance? Can you handle a second job while you're building your portfolio if that's what it takes? Do you want to work for yourself and hire out your services or do you want to try for a staff photographer job?

Your next task is to begin your job search with the goal of getting training, skills, and contacts in your first job that will make it easier to get your next one.

Don't Spend Too Long Finding Yourself

Unfortunately, employers don't reward you for soul searching. So while you should definitely do some thinking and get yourself pointed in a career direction that you like, be wary of waiting too long to get a job. Having a job that isn't perfect is far better than having no job at all. Nothing looks worse to an employer than a long span of time during which you didn't work.

Again, it's not so important that you have the ideal job right off the bat as long as you learn something of value to your career. If you don't work at all because nothing really turns you on or seems like the right place to start, you won't learn anything. It's important to hold out for what you want, but sometimes it's okay to accept a substitute—especially when it may be a not-so-glamorous first job that will put you in line for a much better job later on.

3

GOT SKILLS?

The Purpose of Your First Job

Contrary to what some would have you believe, your first job is not the be-all and end-all of your future in the working world. Your first job is really just the second part of your education, kind of like fieldwork. It's a place where you'll get on-the-job training and acquire the skills and information you'll need to get your second job, when the time comes to move ahead. Your college degree has given you academic background and knowledge of specific subjects. Your first job will give you training and skills that will make getting your second job a lot easier.

It may seem strange to be thinking about your second job when you haven't nailed down the first one yet. But here's why you should keep it in mind. When you're fresh out of school, it's hard to convince employers that you've got the requisite three years of experience in their field. It's not that no one will hire you—it's just that they may not hire you to do the exact job you want. So in order to take the sting out of grunt work, it's important to see it as a stepping-stone to someplace better.

Think of your first job as boot camp. It's not necessarily going to be fun and you're probably not going to be paid a heap of cash. But you will learn something valuable that you couldn't learn in school. When you're certain that you're the lowest paid person on the planet, consider what you're learning on the job—consider it worth something that higher paychecks couldn't buy. You'll be getting training that has value in the job marketplace. Any knowledge, information, and specific skills that you get at your job is something you can take with you when you leave or get promoted. That's why internships have value even though many don't pay you anything.

If you think of your first job as your training ground, a place where you'll be getting paid to learn, it will be much easier to stomach it if the job requires long hours for low pay and puts you in intimate contact with a Xerox machine. If the job isn't one you want to have for the rest of your life or if you decide it's not the field you want to work in later, don't worry. Most likely it won't be. Most people change jobs several times. Use your job as a resource and get one that will provide the best possible training and give you the most options afterward.

Jobs Build Relationships

Your first job is an important networking tool for you. People you meet on the job will often provide you with knowledge that will help you find your next job, or they'll know someone else who can help you. It could be your boss's brother or the person who works in the cubicle next to you, but someone will put you

> "I felt kind of lame calling this guy I knew from my first job 'just to touch base.' I thought it was completely obvious I wanted something since we didn't exactly socialize. But he was really receptive and ended up giving me some great job leads. Your contacts are really important."
>
> —David, 26

in touch with the person who will help you get your next job.

These relationships have value, so if you leave a job, even a job you hate, don't leave the relationships behind. Include professors in the informational loop, and make an extra effort to keep in touch with professors you know personally. Even if it's just to touch base every now and then with a professor you liked and knew fairly well, make an effort to let people know what you're doing and to keep up with what's happening in various industries. For example, you might not love your boss, but by keeping in touch with former co-workers you might learn that your boss has left and new management has revamped the company. You could end up with a new job at your old company.

I Didn't Need to Go to College to Answer Phones

True, answering phones ranks low on the list of things you hoped you'd be doing with your college degree. It can be pretty disheartening when your first job consists of clerical tasks, gofer work, or something you could do blindfolded while standing on your head. But that doesn't make these jobs worthless. On the contrary, sometimes these jobs allow you to be just the kind of fly on the wall that gains valuable information. For example, by answering phones for a congressman, you'd be dealing with different types of situations from those if you were answering phones for a network news station. And by being around different office milieus, you can learn quite a bit and position yourself well for your next career step. Working for a lazy boss can be a great skill-builder for you, especially if you end up practically running things and learning everything you can.

It's common to feel like you're not putting your college degree to good use in your first job. But don't think for a minute that it's useless. The demand for workers with strong analytical ability has increased steadily since the 1980s and college-educated workers are the only group whose wages aren't falling. That's something to keep in mind. Think of your first job as an apprenticeship and add it to the education you've already gotten.

Don't plan on staying at your first job forever. Almost no one I know is at the same job they started in right after college. Some still work in the same field where they began, but most have chosen something else entirely within five years of graduating. This mentality makes it a bit easier to take what feels like menial slave work. You could have the worst job in the world and come away with great computer skills. Chances are, you won't have the worst job in the world anyway. It might not be your dream job, but take a deep breath and get the most you can from it. Then use it to move ahead.

This isn't to say you have to hate your first job or that you have to be planning your departure the minute you start. If you get a job at a company you like or in a field you want to pursue, you should stay by all means. Do keep looking for opportunities for advancement within the company or at a different company within the same industry. And don't let anyone convince you that it's common to work as an unpaid intern for five years before expecting any kind of raise. You shouldn't have to pay your dues forever.

Which First Job?

Remember that your boss isn't the only one who's getting something out of your hours of labor. You're learning about your industry, receiving training, and getting paid some menial amount for it. Get the best job you can. That doesn't mean the highest-paying job or the executive-in-training position. It means the best job you can find that will give you general exposure and allow you to beef up your skills. You also want to put yourself in the best position for meeting people who can give you information and help you figure out where to go next. You need to be on the ball in order for your first job to be all of these things for you. That means asking questions, reading everything at work that you can get your hands on, and taking on every responsibility you can.

You don't have to know at this point what you want to do with your life. So don't get paralyzed if you're still not sure what field is for you. You can still get a job now and position yourself to take advantage of many opportunities later. For the fields described below, you can get a sense of what skills you'll acquire. This should help you figure out where to look for your first job and what it will prepare you to do, whether you choose to stay at the same company or in the same field or whether you decide to apply your skills elsewhere. In either case, the skills you get will enable you to move up in the working world.

You should think of the knowledge you acquire at your first job as a *skill set*. A skill set is really just a way of packaging your knowledge and abilities and specific training for a future employer. That way, you can present your skill set to an employer who needs someone with your specific abilities and pave the way to your next job or your next position within a company.

The career groupings that follow are a way to think about the skills you'll acquire and be able to offer your next employer. They're not a way of limiting you to working within one group forever. Many skills you'd acquire as a teacher, for example, would translate well to a job that requires you to speak in front of groups of people and organize material for presentations. The groupings are meant to serve as guidelines to help you develop the skills you want to have later, for the career you want to have.

Professional Services: Finance, Consulting, and Law

Professional services jobs range from working for a commercial bank to crunching numbers at an accounting firm. Whether you choose an entry-level job in a law firm, consulting firm, or other business that offers professional services, you'll end up with a skill set that is based on analytical thinking.

What Will I Do?

If you're at an *accounting* firm, you'll help with audits, going through business records and making sure they add up. You'll help analyze information for the company by reviewing accounts payable and doing audit testing, making sure checks are accounted for and written properly. You may also help analyze accounts receivable, making sure receipts and invoices are real. Your job may also include analysis of overall sales figures and profit and loss margins. In short, you'll be working with numbers, analyzing company data and creating spreadsheets to illustrate your analysis.

At a *commercial bank*, you might be working in the loan department, helping decide what size credit line a company will receive. To do this, you'll review the company's history and performance and make projections based on your findings. This includes building financial models that show how much the bank should lend at a rate of interest that the company's cash flow can support. You might also think about working as a bank teller. This can give you experience working with people, learning how bank accounting transactions work, and understanding basic investments.

Consultants go into companies and analyze them from the carpet on up. There are consultants who tell companies how to downsize, how to produce more at a lower cost, how to cut back on wasteful spending and streamline their finances. You'll analyze data, write reports, meet with clients, and work in teams.

At an *investment bank*, you might be a research analyst, examining how companies perform within certain industries and assessing their potential for growth. You'll analyze company data and make projections about which companies will make good investments. As an analyst, you'll write extensive reports that your colleagues will use to determine whether to invest in specific companies or industries.

In order to work as an *attorney* at a law firm, you will need to go to law school and pass the bar examination for the state in which you want to practice. But even without a law degree, there are jobs at law firms that will expose you to the workings of our justice system and involve you in legal proceedings. As a *paralegal* you will assist attorneys in preparing cases for court by researching past legal opinions, analyzing case law, and helping interview prospective witnesses. As a *law clerk*, you might fill out trademark applications for clients, help prepare an attorney for a trial, or draft and respond to "discovery," which is the information and interviews some attorneys use when they begin working on a case.

What Skills Will I Get?

In any of these jobs, you'll acquire good analytical skills. This includes understanding how to evaluate company trends and identify what's going right or wrong by looking at numbers. You'll then help people make decisions based on your analysis. These fields teach you to be resourceful because you get information from many different sources and you have to cull through it and produce something relevant and usable. These jobs teach you to write analytical papers and hone your writing skills. You'll learn to look at financial information and assess business prospects, analyze trends, and assess the value of companies.

In any of these fields, you'll get exposure to a variety of companies and businesses, so when you're making your next job transition, you'll have a sense of which businesses you like and you will have contacts at specific companies. Jobs in banking and consulting will give you a broad knowledge of how financial services work, while those in law or accounting will give you a similar understanding of these fields. You'll also come away with the ability to be professional and to talk to a variety of people on many different subjects.

You'll gain a good working knowledge of the financial world— how ventures are financed, what influences stock prices, how companies are valued. By paying attention to details and following through on what people ask you to do, you can learn a great deal. This also means asking if you can attend meetings—your goal is to absorb information and understand the big picture and how it fits with the work you're doing. You'll learn spreadsheet programs, Lotus 1-2-3, and Excel.

At a law firm, you'll get experience interviewing clients and doing legal research, as well as helping attorneys write briefs. You'll come away with good writing and researching skills as well as analytical ability. Firms may specialize in areas like environmental law, employment law, litigation, bankruptcy, sports, entertainment, real estate, women's, or other issues.

How Do I Find a Job?

To find the corporate headquarters of firms in any of these or the following fields, look at the Corporate Yellow Book, available in libraries, or get information at www.leadershipdirectories.com. For jobs in banking, consulting, and accounting, it helps to have a basic working knowledge of spreadsheet programs—you can learn the basics quickly, especially if you know someone who can teach you.

Large companies often have set hiring programs, especially investment banks. These kinds of firms have a set entry point and a training process. Smaller companies typically hire on an as-needed basis. You should consider applying for a variety of positions, if the firm where you want to work tells you they're not hiring. You can learn a lot and get your foot in the door by working in the billing department or in an office assistant job. Also consider temping. You can apply directly to law firms in your area to work as a paralegal, legal assistant, or clerk.

Medicine and Science

Whether you're interested in pursuing a career in research or thinking about applying to medical school, you can get your training in a lab. You'll learn to look at data and think analytically.

What Will I Do?

Most jobs in science/pre-med involve lab work, in which you help with directed research, conduct experiments, and compile data based on their results. In a university lab, one professor directs the research on specific projects. You'll most likely get paired up with a graduate student or a postdoctoral researcher, but what you can accomplish has almost no limitations. You'll learn the scientific theory behind the research and execute the experiments to back it up. You'll compile data and present your findings. Working in a lab will give you a chance to practice the scientific method and see how real tests differ from textbook cases.

Lab work can give you flexibility because you can run your experiments to fit your schedule. If you're applying to graduate school or studying for the MCAT, you'll probably have time to do both. Your lab job could include work as a technician or a researcher or both.

What Skills Will I Get?

You'll be in a setting where you can present your research and get involved in scientific discussions where you critique and defend the research that's presented. This gives you critical thinking skills and an understanding of scientific thinking. You'll learn to troubleshoot, because often your research and experiments don't yield neat test cases and you'll have to come up with new approaches. Lab work will also give you basic computer skills and knowledge of data processing and statistics.

You might contribute to a research project that gets published and get credited. With the skills you'll learn in a lab, you can go on to medical school, continue in research, work in the pharmaceutical industry, or move into the business aspects of the field. Working in a lab will give you great contacts—if you apply to medical school or apply for another research job, you'll be in a good position to ask for information and help.

How Do I Apply?

If you want to apply for a job in a university lab, go to the department where you want to work (or several if you're not sure) and ask for a book describing the graduate programs in each field. They'll tell you about each professor, what projects they're working on, and what they've published. If you find a lab that's published a lot, odds are good that there's a lot going on there. Go to the professor who's in charge of the lab and say you want to help out on a project.

You could also work in private industry, such as biotechnology. Apply to those labs directly. You may start as a lab technician, learning to run experiments and collect data. Also consider applying to university hospitals, which also have labs.

You don't need a heavy science background to get these jobs, but you should understand basic chemistry. Since most research projects take many months to complete, don't apply for a lab job if you plan to leave after two months, because you won't get the most from the experience.

Sales

If you start in a sales job, your first task will be convincing people to listen to you. Whether you're selling stocks, pharmaceutical supplies, insurance, or real estate, you'll learn to read people, to understand their needs, and to pitch your ideas or products effectively.

What Will I Do?

Many sales jobs consist of cold-calling potential clients and trying to get them to listen to you. Ultimately, you want to convince them to use your company's services or buy your company's product. You could work in retail, such as selling clothes, you could sell supplies to domestic or international companies, or you could sell stocks or insurance plans to targeted individuals.

If you work as a sales representative for a company, you'll often travel within your sales territory, which can range from a few neighboring cities to a few countries in Latin America. Your job will include convincing buyers to carry your company's product and coming up with ways to display the product to get the best results.

When you work in sales, you're compensated on a commission basis, meaning the more you sell, the more you make. Some companies are entirely commission-based, while others will pay you a small additional salary. Even in retail sales, you typically receive a percentage of your sales as commission, in addition to an hourly wage.

> *"It's a good personality industry. People who were scared at their first fraternity party aren't going to make good salespeople."*
>
> —*Glenn, 28, started in real estate sales*

In general, you have to work hard and hustle business to be rewarded. This can be a great thing if you have the drive to work hard because you have a practically infinite number of potential clients, and your initiative can earn you good money. On the downside, it can be hard to make your commissions at first and you generally have to get your own leads, meaning you have to research potential clients and call them cold. You have to develop a thick skin for being turned down and learn to move quickly to the next potential sale.

Sales jobs can have good perks, from driving a nice company car to taking clients to sporting events or good restaurants. Your ability to talk with people and make them comfortable is more important than anything else.

What Skills Will I Get?

Your sales skills have value far beyond your first job. Even if you leave the sales field, you'll often find yourself pitching ideas to clients, selling an investor on your idea, or cold-calling or networking to bring in clients. The skills you learn in sales can prepare you to do almost anything. Many business people will tell you that you're always selling, even if you're not compensated as a salesperson.

Sales will develop your persistence, something you need in any field. You'll get proficient at problem solving because you'll learn to look quickly for another way to pitch if the sales technique you're using doesn't work. You'll develop a good ability to read people and know what makes them react. This will allow you to refine your techniques and help get your foot through the door in any situation. You'll get comfortable talking with people and making phone calls.

When you cold-call, your goal is to make an appointment so you can go in and convince someone they want your product or services. You learn to create situations in which both sides, your company and your customer, feel like they're profiting. Sales will teach you to negotiate, another important skill for any job you'll have in the future. Cold-calling teaches you how to do research, how to network, and find your next sale.

Sales can be a great networking job. When you create your own leads, you expand your contacts inside and outside your field. You also get the opportunity to show your business skills to a wide variety of people. This becomes the base for your next job opportunity—you could later get hired by a client or simply get good information about job opportunities. Young people in sales are in a position to make contacts in high business positions. This is great for helping you get your next job because it creates a natural fork in the road: You can either transition into another part of the same industry, such as moving out of real estate sales and into real estate development, or you can transition to the sales arm of another industry.

How Do I Find a Job?

Sales jobs are frequently advertised in classified sections of newspapers and magazines, as well as posted on many job boards. Campus recruiters often interview to fill sales positions. You can apply from ads you see or you can call companies you like. If you want to work for a stock broker, maybe with an eye toward pursuing finance later, you can apply directly to brokerages in your city. Ask if they have sales training programs you can apply for.

Look online for company profiles and information about their products and services. You can typically expect to start on a commission basis, which can have all the joys of an unpaid internship, until you start making sales.

Teaching

The patience, leadership skills, and organization you'll learn by teaching can prepare you to continue in a teaching career or work in many diverse fields.

What Will I Do?

When you teach a class, whether it's kindergarten or twelfth-grade science, you are responsible for organizing and presenting new material, preparing and grading tests, giving specialized help to students, and keeping your classroom in order. This can take a good dose of patience, a sense of humor, and some public speaking skills and organizational ability. You may already know you have some of these skills, but you'll become even better at using them. Tutors and teacher's aides typically work part time, so these can be good jobs to have while you're still in school or while you're interning or working at another job. Substitute teachers work on the days they're needed—you call in each morning.

Once you've gotten some experience, you can take your teaching skills in many directions. One option, of course, is to continue to teach. While some private schools will hire teachers without credentials, you typically have to get your teaching credential in order to get a full-time position. If you decide to get your teaching credential, you need to complete a one-year program, consisting of student teaching and academic classes. Many people in this field also go on to get a master's degree in teaching. The main advantage to this is that public schools will bump up the pay scale for teachers with master's degrees.

Another avenue is to tutor or to teach summer programs, both of which say to an employer that you have an ability to explain and present material. Plus, both will help you decide whether you want to continue in the field.

What Skills Will I Get?

Teaching will help you develop skills like speaking in front of groups, presenting material and explaining it different ways so everyone can understand it, and coming up with creative projects. You also learn to think on your feet and improvise if necessary. These skills have value far beyond the classroom. If you move into a business field and need to present material to groups of people, you'll be well versed in the task. You also learn about people and gain knowledge that will help you work in groups or lead projects.

Working as a teacher's aide will give you a sense of which age kids you like for future teaching purposes. It will also give you hands-on experience with kids. You'll acquire organizational and disciplinary

> *"When you have thirty-two kids looking at you everyday, you learn to be pretty creative."*
> —Liz, 28, fifth-grade teacher

skills, as well as ability in specific areas you might help the teacher with, such as conducting art projects, science experiments, writing lesson plans, or teaching certain subjects. Depending on the teaching style of the teacher you work with, you'll come away with different experiences. Some teachers are more hands-on, while others rely more on lecturing.

How Do I Start?

You can get a job as a *teacher's aide* right out of school by applying to the district where you want to teach. You can apply to more than one district. Typically, you'll have to pass a basic test administered by the district and you'll be assigned to a teacher's aide position within the district, depending on availability. Each district operates differently, so find out what the specific requirements are for your local teaching districts. Most hiring takes place in the late summer or early fall, so you should plan on applying by early in the summer. If you want to be a teacher's aid at a private school, apply directly to the school before their hiring season.

If you want to work as a *substitute teacher*, you need to take a standardized test, much like the SAT, that's administered each year—each state has a different test. You can also get an emergency credential after taking that test, which will allow you to substitute teach while you're waiting to get your test results and your certification.

Another good experience is a *volunteer* teaching program like Teach for America (discussed in Chapter 8). You'll get teaching skills and exposure to diverse situations that can prepare you well for jobs in many fields.

If you want to teach at the junior college or university level, you typically need more educational training. Most university professors have a Ph.D. in the subject they teach, and their career consists of teaching as well as continuing to study the subject, doing research, and publishing papers, articles, and books. You can also teach at this level without a Ph.D., if you're teaching a subject that involves expertise acquired on the job—courses like architecture, art and design, music, journalism, or city planning are typically taught by people who have a lot of experience in these fields rather than intense study of the subject.

Government

Working for the government in Washington, D.C., can give you valuable work experience, knowledge about political issues, and contact with tons of people. The political arena thrives on its young interns and assistants and there are many jobs to be found on the Hill.

In general, if you want to work in Washington, D.C., there are two big categories of jobs you can get with the government: You can work for a federal government agency or you can work as an appointee, such as working for a senator or a representative from the House. You can also apply for government jobs in the District Office in the state where you live. Look in your local phone book for numbers of local government offices and ask about their application process.

What Will I Do?

Most likely, your job with an *agency* will be a research assistantship. You might do some computer programming or get research and information from libraries. You'll be helping people in the agency who are writing political or research texts or working on special projects. Your potential for learning will be huge.

When you work for an elected officer, from the president to a member of Congress, your job is contingent on that person staying in office. You'll typically work as an *aide*. These jobs are easier to get than jobs with agencies, but they're lower paying. The advantage is that you'll meet the senator or other elected official that you work for as well as that person's staff. You'll learn about the state that the official represents, you'll get some computer experience, and you'll learn about political issues.

Your job could entail answering phones, answering mail from constituents, or drafting opinions or issue briefs on specific political topics for the member of Congress or other official for whom you work. You could start in the Senate mail room, assist a press secretary, or help constituents who are planning visits to Washington by getting them tickets to White House tours and other government sights.

What Skills Will I Get?

If you work for an agency, you'll get computer experience, research experience, and a knowledge of political issues. You'll also make a lot of contacts and have direct ties to certain industries, depending on the department you work for and the research you do. You'll get in-depth knowledge of your research topics, plus exposure to many other ideas and good job contacts.

Working in Washington will lay some good career groundwork for you, either because the government official you work for will help you directly or because the experience looks good to employers. Working for a senator or member of Congress is a high-profile job. It's a safe environment in which to learn about the world, train in how to discuss a variety of issues, and gain knowledge about political news topics. You can also get letters of recommendation, if you're thinking about going to graduate school.

Government jobs will give you invaluable knowledge about the world around you, and the experience will show employers that you're comfortable working in the thick of the

> "I moved to D.C. without a job and just started talking to everyone who would give me five minutes. Within a week I got hired as a bartender and within two months after that I found a job as a congressional aide."
>
> —Dominick, 26

country's power center. Washington is a fast-paced environment and you'll become street-smart and knowledgeable and make many valuable connections.

How Do I Apply?

For jobs with government agencies (like the U.S. Department of Housing and Urban Development [HUD] or the Treasury), there's a formal process and a regular hiring period. Generally, there's a nonnegotiable salary that goes along with your position. Find out who handles applications at the agency where you want to work and talk to that person directly. Find out what positions the agency has to fill and what its hiring schedule is. Government agencies are big and it's typical to get the runaround. Make sure you've gotten complete information about application deadlines and get your materials to the right person.

If you want to work as an aide, begin your job search by calling your state politicians' offices to ask about opportunities in Washington or in your state. Some legislators will only hire constituents, but you don't have to work for the member of Congress from your state. When you get called for an interview, make sure you know the legislator's committee membership and policy stance on major issues. You should also be aware of current big issues.

You can apply directly to the offices in Washington. Either send your resume to the office where you want to work, or apply at a congressional placement office. For the Senate, go to the Hart Senate Office Building; for the House, go to the Ford House Office Building, also known as the House Annex II. You'll fill out a formal application, supply your resume, and take a typing test. Think about whether you'll feel more comfortable working for a Democrat or Republican, but don't party-hop—partisan sentiments are alive and well on the Hill.

Be persistent. If it means starting as an intern until you meet enough people in Washington that you hear about a job opening, do it. There is high turnover in D.C. and many jobs. By putting yourself in this milieu, you're stacking the odds in your favor.

What Else?

In addition to appointee and agency jobs, there are many others to be found in Washington or in your state. You could apply to work on an *election campaign*, you could apply to join the Peace Corps (information in Chapter 8), or you could work for a *lobbying* organization. If you support the National Association for the Advancement of Colored People, the National Organization for Women, or an environmental group, consider working for a *nonprofit* organization. All of these jobs give you an awareness about the world and how problems get solved, as well as organizational skills and the ability to work with people.

How Do I Get Information?

If you want to keep current about what's happening in Washington, read *Roll Call,* the semiweekly Capitol Hill newspaper, and *The Hill,* a weekly about the U.S. Congress. Also check out job listings on the Opportunities in Public Affairs Web site at www .opajobs.com.

You can get good information online through Yahoo at www .yahoo.com/Government and find links to the Web sites of all areas of federal and state government.

Technology

There is no getting around the growth in jobs of the technological sort. Even if you didn't major in electrical engineering and computer science, you can still make your mark on the high-tech world. Almost every company on the planet uses computers, which means there are jobs that require basic computer savvy, serious skill, or a passable ability to type.

What Will I Do?

If you are a *programmer*, you will write the computer code that makes the computers do what the company needs them to do. In other words, computers are only as useful as the computer code that gives them instruction on what to do when the user gives them commands.

If you have a job in *Web editing and graphics*, you will work with computer programs like Macromedia Flash and will convert text and images into HTML format using a specific computer language that makes a computer display the characters you type as images, words, and links on the Web. You also might choose to get experience in content editing. This is where the old school meets the new. You will learn how to use programs to edit text for Web publications, which have different requirements than paper publications. Web publications must have easy-to-use navigation to get a reader to the right information without having to use the Back button fourteen times.

Or you might choose a job in *computer networking* or *technical support*. These jobs are great for people who like to figure out puzzles. You'll be faced with computer glitches and you'll need to solve them. You'll also be in charge of setting up networks, or complex configurations of computers within an office or across a multinational company, which enables every employee to communicate with every other via computer.

What Skills Will I Get?

Depending on what kind of technology job you choose, you may learn programming languages like SQL and Oracle or you could learn to be a pro at Flash animation. The key to marketing your new skills when you go to look for your next job is to find ways to make your experience shine next to the competition. If you are applying for a job with the admissions department of a university, for example, your resume will stand out if you have done a little Web editing or if you know a few computer programs like Microsoft Excel and Powerpoint. Even if the university isn't currently offering their applications or admissions guidelines online, they may want to do so in the future. And if you have the necessary skills, it will make you a more attractive hire.

How Do I Start?

Start by logging onto www.webmonkey.com, which bills itself as "the web developer's resource." The site offers tutorials on a huge variety of Web skills, everything from authoring to programming to Web design. If you're trying to decide which skills you need, log on to a career site and look at some of the high-tech jobs to see what they expect you to have for prior experience. If a great-sounding job requires that you have familiarity with HTML and Excel, for example, you could use Webmonkey to hone your HTML skills and buy an *Excel for Dummies* book to learn the basics of that program.

Then check job sites like www.dice.com for technology jobs that will make use of the new skills you have.

Communications

This category of jobs covers everything from broadcast news to public relations, anything from book publishing to film. It's typical to begin your career path in an entry-level job or internship, both of which help you get your foot in the door and teach you the basics. After working in a communications field, you'll come away with good writing and/or editing skills, familiarity with deadlines, and knowledge of the specific industry where you work.

You might start as an intern at a network news station and work your way up to show producer. Or you might start as an intern at one magazine and move to an assistant editor position at another one. Good communications skills are applicable to other fields as well.

What Will I Do?

In *media* jobs, such as working at a news station or writing for a magazine, it's common to start as an intern and move into a paid position after you've earned your stripes. These jobs are known for their long hours and low pay. But don't underestimate what you can learn, even if you're not paid at all. You could work as a fact checker, verifying information before it goes into print, or you might compile lists of sources that the writers can call for quotes or information. You might watch the news wires for new stories or edit copy. If you work in broadcasting, your job might entail helping camera people or typing the anchors' scripts into the TelePrompTer. In book publishing, you could be reading book proposals, editing copy, or helping to create the publisher's catalog of upcoming books.

If you start as an intern or in a junior position in *advertising*, you'll work either with account executives, who handle clients and the media that market a company's product, or the creative staff, who come up with concepts and slogans to convince consumers to buy the product. You might be answering phones, helping to develop creative concepts, doing research on the target market and the products they buy, or helping account executives set up video shoots or print campaigns.

In *public relations*, you'll help write press releases and compile media lists of people who will receive them. These lists of broadcasters, newspapers, and magazines, along with specific names at each place, need to be updated. You'll help out with scheduled media events, making sure the press gets access to the right people for their story. You'll also help compile company information that will be attractively presented to the media in a press kit.

What Skills Will I Get?

Jobs in the *media*—from online publishing to radio news—will teach you how to think and work under deadline pressure, as well as come up with innovative ways of presenting information. You'll learn to write concisely and clearly. Even if your job requires you to fact-check someone else's work, you'll use these skills when you write your own stories later. Plus, you'll see how publishing houses, editorial departments, or newsrooms operate and get exposure either to current events or the specific subject matter of the publication—or even cable station—where you work. This will expand what you know, as well as your ability to speak and write about it. Don't underestimate the value of good writing skills—many jobs require them and many people don't have them and consider you a savior if you can write.

This goes for *public relations* and *advertising* as well. You'll learn to write strong, concise copy and to understand how advertisers think and how they strategize to reach the right market for their product. This knowledge is useful if you decide to go into marketing or another field that requires you to analyze the consumer. You'll learn to sell your ideas, an important skill in this and many other fields. Your contacts in the media will grow and you'll develop good phone skills. The media contacts you develop may be important to you in the future, even if you're not in PR but have a business or product of your own that you want to promote.

How Do I Start?

Newspapers sometimes hire cub reporters to work as stringers, meaning you cover local council meetings and events and write up a small story if anything interesting happens. Many newspapers and magazines have internship programs or they hire copy editors or fact checkers on a part-time basis. Apply directly to the editorial department. In print media, you can also start by freelancing, pitching story ideas or finished feature stories or columns to the editor who handles this material. If you get your foot in the door and the editors like your writing, you could be in line when a position opens up.

Broadcasting is also a place where it's common to start as an intern. Read *Media Week* and check the job boards at film and journalism schools in your area, many of which list available internship positions. For jobs in advertising, bone up on *Advertising Age* and *Adweek*. Find out if there's an Ad Club in your area, go to events and network. If you're interested in the creative side, it's a good idea to design mock ads for existing products to show your creative ability at an interview.

What about Other Fields?

Your first job is by no means limited to the above choices. Anything from performing arts to carpentry offers apprenticeships or entry-level positions that will give you a skill set. You could assist a photographer, read and analyze scripts for a film production company, or work on a movie set. You could apprentice with an architect or a city planner. Fields like these will give you more specific skills that you can only acquire by doing the jobs or helping someone else do them.

In any field you can think of, there are people willing to hire you on as an apprentice. Offer your services in exchange for learning everything you can. That will put you in the best possible position for turning your experience into a career you like. Of course, none of this is easy. It's not easy to work as an unpaid intern, for example, and still have the great apartment and the nice car. But you can moonlight or freelance to pay the bills while you're paving the way to the job you really want. Moonlighting can be a good way to balance a low-paying first job with the lifestyle you want to have. See Chapter 9 for moonlighting ideas.

Remember the Purpose of Your First Job

Keep in mind that your first job is a stepping-stone, the beginning of a path to someplace else. Learn all you can and, most importantly, *don't stay at your first job too long.* If you do, you could end up like those disgruntled workers, ten years your senior, who never left their entry-level jobs, who never managed to get a promotion because they kept xeroxing away, hoping someone would complete their job searches for them. Your first job is by no means your final destination, so avoid letting it become one. You'll find success by moving on, moving laterally into a different industry, moving up in the same industry. Again, this doesn't mean you have to ditch your first career choice—just ditch the internship or the entry-level job in favor of one with better pay and more responsibilities. If the field you start in ends up being your dream career, you should stay in it. Just make sure you're moving forward.

4

THERE'S A JOB WITH YOUR NAME ON IT

How to Be a Breadwinner at Age Ten

I once read a magazine article on salary potential that said you should expect to earn twice your age in thousands of dollars of income. According to that glib little piece of financial wisdom, I was a professional failure at age 26 when my annual income barely topped $20,000. I was earning what a 10-year-old was supposed to make.

The main thing wrong with this equation is that it's infinitely more likely that you'll make $80,000 when you're 40 than $40,000 when you're 20. At this stage of life, there's a certain amount of slack that should be cut for all of us. But according to those who come up with such mathematical wizardry, there's no slack to be had.

So on a further journey into self-annihilation, I tend to compare myself to where my parents were at my age: married, with two small babies, two big cars, a house, a dog, and one income to pay for all of this. Sound familiar? Don't be too quick to sign yourself up for the College-Educated Failures club. If nothing else, we need to cut *ourselves* a little slack.

It's a Process

One very important thing to come to terms with now is that your working life is more than a series of destinations. You are not merely at point A now, biding your time until you get to the next letter in your alphabet. Everything you do from this day forward is part of a process. There are no wrong turns. Even if you change jobs ten times before you're 30, none of your time has been wasted. Don't denigrate the time you spent teaching fly-fishing just because now you've decided to be a computer programmer.

You never know when someone you're working with will have an interest in fly-fishing and will hire you over someone who doesn't. Or maybe you'll end up moderating the Web's most popular fly-fishing chat room.

It's important to stop focusing on destinations. You have plenty of time to reach them and there are a lot of things you need to learn along the way. You might want to run a company someday, but what if you were put in charge tomorrow? Would you know what to do? Part of what you're doing now is building up a series of accomplishments and a means to achieving the end you want.

Sometimes it's hard to see the relevance of bringing coffee to the assistant editor at the music magazine where you're slaving as an intern. But it will get you to the next step in your career. Everything you do is part of the process.

How Do You Find the Jobs?

This chapter will look at ways people get hired and create jobs themselves. There are better ways of searching for a job than using the classified advertisements in the newspaper. This chapter will help you circumvent two of the most tedious propositions known to mankind: reading the classified ads with the growing recognition that you need three years' experience working in the job that you need to get to accumulate three years' experience, and sitting through a session with a college career counselor who tries to explain why stuffing hot dogs into boxes is an appropriate marriage of your degree in economics and your interest in animals. There are better ways to look for jobs.

Square One

The purpose of the preceding chapters was to point you in a direction and get you prepared to pick a starting place. You always have to start at square one. That should be a place that gives you some options, rather than being a lockstep plan for the rest of your life. Once you've found that square, you're ready to begin the process of getting that first job.

Begin by doing your homework, something that unfortunately doesn't disappear when you finish school. Your research will help you find good information that can help refine your choice of jobs, as well as mentors who can give you guidance. The reason you need to do all this homework is that the more information you have, the better you'll be at discovering exactly where you want to work. If you know what you want, you're that much closer to getting there.

Read up on fields that interest you. That means picking up copies of industry or trade publications, just like the people who work in those fields do. Start building a bed of knowledge in a specific field. This will help you in interview situations and, more importantly, on the job. Find out what salaries people make, so you won't be shocked later in a job interview. Make a list of companies you'd like to work for and look for articles about them. Find out how long companies have been around and how big they are. If you're interested in starting a business, you might read *Inc.* and *Entrepreneur*. If you want to go into advertising, you'd look at *Adweek* and *Advertising Age*. And so on.

Some Good Responses to Parental Comments Often Uttered during Your Job Search

Comment: You're way too focused on looking for a job that makes you happy. Work is work. It's not supposed to be fun.

Answer: If I get a job I like, I'll have a better chance of succeeding at it because I'll enjoy going to work each day. And what's wrong with being happy?

Comment: When I was your age, I . . .

Answer: The job market is different, the economy is different, and I'm not you.

Comment: I don't think you have the luxury of sitting around waiting to discover what you want to do.

Answer: I'm not sitting around. And when I know what I want to do, I'll be that much closer to being able to do it.

Comment: I spent over (insert amount) on your education, not to mention the cost of feeding, diapering, and clothing you over the years. Now what are you doing with your life?

Answer: I appreciate all you've sacrificed to provide me with Pampers and a college degree. I plan to do the same for my kids and instill them with the same wonderful values you've given me. That way they'll know it's more important to take my time and be happy with the career I choose than to rush into the wrong thing and be miserable. Thank you for teaching me that valuable life lesson.

Comment: Margie's daughter is an attorney at one of the top law firms in the country AND she's getting married.

Answer: Margie must be very happy.

Comment: Why don't you just call Bill Gates and ask for a job? The worst he could do is say no.

Answer: (Hold your tongue and refrain from suggesting your parent seek therapy for delusional behavior.) Thanks, I'll try that. If it doesn't work, though, I may just go back to my own method of job hunting.

Comment: You're going to be part of the first generation to make less money than their parents.

Answer: Don't be so sure.

Call everyone you can think of. Find out what they do each day and what they know about the direction of their industry. Ask whether hiring is cyclical, meaning it's better to send a resume at certain times of the year when the industry is hiring. You don't have to develop mentoring relationships with everyone you talk to, but it's nice to start building a network of people in your field with whom you can share information. You may end up working together some day.

Use the resources available to you. If you have access to databases through your college campus, check them out. Type in company names and see what articles have been written about them. Use the World Wide Web (more on this in Chapter 6) to get information about specific companies by looking at their Web sites or other sites that include information on your target industry.

Don't forget the good old library. Use its databases and directories to find everything from news articles to addresses and phone numbers for companies you like. Look in the reference section for big directories of industry associations and of specific companies. If you decided you want to work for a Fortune 500 company, for example, you should look at the annual issue of *Fortune* magazine that lists the top companies. Here are some resources you might consider:

- *Adams Jobs Almanac*
- *Book of Lists*
- *Hoover's Directory*
- *Databank of Jobs*
- *Encyclopedia of Associations*

Also look at business databases, some of which require you to pay a fee. Here are some to investigate:

- *Dun's Electronic Business Directory*
- *Moody's Corporate News*
- *Standard and Poor's Industry Surveys*
- *The Thomas Registry*

Go to events related to your field. For example, if you find out about a conference for sports reporters and that's the career you're trying to break into, try to attend. Find out about them from the mentors you've talked with or from the industry associations you located in directories at the library. Look for advertisements in trade publications and be aware of online chats with people in your industry. When you go to events, force yourself to go alone instead of recruiting a friend. That way, you won't have a crutch to lean on and you'll be forced to talk to people.

Don't Flood the Market with Resumes

> *"I sent out 50 form letters which I'd customized to insert the employer's name in each one and got 34 customized rejection letters, four marked "return to sender," and I never heard from the rest. I was 0 for 50 and out 15 bucks for stamps."*
>
> *—Julie, 29*

This used to be the tried-and-true method of job seeking. The idea was that if you sent resumes to enough companies, someone would hire you. This is known as playing the odds or betting the numbers. It's far from successful. Employers receive too many resumes to do much more than crank out a form rejection letter to the masses and call an occasional prospective employee for an interview. Emphasis on the word OCCASIONAL. If it makes you feel better to do a mass mailing or if it gets you up out of bed doing something, you might still consider it. But if you really want to increase your odds, consider the strategies that follow.

Look at Job Listings

One great thing about looking at posted job listings is that the jobs actually exist. It's no longer a matter of blindly throwing darts at a bunch of companies hoping one will hit. The employer is actually asking to see your resume and planning on hiring someone. Why shouldn't it be you?

Your alma mater will have a job board that you can usually use if you're a recent alumnus. If it's been a while since you graduated, you might have to pay to get access to the job boards, so you need to decide if that's worth it to you. The advantage to looking at jobs posted on campus is that the employers who placed the ads are looking for graduates of your school. So you've already met one piece of criteria and are that much closer to convincing the employer to hire you.

Make use of job boards you can access online. Chapter 6 lists some of the good career sites, but be on the lookout for more by using the search engines. An advantage to looking online is that it's a good way to find out about opportunities in other cities. If you're interested in jobs all over the country, check out these two national publications that list jobs culled from dozens of newspapers:

- *The National Business Employment Weekly*, published by the *Wall Street Journal*, is available at newsstands. Or check the jobs database at www.CareerJournal.com.
- *National Ad Search* is also a weekly paper, available at selected newsstands or by calling (800)992-2832. You can access the ads online for a nominal fee per ad at www.nationaladsearch.com.

Also look at trade publications for the industry where you'd like to work. Many have classified advertisements and they often list entry-level or assistant jobs. These classifieds by far outshine the regular ads in the newspaper. They're specific to the industry that subscribes to the publication, so they're a more thorough source of jobs in one field. Many companies who place ads in the trades don't place them in the newspaper classifieds. So the only way to find out about them is to think like an industry insider and read what they read. Often, industry publications have "Help Wanted" sections that list jobs. Check the library for these directories, which list industry publications and newsletters:

- *Gale Directory of Publications and Broadcast Media*
- *Hudson's Subscription Newsletter Directory*
- *Newsletter Strategy Session*, which contains newsletter directories at www.nwsltr.com/nwsltrdir.shtml

Network

The idea of networking somehow conjures up the image of slick hipsters passing handshakes at a party without a glimmer of sincerity. In reality, networking is an important part of job searching and you don't need to employ slimeball tactics to be effective. What you're trying to accomplish is making sure everyone you know is aware you're looking for a job. Don't feel uncomfortable about it. You don't have to make it sound like you're desperately seeking job handouts you couldn't get on your own. You're merely asking to be kept in mind—kept in the loop, if you will. If your attitude says "I want to know what's out there" instead of "Get me a job or I'll pester you till the end of your days," you're more likely to succeed.

Every day, professionals talk to each other and find out what's going on in the industry, who needs what, and where there are opportunities. That's why they might know about job opportunities before they ever make it onto job boards or into newspapers. The reality is that many of these jobs open up and get filled before you ever hear about them. That's why you need to network. Let people know you're looking and they can keep you in mind when opportunities arise.

One phone call sometimes isn't enough. Without badgering people to death, touch base from time to time and inquire whether they know about anything interesting. This conveys that you value their opinion and think they know what's up in their industry. You'll remind them of your presence and your desire to find a good job without asking them outright.

There is one special proviso, however, that goes along with networking: You need to know what you're looking for. It's not enough to say you're merely looking for a job. One of two things will result. Either the person you're talking to will have no idea what kind of job to keep you in mind for and will not ultimately help you, or the person will find you a job that will be simply that—a job—and probably not remotely close to a job you'd want.

When you're networking, remember that people are busy. They don't have time to help you figure out what you want to do or what kind of job best suits you. You need to tell them, in fifty words or less, exactly what you want to do and exactly what skills you have. That way, when they hear about a job, they can represent you well to the employer.

Networking also means more than talking with people you know. It means getting on the inside of an industry, joining professional organizations, and going to events. Many jobs result from being in the right place at the right time. Make an effort to put yourself in the right places.

> "I spent two years actively searching for a new job. In the end, it was not one of the countless want ads I responded to, but an old friend who heard about an opening in his firm. Always remember that the key to finding a new job is telling everyone that you are looking."
>
> —Ben, 29

Interview for Information

Informational interviews can have many benefits to your job search. First, they're a way for you to find out, firsthand, what it's like to work in a particular field. Second, they're a way for you to ask questions in an interview situation where there's no job at stake. It's good to practice your interview skills without having to worry about the other six candidates sitting outside the door waiting for you to blurt out the wrong thing and leave the job for them. Third, they may lead to a job.

Informational interviews can be a great way for you to get your foot in the door. You get a chance to show up in person, dressed for success, and you might meet the person who could ultimately hire you. An informational interview is a much better tactic than sending a resume cold. Even if the company isn't hiring and doesn't plan to, your informational interview can make a more lasting impression than pages listing your accomplishments.

Treat an informational interview like one that could lead to a job. That means doing your research ahead of time rather than waiting until the interview. The more prepared you are, the more specific questions you can ask. Your interview will yield a lot more information if you come prepared. Plus, appearing knowledgeable and thorough in your research reflects well on you. Make good impressions everywhere and you never know what will happen.

How to Set Up an Informational Interview

Getting a company to grant you an informational interview can be tricky. Firms don't have time to conduct tons of interviews, so you have to pick your prospects carefully. Sometimes it's better to take a subtle approach. Don't call and demand an informational interview. Call and say you'd like some information about future opportunities with the company in a SPECIFIC area and find out who handles these things. You may get put in touch with a human resources director, but don't assume you're being placed in the circular file. This may be the person who initially screens applicants or who ultimately does the hiring. Either way, you can get valuable information from almost anyone at a company. Ask for a meeting with anyone who will take the time to talk to you.

If you've done thorough research, you might have come across some names of specific people in the company who work in the areas that interest you. Call them up and tell them you're trying to get some information about how to get started in that field. Ask if you can have twenty minutes of their time, at their convenience. Say you want to know how they got started and where they see opportunities for people just starting out. Ask about the career path for someone starting out in the field. Find out what they like and dislike about their jobs. Everyone likes to be asked for their opinion and advice.

Here is where you can combine interviewing with networking and set up informational meetings with contacts, friends of friends, friends of your nearest relative, or anyone else willing to fill your ear.

Once you've talked to someone, they've already invested something in you: their time. Some people want their investment to pay off and might make additional efforts to make sure you know about job openings. Other people are happy to talk to you but make it clear they can do nothing more to help. Consider their time and advice valuable either way. Ask if you can check back with them if you think of more questions. And abide by the cardinal rule of informational interviewing: Always send a thank-you note within the week, preferably later that day when you get home. Keep it professional and brief, thanking your interviewer for his or her time and expressing how valuable the information is to your job search. Don't jeopardize what could be a good career relationship by omitting something so simple as a gesture of thanks.

The smaller the company, the easier it is to get in touch with a real person. Some small companies have tremendous growth potential while others intend to remain small. Ideally, you'll interview with the companies that plan to grow. But for information purposes, anyone who's doing something that interests you is worth contacting. You can never learn too much or be too prepared before you walk in the door for your real interview.

Target Specific Companies

One of the best job-hunting methods sounds too easy to be believed. You don't need to buy crystals and beads and run through creative visualization exercises for this to work. It's just a matter of simple geometry. If you start at point A and you want to get to point Z, you can usually figure out a way to do it, no matter how difficult or time consuming it ends up being. But if you don't know where Z is, it's pretty hard to find it. And the more Zs you can come up with, the better your chances are at making the trip from A to Z.

Of course, you'd like to end up in your dream job right now, without having to go through unpaid internships, wrong turns, and low-paying, work-your-way-up positions. But all those things are part of the process that gets you to your destination.

Make a list of the work skills that best apply to the jobs in that field. The come up with a list of companies you're interested in who really need your skills. Write to them and tell them how you can meet their needs. But don't just write to the human resources person at each firm. Take the approach outlined in the section on informational interviews. Look for specific people within the company who would benefit from having you there.

For example, say you're targeting an investment bank and you may want to be a research analyst for the high-tech sector, specifically telecommunications, because you wrote your college thesis on how changes in technology will impact telecommunications in the future. Find out which investment banks have analysts in telecommunications and find out who is in charge of hiring them. Direct your letter and resume to that person, citing how your knowledge of telecommunications can be an asset. Yes, you should be that specific.

Find out if firms are facing particular challenges. Using the above example, maybe you'd target firms that have no telecommunications analysts but would like to move into that sector. Offer your knowledge where knowledge is needed and you could land an interview. Your odds are infinitely better than sending a resume cold when you're not even sure what the company needs.

Make yourself an asset and fill a need. Employers are looking for a match between their needs and the qualifications of a candidate. So the better you are at pinpointing their needs, the better you can be at making sure your qualifications fit them.

Use Campus Resources

Whether it's a month or a year before graduation, or several months afterward, you should make use of your college career center. Find out if you can access the career center online to look at job boards and find out about upcoming career fairs and seminars.

Visit the career center in person. Set up an appointment with a counselor and present your career objectives. Counselors can administer the personality tests that pinpoint career directions for you. They can help you plot career strategies and some even conduct taped mock interviews so you can evaluate your ability and work on problem areas.

Bear in mind that career counselors are not job placement personnel. Don't go in expecting a career counselor to find you a job. Instead, expect to get information, alumni referrals, access to job boards, and a real human being to give you feedback about your job search.

Make sure you're on the mailing list of both the career center and the alumni association so you can be kept informed about upcoming events, lectures, and career fairs in which recruiters come to campus for interviews.

If you don't live in the same city as the college you attended, find out if there are affiliate programs in your city. You can also find a career counselor in your area by calling the National Board of Certified Counselors at (800)398-5389.

Don't feel like you need to sign up with the first counselor you see, especially since you'll be paying for their services. Ask for referrals and trust your gut. Look for counselors who specialize in areas that pertain to you, such as catering to young college graduates or people in certain industries.

Check Out Alumni Associations, Mentors, and Referrals

The alumni association is a good place to start. Ask if there is a formal mentoring program, in which alums from your school sign up to provide advice and guidance to those following in their footsteps. Some schools have their alumni organized in binders according to profession, while others have more informal ways of keeping

> *"I asked a favorite professor how he got his first journalism job and he harkened back to the time when he was returning home from the [Korean] war and he called up the* New York Times *and asked for a job. The rest was history. I thought about calling the* New York Times *and just asking for a job, but I sensed I might be ridiculed."*
>
> —Sarah, 28

track of alums. Regardless of your school's organizational technique, you can look for a few graduates from your alma mater who are working in fields that interest you. Think of your fellow alumni as sources of information first, jobs second.

Age and experience offer different benefits. If you choose a recent graduate, you have a better chance that your mentor will be able to relate to the trials and tribulations of searching for jobs because it hasn't been so long since he or she was out searching for jobs. There might be a sympathy factor as well, since your mentor knows how tough it is out there. Plus, a recent graduate will be able to tell you about lower-level positions with the company, and the likely experience you'll have your first years on the job. On the other hand, a young mentor might not be in a hiring position or one of influence. So while you can learn a lot, your great relationship with your mentor may never lead to a job.

There are pitfalls to choosing someone too senior as well. Certain bits of counseling might best be taken with a boatload of salt because you may not get advice you can actually put into practice. Times change, so make sure your mentor can give you advice about how to get into your chosen career field today.

Don't forget to attend alumni events. Even if you live in a different city than your alma mater, call and ask about alumni associations in your area. These events are good places to network and they can be fun—there's no reason why your job search can't be fun, at least part of the time.

Intern Your Way into a Job

Intern. Slave. Gofer. Bottom feeder. Low face on the totem pole. Grunt. Lackey. The flattering monikers abound. What was once the domain of students looking for independent study credits is now the stomping ground of college graduates pursuing that coveted but elusive entity—EXPERIENCE.

You need it if you want a job, but how can you get it? Gone are the days when a plucky kid out of a Dickens novel could just up and get a job by displaying only wit, verve, and ingenuity. Today, you must also display experience. Internships can work well in this area, mainly because they're easier to get than entry-level jobs. The reason, of course, is that you don't get paid.

Despite the demise of slave labor, companies can get away with hiring employees and paying them nothing. Welcome to the world of interning, if you haven't visited this spot sometime during college. You can find internships in fields anywhere from journalism to politics, and in some fields it's almost expected that you've completed one or several internships before you've earned your stripes. Some companies do have formal arrangements to hire a certain number of interns per year for pay.

Most internships offer experience in your career field as the main reward for your long hours. This is one career strategy you have to weigh against your need for cold hard cash right now. Granted, you could specifically target the paid internships, but the competition for them is as fierce as that for entry-level jobs.

If you choose the internship route, you don't have to go overboard. There's no need to work 40 hours a week as an intern when 15 or 20 will give you the experience you need. Plus you'll be left with some time to earn enough for food and rent. You also don't need to make a career of interning. Try to set a limit at the outset, say three months, after which you can be considered for a real job. If your employer won't even commit to considering you for a permanent position, this is something you should find out at the outset.

While you're at your internship, try to pave the way to a job for when you're done. Use the new contacts and resources to your advantage. Once you've developed a good rapport with your co-workers, they'll want to see you pulled out of the intern chair and into a real job (as long as it doesn't threaten theirs). For example, if you're interning at a radio station, talk to advertisers, producers, and anyone you can who knows the various facets of the business. Try, however, to be discreet and use some judgment. You shouldn't make a big production out of your job search on the first week of the job when your boss is strolling by.

Temp Your Way to the Top

There was a time when doing temp work was, well, a temporary thing. It's generally perceived as a good way to make some money in between jobs by using your typing and phone-answering skills. But temping can also be a way to get your foot in the door of a company where you want to work. Temporary employment agencies also work as de facto permanent employment agencies, matching job openings with candidates to fill them. You might start in a temporary situation that will become permanent if you and the employer hit it off.

It's a career strategy similar to taking an unpaid internship with the hope you'll become a permanent staff member after a trial period. But unlike internships, temporary positions offer you a paycheck. Even if a temp job doesn't lead to a full-time position, it can add skills to your resume that will help when you apply for the next job.

Temp firms can place you in specific industries that need temporary workers for more than just clerical duties. Accountants, writers, lab technicians, and computer technical specialists can find jobs through temp agencies. Look for temp firms that cater to specific industries, from finance to entertainment.

Whether they find you a job or not, you shouldn't have to pay a temp agency. There are plenty of temporary employment services out there that don't charge you a fee, so stick with those. Temp agencies make their money from the employer, so don't feel like they're working themselves to the bone without being compensated. To find a temp agency that places people in the industry where you want to work, call some companies in that industry and ask which temp firms they use.

Tell Employers What Job You Want

Here's what no one told me: You have to be specific. Give people a reason to hire you or grant you an interview or let you into graduate school. It's not enough to say you're really interested in their firm or you know you'd really enjoy the field of advertising. How many cover letters do you think they get that say, "I have no interest in a position at your firm and the thought of working in advertising makes me sick"? Novel approach, but probably not one that leads to a job.

Specifically define what you want to do on the job and what skills you can offer the company. Do more than merely say you want to work in consulting at a Big Six accounting firm. Come up with a few specific companies and positions that interest you. Then find out who does the hiring and whether the company looks for people year-round or during specific hiring periods. There's no sense beating your head against a wall in June if the company only hires once a year in March.

Find out if there are any open positions. Your attitude should be that if the company is going to hire anyone, even one person, it should be you. Why shouldn't it? Then, before you ever set foot in the office for an interview, rack your brains for all the reasons you should be hired. You don't have to make things up. Think about your abilities, the ones you defined in Chapter 2, and figure out which ones will be most valuable to the company where you want to work.

If the company isn't hiring at all, you're back to the numbers game, banking on the laws of attrition. That doesn't have to mean the end of your career search with this company. It just means you have to change your tactics so that you're in the right place at the right time when the company IS hiring.

Be Persistent

> "After calling the director of a news radio station, not to the point of annoyance but definitely under the definition of persistence, I finally was brought in for an interview. The first thing the news director wanted to know was, 'Why me? Why did you keep calling me?' He'd called me in simply because he was tired of saying no. Wear them down!"
>
> —Kyle, 24

Pick twenty or so places where you'd most like to work and send a letter and resume, follow up with one phone call, then another and another.

One good tactic is to find someone at the company who does a job that interests you and to target that person with your cover letter, resume, and phone call. Avoid making it sound like you're aiming to send that person into early retirement by actually taking over the job he or she does. But if someone who doesn't receive many letters or phone calls hears from you and takes an interest, you could end up with an insider pulling for you at hiring time and letting you know when opportunities arise.

More Advice

1. When someone gives you a referral, an opportunity to send a resume, or an offer to read a proposal or business plan, you should follow through immediately. This sounds obvious, but people often let days turn into weeks and each day that elapses increases the chance for something to go wrong. Things can change. People leave their positions, the climate of the com-

pany can change, the job opportunity can get filled, the person can forget the phone conversation you've just had. Don't miss the boat.

2. Do SOMETHING every day. It could be something as minor as sending out one cover letter and resume or calling someone your friend referred you to or taking all the scraps of paper with phone numbers on them and organizing them in a business Rolodex or entering three months' worth of tax information into a computer program—every day, do at least one thing that will help you find a job.

3. Just because something hasn't been done a certain way before, it doesn't mean *you* can't do it that way now. Never be dissuaded by someone who tells you there's only one method to a certain career end. And don't be afraid to take a chance on the uncharted course. For everything that exists now, someone had to do it first. That someone could be you.

4. Establish a routine. Even if the routine entails getting up at five A.M., when you know you won't be distracted by the urge to make phone calls, and then taking a nap at three o'clock. As long as you do it every day, you'll learn to work when it's work time and take a break when it's not.

5. Ruts are easy to come by. You can always find one without looking for too long. So if you're in a job that feels like a rut and are tempted to try something new, do it. You can always go back to the routine—if not in your old job at your old company, than an equally rut-like job elsewhere.

6. Be a professional. This means not having an audio clip from *SpongeBob SquarePants* on your answering machine. It means investing in some business cards, even if you don't yet have a business or a job title. People need a way to find you (though sometimes only to ask you on a date) and you don't want to pull out a Gap receipt and write your number down with an eyeliner pencil or a ballpoint pen that bleeds.

7. Never take rejection personally. If someone doesn't have room for you at a company you're interested in, it's not a reflection

on your skills, intelligence, or personality. Rejection is just a nine-letter word that means you'll need to keep looking. That's all it means.

8. Learn who you can count on for moral support. Never call a friend whose favorite pastime is sharing misery. It may love company, but . . . Moms can be excellent morale boosters. They don't have to approve of, understand, or be cognizant of exactly what kind of job you're searching for—they just have to tell you you're wonderful and reassure you things will work out. Sometimes it helps to explain these parental job requirements to them.

9. Develop a noise filter. You'll hear a lot of it, everything from, "You have to specialize, no one will hire someone whose skills and interests aren't clearly defined" to "You have to become a Renaissance person, no one with only one set of skills is a desirable employee." It's all true and none of it's true. But it can be distracting, right when there are more important matters at hand.

10. Lighten up. Your career is important but it's not worth creating an ulcer. You are employable. You will find a job. So on those days when you're wringing your hands and wondering why no one has called you back and thinking about buying a case of Top Ramen or turning off your heat to save money, remember that this is all just some grueling test designed by the deity of suffering and, eventually, you'll pass and move on to the next of life's little challenges.

Don't Settle

It's not lack of spine. It's just the oft-grim reality of the job market that can make you stoop to consider accepting a job that's below your standards. You graduate and people tell you the job market is bad or that you're going to have to get an unpaid internship or something. But you don't really want to believe it. You hope that you'll be the exception. Someone will surely offer you a job as soon as she sees your sterling resume and you'll be able to circumvent the job search nightmare. Then you get some rejection letters. Or you come home from a job interview where you're one of thirty candidates and you feel like it didn't go that well.

Then, instead of holding your ground and waiting for a great job at a great company to open up, you start aiming for a less-than-great job at a mediocre company. And if that doesn't come through fast enough, you're down to a completely demoralizing job at a company no one's heard of. Short of paying someone to let you have a job, you've reached the low point of your job expectations. What happened to the pride you once had in your status as a graduate of a great college?

Keep your standards. The job market may be tough, but

> *"Talk about lowering your standards; I remember answering an ad from the career center that wanted someone to go into crop fields and mark plants with four-digit numbers. I thought my college diploma at least made me qualified to do that. The woman on the phone asked if I had any allergies because we were going to be around a lot of dry grass and pollen. Plus, she said, it was really important to stay hydrated because we'd be in the fields under hot sun for hours and it got kind of hard to label the plants correctly if you were delirious. I'm allergic to about every plant under the sun and I didn't want to go passing out in a field somewhere, but I was actually considering this job because it sounded like I could get it. It paid seven dollars an hour. Somewhere during our conversation, the voice of reason screamed loud enough that I hung up the phone."*
>
> —*Jeff, 24*

you WILL find a job that uses your skills and abilities. If you thought you were going to get offered an executive position with the first company that received your resume, you may have to bring your expectations down a notch. But short of that, you have every right to expect to get a good job. Be prepared to give it some time and make some sacrifices in what you thought you'd be paid, but don't give up. And don't settle.

5

RESUMES, COVER LETTERS, AND THE LIKE

Your Marketing Tools

It seemed like an oversight to give you all this information about job hunting with no mention whatsoever of resumes and cover letters. Herein lies the purpose of this chapter. But if you need more thorough information on the subject, include that in your job search research. Here you'll find the nuts and bolts you need to know before you can contact your targeted companies and tell them how your skills meet their needs.

Resumes

Your resume should fit on one page of nice-looking paper. Choose either cream or white and look for good quality paper at a local print shop. You can buy a ream (500 sheets) of the paper you choose and photocopy your laser-printed resume onto the paper yourself. Use the same paper when you print out your cover letters and everything will match.

Although you'd like to show your potential employer that you have a unique sense of style and verve, your resume is not the place to do it. Use a plain font like Courier or Times. Palatino is about as fancy as you should get. That way, if anyone ever asks you to fax a resume, you'll be sure it's readable.

Your resume should have your name and address centered at the top, as well as a phone number where you're most likely to be reached. If you're moving, list a permanent address, like your parents' house, if you don't know where you'll be after the move. Don't clutter your resume up with fax numbers and multiple phone numbers, but if you have an e-mail address or Web page, let employers know where they can find you online.

Finally, don't try to craft one perfect resume to fit every type of job that interests you. You might have two or even three different versions that highlight different aspects of your work experience and activities. Keep them on your computer so you can change them if necessary.

The Format

There are as many philosophies on how to write a resume as there are cable channels. As long as you avoid the major pitfalls like spelling errors and unreadable fonts, you'll be fine. Although you don't have to include every category listed below, you should think of them as ways to best express your abilities. Whichever ones fit best should go on your resume. The basic order of subject headings on your resume should go something like this:

- Objective statement
- Education
- Work experience
- Activities/interests
- Awards
- Skills

When you format your resume, clarity should be a top priority. Use devices like bold type for your subject headings or bullet points to list job responsibilities, awards, or skills. Instead of writing out long descriptions that clutter up the page, keep things simple and readable. Don't write a paragraph describing your last job when a few bullet-pointed descriptions will do. And if you only have one item for the activities, awards, or skills category, you might think about omitting the category and fitting your accomplishment into one of the other sections.

Your Career Objective

The objective statement is not mandatory, but it can be a good way to specifically state your career objective. If you have a lot of work experiences on your resume that seem to show the career direction you're pursuing and you don't have room for the objective, it's fine to omit it. You can always explicitly state your objective in your cover letter. But if you want to tell a prospective employer exactly what your career goals are, don't hesitate to put it in a statement at the top of your resume.

Make sure to be specific. It's not enough to say, "I'd like a fulfilling career in the entertainment industry," for example. You should pinpoint exactly where you'd like to go within the industry. Instead, say something like, "I'd like to do camera work on documentary films."

Education

You should consider putting your education at the top rather than the bottom of your resume because it may be your most comprehensive and significant accomplishment thus far. If you think your work experiences will make a bigger impact than your education, don't hesitate to put that section first.

Under education, include the college you attended and your graduation date or your projected graduation date. Put down your major and any minor areas of study. If you wrote a thesis, include that information, and if you graduated with any honors or won any awards or scholarships, include that here as well. The general rule is that if your GPA is a 3.5 or above, you should include it.

Don't expect employers to understand abbreviations. They're not stupid, but if you write "UNC at Chapel Hill," they might not immediately recognize that as the University of North Carolina. Don't make employers work. If your major was electrical engineering and computer science, don't just put EECS and expect everyone to figure out what it means. The same goes with awards you've won and organizations where you've worked. Instead of saying you won the Dominick Award, explain that it's an award given to the winner of the freshman writing contest.

Work Experience

Your work experiences should be listed chronologically, starting with the most recent job you've had. Don't despair if you don't have a lot of work experience. This section need not include only jobs you were paid to do. List volunteer jobs, internships, research assistant work, or other work you did for school credit. Feel free to deviate from the chronological method if you think it makes a better presentation of your experiences. For example, if you worked three summers as a volunteer firefighter and had intermittent volunteer jobs in the health-care field, you may decide to group the health care jobs together and list them first if you're applying for a job in a hospital.

Any job that gave you relevant experience should go on your resume somewhere. Try to give an employer a sense of what you did at each job and how it applies to the job you're seeking. You can use bullet points and list your job duties, or put them into a short paragraph. Don't feel the need to use complete sentences here. Use good descriptive verbs and say things like, "Completed case study on how city sewage runoff affects wetlands habitat, rescued and cared for baby swallows, edited local newsletter sent to 2,000 members."

Activities/Interests

This sounds like a list of things you did at summer camp when you were a kid, but it may have a place in your resume. This is where you list or describe special interests that may catch the eye of a recruiter or interviewer. For example, the last two summers

Stacy Kravetz
1 Hire-Me Place
Noslacker, CA 90000
(310)555-1212

Objective: To work on a wildlife preservation team, helping to create graphical computer displays to document population growth

Education: B.A. Utopia University, 1996
              Major: Botany
              Minor: 18th-Century British Literature
- Participated in group honors thesis project, which consisted of creating wildlife preserve for endangered local wildflower colony and documenting growth patterns
- Received Harry S. Truman Award for Original Poetry

Experience:

Volunteer *January 1995–Present*
Banana Tree Wilderness Foundation
- Planted trees in urban communities
- Conducted letter-writing campaign to government officials for local banana tree preservation
- Planned and supervised neighborhood cleanup event

Intern *June 1995–August 1995*
The Wildlife Farm
- Fed and cared for endangered species of coyotes and deer
- Compiled data on animal life spans in various regions to be used in Wildlife Farm newsletter and possible upcoming publication in *Wild News on the Planet* newspaper

Seamstress and Office Manager *June 1994–August 1994*
Manny's House of Fabrics
- Sewed the hems on floral draperies
- Created computerized filing system for inventory
- Assessed customers' needs and helped them choose color schemes and fabrics for furniture and draperies

Manager *June 1992–August 1993*
Nora's Hoagie House
- Managed 16 employees on graveyard shift
- Set up and managed office filing system

Skills:
- Computer programs: Microsoft Excel, Microsoft Word, and Word Perfect
- Completed 60 hours of wilderness first-aid training

that you spent cycling across the country for charity should definitely go in this section of your resume because they show a lot
about your commitment, altruism, and cycling ability.

Your activities and interests don't have to qualify you for the
Nobel Peace Prize to make it on your resume. If you're an avid
photographer, botanist, cooking enthusiast, or any other hobby
that sets you apart from the crowd, put it on your resume, especially if it's relevant to your career objectives.

If any of your experiences showed leadership skills, like if you
were captain of the squash team, here's a good place to make note
of that as well. If you decide to leave off an activities category, you
can fit some things you've done into the awards or skills section.

Awards and Skills

The awards section is pretty straightforward. It should include
any academic awards you've received since you started college.
Also include nonacademic awards, such as president of the Speech
and Debate Club or winner of the campus newspaper's photography contest. An alternative is to list awards under education.
Again, it's up to you.

Skills are also straightforward and easy to bullet point or list.
Include specific computer programs you know, foreign languages
that you speak or read, and any additional abilities that will be relevant to your career path.

So How Will My Resume Look?

For reference, here is what my resume might look like—some
details have been changed to protect the innocent (me). Again, this
is the chronological method, but there are others you might
choose to better display your experiences.

How's Your Spelling?

One great way to turn off a potential employer is to load your resume with typos and grammatical mistakes. Even one spelling error can be enough to land your resume in the Dumpster. Make use of computerized spell checking, but don't trust it completely. If you've read your resume over too many times to be objective, enlist the help of a literate friend who may notice an error you missed.

Electronic Eyes

Gone are the days when you could guarantee that a real human being sat poring over stacks of resumes looking for a gem in the crowd. Now many companies use electronic scanners to select candidates who list certain qualifications on their resumes. Of course, not all companies let the automatons do the scanning, but in case you apply to one that does, make sure your resume is ready.

Whether you're sending your resume via e-mail or snail mail, expect that it might get scanned for keywords. Make sure your resume has the keywords that best apply to your skills and the type of job you're seeking. The objective statement is a good place to use keywords that describe what you're looking for in a job, even if you don't yet have the experience. That way, the scanner will pick up your resume regardless of your qualifications. (For more on keywords, see Chapter 6.)

Cover Letters

By now you've narrowed down your list of recipients of your cover letter and resume. You've decided not to flood the market and you have a good idea of who needs your skills and experience. Now it's time to let them know.

Your cover letter is a chance to tell the employer something

Six Things to Avoid Putting in Your Cover Letter

1. *I'd really like a position with your company.* How many people do you think they hear from who don't really want a job and are fervently hoping for a rejection letter?

2. *I find the field of sticker manufacturing (or job of choice) exciting.* Like you'd be applying for a job if you thought the field was infinitely stagnant and boring.

3. *Per your ad . . .* This is not great grammar, plus it sounds stilted.

4. *I have no experience but I feel I could learn quickly.* Don't talk about what you can't do or haven't done—talk about the experience you do have and how it will help the company meet its needs.

5. *As you can see by my resume, I've had many job experiences.* They'll see your resume and your experiences without your directing them to it. Instead, expand on parts of your resume, telling how an experience has prepared you for the job.

6. *To Whom It May Concern / Dear Sir or Madam:* Know who you're sending your resume to and address that person by name and title, as in:

June 25, 2003

Joe Bob Beatty
Executive Vice President of Marketing
Zygotes Unlimited
111 Zephyr Drive
Sunny Shores, TX 00010

Dear Mr. Beatty:
Your dynamite letter comes next and Mr. Beatty swoons.

Mr. Beatty might be anyone from the human resources director at a company you like or the friend of your parents who suggested you drop him a resume. If your research has produced names of peo-

ple who head the departments where you want to work, write to them instead of the human resources director. There's a better chance your resume will get seen by someone who matters if you target your letter to that person.

---

about yourself that doesn't appear in your resume. In other words, don't say, "As you can see from my resume, I went to Yukon U." Instead, use the opportunity to introduce yourself and explain how you became aware of the company—either through an ad or a personal contact—and explain why you're interested in the job. This should be about a three-line paragraph.

Your second paragraph should explain exactly why you're a good match for the company and its needs. Here's your chance to show you've done some research and have fully considered how hiring you will benefit the company. You can go into more depth about one or two items on your resume if they're especially relevant. Again, this should be about three sentences. Restrain yourself.

Finally, you wrap it up. Short and sweet. You express thanks for the person's consideration and say you'll phone in a week or two to find a convenient time to meet. That way, you can follow up and not feel weird about it, because your letter said you intended to call.

Sign it "Sincerely," and don't forget to pen in your signature and include your resume. If you can get your computer to print an envelope, great. Otherwise, hand-write the address and put it in the mail. Even if a job listing says to fax a resume, include a cover letter with it. When faxing, it's a good idea to mail along a clean copy as well, if an address is provided.

Your Follow-up Call

Don't be timid and don't worry that you're being annoying. Just call, say you sent a letter to the person you wrote to, and ask to speak to that person. If you get an assistant who offers to take a message, that's okay. Just don't hang up without asking a few innocuous questions about when might be a good time to reach Mr. Beatty and what the status is of the job opening. If you're nice, you can get some good information from an assistant.

If you feel like you're getting nowhere, try a different approach. Tell the assistant you really like the company and you'd like to know if Mr. Beatty could spare a few minutes to answer some of your questions. If this flies, you might talk to Mr. Beatty on the phone or you might get a full informational interview. Either way, your foot's in the door. That may be all it takes. Sometimes people are so busy that even though they desperately need to hire someone, they just don't have the time to go through the process of doing it. Help them along.

The one thing to avoid is pestering Mr. Beatty and his assistant to death. There is a point where persistence becomes annoyance. Don't reach that point. Generally, you can do this by calling no more than once a week.

Interviews

The best way to prepare yourself for an interview is to know what to expect. You don't want to walk in expecting a casual chat only to find a six-person panel waiting to interrogate you. Depending on the industry, different things may be required of you at the interview. If you're interviewing for a job as a software programmer, for example, you may be asked to do some programming or answer technical questions. If you're interviewing for a writing job, you may need to take a writing or copyediting test. The idea is to be mentally prepared.

Expect to be asked an array of questions ranging from personal questions, like How did you choose your major?, to problem-solving questions. If the thought of being asked questions about yourself makes your skin crawl, you'll have to try the agony method of learning to talk animatedly at will. Embrace those fam-

> *"When interviewing at a company, try to find out about the corporate culture first. Try to find out how people in that company dress, whether it's really corporate business attire, casual clothes, or funky. Most perceptions about you are made instantaneously, and one comment I hear frequently is 'I'm not sure that person would fit in here.'"*
>
> —Rachael, 25

ily functions where Uncle Ozzie will ask you what you want to do with your life and why you spent last summer teaching scuba when accounting is really your passion. You'll learn quickly.

When you're being asked dry interview questions, it's easy to give stiff, dry answers. If you can make your interview more like a conversation and less like an interrogation, you'll feel more relaxed. If any of your answers would be enhanced by an anecdote, use the opportunity to break the ice and let your personality come through.

Interviewers aren't trying to trick you or make you squirm. Sometimes they're just not that good at it themselves and they ask questions that don't yield thoughtful, interesting answers. If this is the case, don't let it penalize you. Be charming, try to put them at ease, and you'll end up having a better interview.

The interview is also a place to let your research pay off. You can show your knowledge of the challenges the company faces and discuss how you're well suited to serve the company's needs. Use the opportunity to expand on portions of your resume, especially on experiences that directly relate to the challenges you'll face on the job.

Sometimes the hardest thing is saying what you think instead of what you think the interviewer wants to hear. It's especially tough if the interviewer asks something like, "So what do you think of our strategy of using ant colonies as test cases?" You might not understand the strategy or you might think it stinks, but you think the interviewer wants to hear praise. In fact, the interviewer just wants to hear what you think. You can ask a few questions about the thinking behind the strategy or its results so far before you give your answer. By asking the interviewer to tell you more, you can gather more information to help you answer *and* give yourself more time to come up with something to say. The point is that you should think for a moment, be tactful, and say what you really think.

It's never a bad idea to take a moment to think. You'll avoid saying the wrong thing as soon as it pops into your head. You'll also appear pensive, thoughtful. Not bad when you really just need a minute to come up with an answer.

Don't be overly sensitive and try to read too much into the interviewer's expression after an answer to a question. Assume you've answered brilliantly and smile. It will be convincing and show confidence even if deep down you feel like crawling under the desk.

> *"A friend of mine was interviewing for a law firm position and was the final candidate for that interviewing day. In the final minutes of the interview, he gracefully stood up and reached for the interviewer's hand. In his effort to give the interviewer the strong, firm handshake that would project his confident, yet easygoing style, he knocked a pitcher of ice water that was sitting on the interviewer's desk, emptying its contents all over the interviewer and the notes and resumes from the 15 or so interviews that had transpired that day. Moral: 'Well, I guess that takes care of the competition,' is not a good reply in this case."*
>
> *—Abby, 24*

Before the Interview

Before you set foot in the office of your prospective company, call to confirm your appointment. Ask for directions if you're not sure how to get there and find out where you can park if you're driving there. Dig out the information you copiously researched on the company and on the industry as a whole (or do the homework now), and familiarize yourself with these background materials.

Go over a few questions you'll ask when given the chance. You don't want to stutter and wheeze when the interviewer turns the tables and allows you to ask questions. Ask about a typical day on the job. Ask what the career path is for someone starting in your prospective position. Find out where people are who started in that position three to five years ago. Ask about where the industry is going.

Leave discussions of salary to the interviewer. Don't ask about benefits either. When you're first starting out, you probably won't be negotiating these things. You'll just be told what the norm is for the job.

If you have a nice-looking folder or a briefcase, bring it. Put a couple extra resumes inside as well as paper and pens. You never know the direction the interview will take. You may end up talking with someone who hasn't seen your resume and needs a copy. What starts as an interview could turn into a first-day orientation if all goes well. In that case, it would be nice to take some notes. If you don't have a briefcase or leather-looking folder, better to bring nothing than try to produce a makeshift replica from a torn PeeChee folder.

Bear in mind as well that not all interviews are formal. You could be meeting with suits at a Fortune 500 company or a couple of people dressed casually in a TV production office. Know the standard for your industry so that you can dress and approach the interview accordingly.

Preparing Yourself

Bearing in mind that the most difficult question to answer is often the most basic, you can prepare yourself by thinking a little before the interview. Often the question "Tell me about yourself" is met with near total paralysis. Somehow the only thing you can think of is where you were born and when. Later, when the postinterview floodgate opens in your brain, you think of all the things you should have said. Here are some questions to ponder before your interview:

- Tell me about yourself.
- How did you get interested in this field/this company?
- How did you choose your major?
- What classes were your favorites?
- What are your short-term work goals? Your long-term goals?
- Tell me about (something on your resume).
- What do you do for fun?
- What do you read? What is your favorite book?
- What do you want this job to provide for you?
- What are your strengths and weaknesses?
- What can you contribute to this company?
- What was the most difficult decision you've had to make?
- What person/experience has influenced you the most?
- Why should I hire you?

You need not write out complete answers to these questions. You should just use them to build your confidence before an interview. You can come up with great answers. You can dazzle the interviewer. You can get a job.

Your Benefits

When your potential employer waves a sickeningly low salary figure before your eyes, you may be tempted to scream in protest. Remember, however, what your first job means to you in terms of training and skills, and don't forget to consider other benefits that may go along with your wages. Consider the following benefits to be value added to your paycheck:

- Health insurance that you don't have to buy yourself, disability coverage
- 401(k) or other pension plan, especially when the company matches your contributions
- Driving expenses, including mileage reimbursement or a company car

- Travel expenses that mean you don't have to spend your paycheck while you're on the road
- Personal days, sick days, and vacation days with pay
- Stock options, which can still be quite valuable despite the dot-com debacle

Thanks Again

One final note is about the final note: the thank you. Write one immediately to anyone you meet with, as a show of competence and a reminder of who you are. Don't use your thank-you letter as a pitch to get the job. Brevity is the soul of wit, as Shakespeare was wise enough to note.

Job Insecurity: Be Prepared for Change

When you start a new job, think of it as a temporary place on your career path instead of a permanent one. Work for the company but also work on your own career. The skills you develop on the job can serve you well in the future at other jobs or in a better position at the company where you currently work. This doesn't mean you should be disloyal to the company you work for, but you should always be thinking about where you want your career to take you.

Don't be afraid to take your toys and go home. You should never feel so desperate to have a job that you're afraid to leave a bad one. Keep a stash of emergency money that will give you the freedom to quit and look for something better. It might take some time to build this up, but once you do, it will give you the freedom to hold out for what you want. See Chapter 17 for strategies on creating a financial cushion to tide you over between jobs.

Develop your skills. Keep a list of all the job responsibilities you have and the projects you work on. Sometime down the line, when you're interviewing for your next job, people will ask what you do at work. It's easy to forget that you did a special project for the president of the company or that you were put in charge of all correspondence within your department. You might even consider keeping a portfolio of samples of your work. A future employer may want to see your samples or you may just need to refer back to them later when you're working on a related project.

6

IT'S A WIRED, WIRED WORLD

Hyperlinking on the Web . . . What!?

A long with all the new technology that allows you to surf conveniently at your desk comes a barrage of new terms that may seem a little confusing. Your computer is your direct connection to people, jobs, and information from around the globe. But first you need to be able to navigate this world without sounding like your grandparents.

Here are a few basic pieces of information that even the savviest of surfers don't necessarily know: the *Internet* is the global computer network, which connects millions of computers and computer networks around the world via telephone lines. The *World Wide Web* (the Web) is a system that operates over the Internet. The Web allows you to jump to information you want by clicking on a link or highlighted portion of text. This is called *hyperlinking*. In order to hyperlink, you need to surf through *hypertext*, the documents on your screen that contain links. The links take you to a variety of data, from additional text to graphics, sound, or video clips.

A *Web site* refers to a business or organizational presence on the Web, which can be found by typing a Web address, known as a *URL* (uniform resource locator). *HTML* (hypertext markup language) is a language programmers use to create pages on the Web. You can send *e-mail* (electronic mail) in the form of typed messages from your computer to a recipient's mailbox, which is where your message will be read.

Job Searching on the Net

You're armed with a computer and either a high-speed modem or a digital subscriber line (DSL). In other words, you're ready to expand your job search into cyberspace. Using the Internet for your job search is especially useful because you can do it any time of day, from the comfort of your desk at home. This means that even if you have a job or classes during the day, you can make use of your nights to search for something else. In order to make the most of your online job search, you need to know what you're looking for, where to look, and how to choose between service providers. Ideally, you should have a Pentium computer that can run Windows or a Macintosh with OS X. Your modem speed should be at least 56K bps (bits per second). And you should have a word processing program such as Microsoft Word.

While more and more companies have their own Web sites and the capacity to receive electronically sent resumes, not every company that interests you will necessarily be Net savvy. Don't feel like all of your job searching needs to be done online, but do consider it a viable option. There are many great online resources to enhance your job hunt.

There are primarily two ways you can get online information: through an *online service* (America Online) or through an *Internet service provider* (ISP). The two types of access differ mainly in price, services offered, and ease of locating information.

The AOL Dilemma

AOL synthesizes large amounts of information into easy-to-read categories. The benefit of an online service is that it provides its own content, in addition to giving you Internet access. You'll get news, online editions of magazines, newsletters, and newspapers, as well as stock market quotes, chat rooms, e-mail, games, and services like travel and shopping information, technical support, and Web access. AOL does the choosing for you—its editors have decided what news to post, which magazines to provide, and which chat rooms and discussion groups you can access.

When choosing between an AOL account and an account with an ISP, you should consider how valuable it is to have AOL's content presented to you. Do you want to read the articles and browse the weather reports on the home screen AOL presents to you? Or do you want to set up your own home page through your Internet service provider and select the combination of news, weather, stock quotes, or whatever you want? It is certainly a matter of personal preference. Pricing is pretty much the same no matter how you set up your online account. Some people prefer to use AOL when they are getting their feet wet in the online world. Others feel comfortable navigating the online world alone. It's up to you. You can get software to install AOL by calling America Online at (800)827-6364.

Once you've installed the online software onto your hard drive, keep the CD-ROM. You never know when you might want to get access to your online account from another computer, such as the one at work. If you keep the CD-ROM, you can reinstall the program on another computer and use your password to sign on. You'll also be covered if you need to reinstall the software in the event your account gets corrupted.

Internet Service Providers

Internet service providers typically give you flexibility of software, such as different e-mail programs. Expect to pay about $20, give or take, for unlimited Internet access. Every major city provides Internet access through a local phone call to at least one access provider. If you're up for getting a little more Net savvy, you can sign up with an ISP and typically have unlimited access for a flat monthly rate. The service providers give you Internet access but they don't provide their own content, meaning that they don't organize material, such as news briefs, or have writers creating original content just for them—this is the main difference between ISPs and AOL.

What ISPs do provide is a means for accessing the World Wide Web and Web-based chat rooms. Most services provide e-mail and some also have newsgroups or let you create your own Web page.

After you've found sites you like and plan to revisit, you can design your own *bookmark* or *hot list*, which keeps track of the addresses for easy access the next time.

When you choose an Internet service provider, make sure you can sign on at the fastest speed your modem can support. Also sign on with a local phone number to avoid toll charges. If you travel a lot, find out if there's an 800 number you can use or a local dial-up you can access in your destination city so you won't pay the toll to call your regular number from out of town.

Also find out if technical support is available online or if you can call an 800 number, rather than paying for the call. You can get a list of most of the Internet service providers on the Web at www.thelist.com. Below are some good Internet service providers:

- AT&T WorldNet   (888)368-3728
- MSN   (866)900-6768
- Juno   (800)654-5866
- NetZero   (800)333-3633
- Earthlink   (800)395-8425

Speed and High Speed

Next you have to decide whether you are patient enough for the speed provided by your 56K modem or whether you need more. If you are used to the fast access to Web pages provided by a campus T1 line, surfing with a 56K modem can feel like the online equivalent of snail mail. Do you feel the need for speed?

If you do, you'll most likely choose between a digital subscriber line and a cable modem. In some cases, the decision is made for you. Cable companies serve specific areas and if you are outside that area, you may opt for DSL. By the same token, not all companies that offer DSL serve all areas. So check with your provider to see what your options are.

What you get when you opt for speed is an instant connection, without having to dial in every time you want to go online. You also can download and e-mail large files like photos or MP3s much faster with a high-speed connection.

Cable modem access is offered by whichever cable company serves your area, while DSL is offered by some ISPs or phone companies.

Don't Surf Up a Creek without a Paddle

Once you have Internet access, you need to avoid getting lost or distracted. If your job search takes you to the World Wide Web, where job listings abound, you need to make good use of your time so you can spend it sending resumes, not aimlessly searching for Web pages.

The main surfing tool is called a browser. Browser software helps you navigate the Web and is usually provided by the Internet service you subscribe to or it comes with your computer. Most people use Netscape or Internet Explorer as their browsers.

There are several places you can look for job information. The World Wide Web has home pages from different companies as well as sites geared specifically to matching you with employers who post jobs. You can also look at newsgroups, which are places to exchange information with people who have common interests—they're basically discussion groups and can be good job networking sources. Look at www.usenet.com to find a newsgroup on a topic that interests you.

Directories and Search Engines

A *search engine* or *search directory* can take the guesswork out of online searches. A search engine is a Web site that lets you search for other Web sites by typing in a keyword or selecting from a topic list. Directories are lists of Web sites that can also be accessed by keyword, sometimes accompanied by reviews or picks from the editors who compile the directories.

Following are some good search engines and directories that will make Web surfing infinitely easier. Yahoo is a good place to start because it has links to other search engines, so if you want to search further, you can do it through Yahoo without entering another URL:

- *Yahoo*, at www.yahoo.com, is the oldest directory. It lets you search by its list of topics or the keywords you type.
- *Google*, at www.google.com, is so good and so popular that it has spawned its own verb, to google. Example: "A friend of mine set me up on a blind date so I googled him (typed his name into google.com) to see if I could find out anything about him before our date."
- There are many other search engines out there, but if you've tried searching on Yahoo or Google, you've most likely gotten thorough results. The search engines below have been around for years and also offer good services, including things like news, job listings, and shopping.
    www.altavista.com
    www.excite.com

www.lycos.com
www.webcrawler.com

Using Online Tools

Once you've got your searching skills up and running, you can use them to do research before you begin your actual job search. Look for Web pages of companies you're interested in working for, and search for sites with information about certain career fields or information you need for your job search.

For example, if you live in Topeka, Kansas, and you're looking for information about how to write a resume or if you're trying to find resume-writing services, use "resume AND Topeka" as your keywords. If you typed only "resume," you'd end up with thousands of resume-related Web sites, including online resumes other people have posted. You need to refine your searches to make them more specific.

> "I was living in New Jersey and looking for jobs in California and Boston. I bought a modem and some fax software, which was a key component in my online search. I looked at jobs through Monster, flew back to California and got a job at Oracle, a software company. The Internet is also a great tool for getting research about companies. When I was living in the boonies, I could go to companies' Web pages and do research. It won't replace cover letters and networking, but it's a good component of your job search. When I was moving from place to place, the one constant was my e-mail address, so people could always find me."
>
> —Greg, 25

The Online Job Search

Every day, new Web sites are added, and with them are more job listings and career information for college graduates. This can only be seen as a positive thing when you're beginning your job search. Some list classified ads, others give you access to the job boards at college career centers, and still others have jobs posted by employers. As of this printing, the following are good sites to check out.

- *Your alma mater.* Start by looking at the Web site for your school. There's no rule that says your college career center becomes obsolete in a high-tech world. The Web site for your college can yield career opportunities through alumni connections and access to the career center. If you don't know how to find your college online, use a search engine to find the URL for your school's Web site.
- *America's Job Bank*, which touts itself as the largest pool of active job opportunities, is a good source of over 250,000 job listings in the private sector. Five percent of its listings are for government jobs. In addition to being available on the Internet, America's Job Bank can be found electronically in public libraries, schools, and universities. You can find it at www.ajb.dni.us.
- *Vault.com* specializes in jobs in the finance and consulting industries as well as offering job listings in law and jobs for candidates with M.B.A. degrees. The site also offers company research and profiles.
- *Wetfeet.com* offers industry and company profiles as well as information on salary and interviewing. The site has job and internship listings as well as career counseling advice.
- *Hoover's Online* requires you to pay for certain services, but it has a very thorough database of company profiles, including financial statements and stock quotes. It has listings of corporate Web pages as well as job listings. Go to www.hoovers.com.
- *Monster.com* is one of the largest job search sites. Monster provides a job database that you can access by job title, company, career field, or location. It lists employer profiles, entry-level and more specialized job opportunities, and an online career center with job fairs and advice. You can also post your resume.
- There are as many job Web sites offering job listings as there are ways to fit the words "job" or "career" into a Web address. Here are some of the better ones:

www.flipdog.com
www.careerfile.com
www.career.com
www.careerbuilder.com
www.hotjobs.com
www.employmentguide.com

- There are also job sites that focus on specific career fields. These sites are useful for candidates who already have experience in certain fields or who want to search for jobs within only one industry. Some of the industry-specific sites include the following:

www.engineer.net
www.dice.com (technology jobs)
www.journalismjobs.com
www.medicaljobsonline.com
www.govtjobs.com
www.lawjobs.com
www.k12jobs.com (elementary school teaching jobs)

Resumes Online

Posting your resume online is a slightly different proposition than sending it in the mail. First of all, it will look different. You can e-mail your resume as an attached file and it will look the same, but many employers don't like this because they have to download it, and because opening attachments risks the spread of Web viruses. The other alternative is to e-mail your resume in the text window, but it will look different than it looks as a regular document.

The best way to design your resume to be read online is to e-mail it to yourself so you can see what it looks like. Then make changes until you come up with a version that looks good when sent. To do that, you'll need to redesign it in a format that can be read online. This means changing it to plain text and reformatting it to fit the constraints of an online document. In other words, online mail programs won't read bullet points or boldface type, so you'll have to come up with alternatives if your paper resume has them.

If you don't want to custom design your online resume, there are other options. Many career sites that provide resume posting also help you design your resume. Often, they include boxes that you fill in with your name, address, past job titles, and descriptions. Then your resume is ready for posting.

Before you post your resume, look at job descriptions you find online as well as the keywords that lead you to the jobs. Since employers will be scanning resume databases using the same keywords that are in their job titles and descriptions, make sure to include these keywords in your resume so it will be found. For example, if you used the keywords "graphic artist" to find jobs, be sure to include the words "graphic artist" on your resume so employers will find you with their search.

If you don't have any past experience in a field you want to enter, you may have trouble writing keywords into your resume that reflect the job you want. Here's where you can make use of the objective section of your resume, packing it with keywords for the job you want. When describing your past job titles and duties, give brief summaries, also using keywords where possible.

Where to Post

Now you have to consider where to post your resume. Choose a database that gets good exposure, one that's visited by as many employers as possible. One thing to remember is that once your resume goes into a database, you don't know who might see it. Find out who has access to the database and whether anyone can see your resume or whether the employer has to match job descriptions with your qualifications. Avoid putting your home address on your online resume, for confidentiality reasons, and list only your e-mail address.

There are enough services out there that allow you to post your resume free of charge that you shouldn't have to pay to post. Also make sure the service you choose won't charge you to update your resume. Find out how long it will be posted and how you can delete it once you find a job.

Your Own Web Site

As more and more people become Web savvy, having your own Web page may be akin to having a business card. Your resume can refer potential employers to your personal Web page that will tell them more about you than merely your curriculum vitae.

First you need to register an Internet domain. It can be something as simple as your name with a dot-com attached or you can dream up something that speaks to who you really are. You can register a domain at one of the following sites:

- www.register.com
- www.networksolutions.com
- www.domains.yahoo.com

Several of the Internet service providers allow you to create your own Web site. If your Internet service provider offers you a Web site as part of its services, you'll probably get programming information from the ISP. Another alternative is to create your own page by learning the HTML programming language through Web-based tutorials or books. This can be pretty time consuming, and if you don't need this computer language for work, you may not want to spend time learning it. If learning to use HTML gets you all revved up, check out www.webmonkey.com to learn how to design your own Web page.

One alternative is to hire a company that designs Web pages and have one custom-made to suit your needs. Look for a Web designer who will maintain your site or update it at regular intervals.

Once you have a Web site, you need to decide who will see it and how you want to publicize it. Depending on your objectives, you may want to be selective about who knows your URL or you may want to actively publicize your site. For example, if you start a business and you want to give people maximum exposure to your site, consider listing yourself on a search engine. You can submit your URL to search engines yourself or use bCentral (www.submit-it.com), which submits your URL to major search engines for $79 or more, depending on how many search engines you want it submitted to.

Alternatives

If you don't have a computer at home, you can still make use of the Internet for your job search. One way is by making use of an alternative Web-friendly device. A cell phone perhaps?

While it might seem like an extraordinary splurge to buy a cell phone with all the bells and whistles, it can be a useful, even economical, way for the computer-lacking to surf the Web. This can be a good solution for Net surfers who do all their computer work at the office and don't have use for a PC at home but who still need to access e-mail and surf the occasional Web site.

The drawback to Web-enabled devices is that you typically can't download information you retrieve from the Net. So for extensive researching where you don't want to sit in front of your phone, copying down articles and information onto notepads, you might opt to borrow a friend's computer, head to the nearest Internet café, or go to the library. But for looking at Web pages, chatting, or looking at news or job listings, an enhanced phone might be all you need.

7

GOING SOLO

Build a Better Mousetrap

S ometimes you'll find it tricky to convince a potential employer you've had five years' experience in a certain field when you've barely been out of school five months. It's one of the ironic catch-22s of the working world: You need experience in the job that you need experience to get. It's times like these when you might decide to can the idea of working for someone else, and sign up as your own employee. According to the U.S. Bureau of Labor Statistics, there will be almost a million more self-employed workers by the year 2005. You could be one of them.

It's not as daunting as it sounds. This is a time of life when you don't have that much to begin with, so you don't have much to lose. In other words, what's the worst that could happen? You spend a few months researching an idea and trying to get if off the ground, and if it doesn't work, you're no worse off than when you finished school. So why not give it (whatever it is) a try now?

Self-Employment

Clearly, going it alone is not for everyone. But with the corporate downsizing trend leaving more and more workers without the promise of the pension fund and the gold watch, you should consider the growing freelance market as a very viable opportunity. For example, newspapers and magazines, which formerly employed large staffs of writers and photographers, now function with small core staffs. They use freelancers for individual assignments and keep their operating costs down. Often these are the same writers and photographers that used to be staff employees. The good news for graduates wanting to enter a field is that they too can compete for the freelance assignments and there are increasing numbers of them. First you have to decide whether to start a business or small venture or to do independent projects for a handful of people or companies.

QUIZ: Is Self-Employment for You?

While having your own business or working solo gives you almost limitless potential for financial rewards, there can also be insecure periods, days when you don't feel like working, and stress over whether you're going to make it. Answer the following questions to give yourself a sense of how much you'd like to be self-employed and how well you could handle the ups and downs.

1. When you're just starting out, where do you plan to locate your business?
   a. In a plush high-rise downtown.
   b. In a modest office space that you still can't afford because you have no revenue.
   c. At home or in the garage at your parents' house.
2. How many hours a week will you work?
   a. Forty hours a week.

b. Sixty hours a week.

c. As long as it takes.

3. If someone asks if you could do a project you've never done before, you will:

   a. Say no.

   b. Admit you've never done it before but say you'll try.

   c. Say "Of course, no problem, when do you want it?"

4. When the phone rings, you will:

   a. Try to get the dog to stop barking long enough to talk.

   b. Say "Yo."

   c. Say "Hi, this is Bill," as though you work in a busy office.

5. If someone wants to meet with you and your office looks like a garage because, well, it is a garage, you will:

   a. Meet there anyway and try to sweep first.

   b. Say you'd rather do all business by phone because you abhor human contact.

   c. Suggest meeting at the caller's office under the pretense that it will be more convenient for her.

6. If someone is hesitant to hire you or buy your product because you're a newcomer, you will:

   a. Walk away.

   b. Offer it for free.

   c. Offer it on spec with the understanding that if it's up to par, you'll be paid for it and future work.

7. If someone says he can't afford what you're charging, you will:

   a. Call that person a cheapskate and leave.

   b. Feel sorry for the person and work for free.

   c. Make sure your prices are within the ballpark for your industry, then offer a price break on a one-time trial, as a show of good faith.

8. If your bills arrive in the mail and none of your clients have paid you yet, you will:

   a. Skip the country.

   b. Refuse to pay since you haven't been paid.

   c. Send a reminder notice or call the people who haven't paid you and find out the "status"—specifically, when you'll be paid in full.

9. If you need start-up capital for your business, you will:
   a. Rob a bank.
   b. Charge to the limit on your credit cards before checking other sources.
   c. Write a business plan and try to find investors, and if that doesn't work, borrow money from your parents or another kind relative with whom you've worked out a repayment plan.

10. When you have nothing to do at work, you'll:
    a. Watch soaps.
    b. Cry.
    c. Call people for information or advice and drum up future business by letting people know you're out there, ready to work.

11. If you need to make a long-distance call, you'll:
    a. Call whenever you feel like it and figure it's a business expense.
    b. Call when you know the person will be at lunch so they'll have to call you back and pay for the call.
    c. Get up early (if you're calling from west to east) or stay at work late (vice versa) to get the cheapest rate.

If you chose the last answer to the above questions, you've got the right instincts to consider working solo. Take the answers to heart when you take on your own business.

Your Boss

Before you venture forth with your entrepreneurial plan, do a final self-assessment exercise to make sure you want to be your own boss. This means vowing to provide yourself with a certain degree of self-discipline. It's okay to let yourself take breaks and work at odd hours, especially if your work doesn't require you to be by the phone from 9 to 5.

You can be a nice boss. There's nothing in the self-employment handbook that says you have to crack a whip. Keep yourself on some kind of schedule but don't make yourself feel bad if you haven't gotten enough work done on a given day. Remember that there would be plenty of days at someone else's office when you'd while away the hours and have nothing to show for your efforts. Sometimes that happens when you're working for yourself. As long as it doesn't happen every day, it's okay.

In fact, on days when you just can't seem to get anything done, don't agonize over it and sit miserably at your desk all day. Get out, work out, go somewhere, and don't even think about work. Figure that the next day will be better after you've gotten a good dose of air and had some time away.

Becoming a Professional

Professionalism is very much in the eye of the beholder. If you put forth an image that's smart and businesslike, that's how you'll be viewed by everyone else. Conversely, if you don't pay attention to the details, it will show. Start by getting yourself some letterhead stationery on the same paper as your resume. This doesn't have to be an expensive investment. If you have access to a computer graphics or desktop publishing program, you can design the letterhead yourself. The same goes with business cards, which can be copied onto card stock and cut apart with a paper cutter at the copy shop.

If the do-it-yourself method isn't an option, call a few copy shops nearby and get prices, including business cards while you're at it. In either case, your letterhead and business card should include your name, address, and phone number. Be sure to include an e-mail address, Web site address, or fax number if you have them.

Get as creative as your career field permits. If you are in an artistic industry, you might choose a funky logo or more avant-garde font. In a more conservative industry, stick with the basics and stay away from the overly cute. You can save some money by sticking to black and white, even if you do go with a logo. This way, you can photocopy your letterhead onto the paper of your choice for just a few cents per page.

Why all the concern about image? It's not just a superficial need to look good. Rather, when you send out a letter, it's often the first impression the recipient has of you. So you should make that impression a good one. Look like you know what you're doing, even if you're flying without a net. Perceptions can carry you a long way, so disguise your neophyte status with professional-looking letterhead stationery.

The same goes for your business card. When you leave your card with someone you've met, you're making a professional impression. It's infinitely better to hand someone a card than to scribble your phone number on the corner of a placemat or the back of an ATM receipt. Plus a business card makes it that much easier for that person to find you later.

The Rise of the SOHO

Because people like to have cute, fun acronyms for everything, there is one for the small office/home office that's the new way to launch a business: SOHO. So if someone asks if you have a SOHO business, they're not inquiring whether you own an art gallery in New York City. The benefits to having a small office or a home office is that you can keep your overhead low while you're starting a business and take advantage of technology that allows you to teleconference and fax to people all over the planet.

What that means for you is that you can work at home or in a small office and be taken seriously. You can use your home to get a business idea off the ground or you can make your living—or part of it—by freelancing or working as an independent contractor. If you can deliver the product of your efforts by fax, e-mail,

---

Six Popular Home-Based Businesses

1. *Computer consulting and programming*
2. *Web page designing or content editing*
3. *Financial and business consulting*
4. *Health-care services*
5. *Public relations and advertising*
6. *Journalism and other freelance writing*
7. *Graphics and interior design*

---

direct modem, or FedEx, you can work on projects for a company in a different city altogether. A growing number of fields support SOHO businesses.

How Do You Start?

Sometimes it's intimidating. When people talk about successful businesses that were started by people in their twenties, it conjures up an image of a young Bill Gates. Not everyone with a product to sell or an idea to turn into reality has to create the next Microsoft. The profiles of the start-up businesses below will give you some ideas of how young people started businesses right out of school. They all started with an idea, a desire to own a business, and a feeling that it might catch on.

Fill a Need

One way to pave the way for your success is to start a business in a field you know well. It makes it that much easier to learn about your target market when you're part of it yourself. If you've spent the last three years reading online magazines and you've yet to see an online magazine about sports, you might identify the need for one and see yourself and your friends as exactly the market such a magazine would target. So when you think about starting one yourself, you already know quite a bit about your audience and what they want from an online sports magazine.

Prophet Brewing Company was founded in 1994 after Scott Yara's partner and fraternity brother, Greg Shapiro, returned from a trip to Europe. He had tasted Belgian lambics, which are light fruit ales. They knew microbrews were popular in local pubs and saw an opportunity in the marketplace for fruit-flavored beers. Estimated sales for the company's first year were $3 million.

> *"You never realize what it's going to be like to ask someone for a million dollars."*
> —*Scott Yara, 23, owner of Prophet Brewing Company, a microbrewer of fruit ales*

A lambic is like a polished sparkling wine. It uses brewer's yeast like a beer and goes through a fermentation process of sixteen months. We saw where the microbrew market was—it's a market for specialized, hand-crafted beers. We saw a middle ground for high quality without producing a dark, distinctive beer. We looked at what our friends were drinking and decided the market was there.

We used to sneak into local home-brew clubs to find out how it was done. We tried brewing the beer ourselves, but it tasted terrible. If you're brewing a heavy, dark beer, you can mask any inconsistencies with the strong taste. That's what most home brews are like. But fruit beers are light, so you can taste any imperfections. We were pouring raspberries into these mixtures and it tasted awful.

Greg and I took leave of school for a quarter and met with local brewers. We hired some to do contracting. A friend knew a guy who founded a fermentation school in Davis and we hired him as a consultant to create some new recipes.

We went through a fifteen-month process of developing recipes and learning how to enter the market. We went to the library and read industry journals and learned about packaging and licensing. We had no capital to build a manufacturing plant. Then we found out that Samuel Adams contracts out—brewers will lend you their facilities since they're usually not using them to full capacity. They'll let you have use of their facility for a flat fee.

We got connected to a wholesaler through a friend and that's how the *product gets distributed. It's a slow-growth industry, mostly family-owned businesses. We pooled our money and came up with $40,000 of seed capital, which we used to pay for art for the labels and to open a business account.*

No venture capital company from Northern California is going to give $1.5 million to a couple of guys to start a fruit beer company. We started hunting for capital. Everyone always says you should go to your family or your friends, but we didn't want to do that. We wanted to build our own network of financing. But when you're 22 years old, you don't know who you're talking to. They say they're interested, then the check doesn't come.

I snuck into graduate business classes at UCLA and befriended a professor. He helped us write a business proposal. The first two companies didn't come through, but now we have our financing.

We have eight wholesalers taking the product statewide. Right now we're selling our product from Monterey to San Diego. I think part of the appeal is that we have that Gen X entrepreneur thing. We have orders coming from several large market chains, but we don't have the money to produce the inventory yet. So we're going to grow slower than we could.

Do What You Like

People often say that if you do what you like and do it well, eventually you'll succeed. It's been proven time and again and it's certainly a valid criterion to use for deciding on a business for yourself. Sometimes your business starts as a hobby and then turns into a full-time profession.

> *"You could have the best idea in the world, but if you don't manage your money right, you'll be in trouble."*
> —Debbie Braun, 28, owner of Well, Naturally!, an organic soap company

Well, Naturally! was founded on a shoestring budget. Today, the company produces a catalog and nearly a dozen hand-crafted organic soaps using ingredients like lemon, aloe, rosemary, carrots, and oatmeal. Future plans include a line of bath products and lip balm.

It started as a hobby. I was using all these products that said "all natural" and I'd never even heard of half the ingredients. So I started reading about herbal cosmetics and found out you could make them yourself. I got some books from the library and started making some of the recipes in my kitchen. I thought they were better than what was out there. So I started thinking this could be my business.

I got a lot of information online. I found out who makes soap and what their resources are. You can get tons of information online if you look.

I got my business license and started selling soap. First I was just giving it to my friends to try out and giving it as gifts. I just kept talking to people and telling them about it. Also, I have a Web page, and I just signed up with a search engine so people can find me. Then, around the holidays, I started getting some orders.

I have a catalog that I did on my computer. I wanted to keep my overhead down so I tried to do as much as I could myself.

Sometimes I think, what am I doing? I must be a total lunatic. I'm still figuring out how to do business. Right now I'm mainly selling through the catalog, but I'm planning on selling through stores. All the soaps have vegetable products and essential oils and herbs.

Do What You're Good At

All those years that people have been telling you what a great party-thrower you are, did you ever think that could be your career? People who open catering services or do events planning for corporations or nonprofit organizations do exactly that. Or when you used to sit and doodle lifelike caricatures of your professors, were you polishing your skills as a cartoonist? Sometimes you pick a career, other times a career picks you.

Seth Epstein's company, Fuel, creates graphics used in commercials, television show openings, network identifications, promos, and titles. Their clients

> *"It's better to start with no money. It makes you resourceful."*
>
> —Seth Epstein, 28,
> *principal/director of Fuel,*
> *a company that produces*
> *creative designs for digital video*

include major networks, advertising agencies, and production companies. The company grew from the ground up and was acquired by Razorfish, a unit of SBI and Company. Seth started with an art major in college and a few pairs of hand-painted jeans.

A lot of times friends will tell you what you need to know. When I was in college at U.C. Santa Barbara, I was painting on jeans, old Levis. I gave a few pairs to my sister and she was wearing them around. And then her friends wanted them. A friend of mine said, "You should do something with this." Sometimes you don't see it.

A manager from Nordstrom saw the jeans that my sister had and said I should come in. I made a couple of prototypes and took them to the Nordstrom buyer. She asked if I had style numbers for them. I said, "What are style numbers?" They're the most basic thing you need to know if you're going to sell clothes. So she knew how clueless I was. But she bought on the first day. Then I called another store I liked and asked to meet with the buyer. They ordered that day too. So on my first day, I sold $10,000 worth of clothes.

They wanted them in two weeks and I told them I could do it. I painted every pair in my fraternity room and delivered them myself. Nordstrom kept reordering.

I didn't really know what I was doing, but that doesn't really matter. You don't have to know. The point is, can you do it?

My grandma gave me some money and I just spent it instead of using it for the jeans. I didn't have budgets or accounting. I didn't really know, but I didn't reach out for help. I decided to automate and do screen printing. But I wasn't efficient at costing things out. I thought I was making money when I wasn't.

Then I thought I should design my own jeans. I thought the company would just get bigger. I borrowed money from my family and learned about how jeans get made. I went to trade shows and talked to people. Then I found a place to make them in L.A. This was right around the recession in the early nineties.

Nordstrom cut their orders, so I just had a bunch of boutiques to sell in. I ended up with all this back inventory. I ended up selling them at yard sales in Santa Barbara. But I still did print design to survive.

I was working out of my sister's garage doing tiny design jobs and screening designs on T-shirts. I was doing everything, whatever design job someone would give me. Now I see that I lacked focus. When Fuel took off, it was because we were doing one thing only. It's not just design, but what kind of design? Not just television, but what kind? Do we do infomercials? No. Do we do Web sites? No.

It's what I call a process of exploration. You have a desire to create something and you talk to anybody and everybody. Just pick up the phone and call—people will spill their guts.

I met someone who was doing digital video and got interested in it. I talked to everyone, found out who was doing what, what they were reading, where they got their resources. I saw how digital video worked. With all the money I had, I bought computer equipment, one piece at a time. One thing I learned from doing the jeans is make sure you can generate revenue. Don't get too big without the foundation.

I got around people doing digital video. The faster you can expose yourself, the faster you'll move. Since I was around, I got included on projects. I did an interactive CD for Sony and one for IRS records. Then I hooked up with some video producers and did freelance design for TV. I saw how it was done: how they met with clients, how they delivered, what trade shows they went to, what magazines they read.

I started my company, Fuel, in 1995. My first project was for the FX network. I did some graphics for one of their promos. Then I got a project with UPN and did a station I.D. for them with claymation. Someone came and said she liked what I did and offered to work for me for free. So I had an intern. I started getting more projects and the company grew. We're in a new office space and growing. Our business has increased unbelievably in the last year. Sales for the first year were over a million.

Finding a Business That Suits You

Now that you've decided to start a business or work for yourself, you need to figure out what to do. Most likely, you've got skills or ideas you want to try out in the marketplace.

Your business idea doesn't have to be mainstream as long as you see a need for it. For example, in an outdoor shopping area in L.A., there's a guy whose business is making wax molds of your hand in any shape. Does this guy have his hand on the pulse of a great consumer need? It's hard to say. But every weekend there's a line of people waiting to realize their favorite hand gesture in wax. So don't be afraid to go for it.

Get Educated

The first thing you should do is get educated. Learn everything there is to know about your business, whether that consists of collecting a list of companies where you'll target market your computer consulting services or finding out how cotton jackets are made. Find out what other products or services are out there like yours and what the company owners did to get started. Conduct informational interviews just as if you were looking for a job with a company. Ask questions, do research online and at the library, be thorough.

Try to find a mentor, someone who's been there before you. You'll end up with a valuable information source and a contact in your field. Your mentor can also be a life saver on the days you're tempted to quit because business isn't going well. Everyone goes through this. You will prevail.

The Road to Self-Employment

If you want to start a company, you need to make it official with the IRS. Call your local chamber of commerce and ask if they have business consulting services—many do. Most likely, you'll pay a visit to the city clerk's office to get a license. The cost of business licenses varies, depending on the type of business. If you'll be charging tax on your product, you need to get a resale permit— it's free—from the State Board of Equalization.

You can also get a DBA, which stands for Doing Business As.

Web Sites for SOHO Businesses

- *The Home Office Association of America has SOHO Central online, which profiles businesses that function well as home offices and provides an online newsletter and tips for members— www.hoaa.com/main.htm.*
- *Business@Home provides resource information and articles on home business issues and a discussion forum—www.gohome .com.*
- *Homeworks has advice and tips from Sarah and Paul Edwards, home office experts—www.homeworks.com.*

It's an official way to register your business name with the county where you're doing business. Typically, you get this at yet another office, most likely from the county clerk. The rules vary by city, so start by calling the chamber of commerce to get pointed in the right direction.

Technically, anyone who does business is required to have a license in the city where they do business, whether you own a store or design graphics on a freelance basis. Many independent contractors who receive 1099s at year's end aren't licensed, but cities discourage it.

Marketing Yourself

There are many outlets for exposing yourself and your business to the world. And while it would be nice to take out a thirty-second ad during *Survivor* to target your optimal demographic, that might cost a little more than you have in your wallet this week. There are many less expensive methods you can employ.

Before you do anything, take

> *"You have to start knocking on doors. If you don't knock, how will people know you're out there?"*
> —*Chris, 27, independent television producer*

inventory. This doesn't mean you should count the condiments in your refrigerator or rearrange the contents of your pencil jar. Take an inventory of what you have to offer. You need to be able to specifically describe the kind of work you do and the services or products you offer to the public. You need to know why people should hire you and what you can do for potential clients.

Write a brief *press release* about yourself and your company and send it to local publications. If there is a small business editor, address your press release to that person. You never know what kinds of stories reporters are working on, and if they have your name in front of them, you may be included in an upcoming article. When you send your press release, don't just give basic information—try to come up with an interesting story angle.

You can also get inexpensive postcards printed and send them to targeted people and businesses. You can create them yourself using a computer graphics program or have a local print shop whip them up. Postcards cost less to mail than flyers in envelopes. You can put an interesting design on the back and a basic description of your services or product on the reverse, alongside the address. Doing a *targeted mailing* is a way to advertise yourself to potential clients, not the world in general. If just one person keeps your postcard and calls you, it's worth the effort. If you perform an artistic service, you should put a sample on the front of your card. Be creative. If you're a writer, put some interesting pieces of prose or a paragraph from an article you've written. If you manufacture T-shirts, picture them on the front. Don't hesitate to send these cards to friends. Your college roommate might be a struggling production assistant at a film company today, but two years from now she could be in charge of a movie premiere and order the screen-printed T-shirts from you. In a few years, your friends can be your clients and your business partners.

Cold-calling can also yield surprising results. The idea is to let people know you're out there. You never know if someone is floundering around, trying to find someone to design a Web page, when the phone rings and you announce that you're a Web designer. People reward initiative. You might get a response like,

"We don't need anything like that now, but we might in a few months." If so, urge the person to keep your number and follow up in the coming months, just in case. Also send along one of your postcards.

Think about going *online*. You can raise awareness for your products and services through newsgroups and possibly get referrals that way. Web pages are coming down in price and you may be able to get one through your Internet service provider. Your homepage should contain keywords that make it easy to find using a search engine. For example, if you write cookbooks, you might contact a cooking Web site. They might feature a new cookbook each week and you could get exposure that way. If you have a product, you might consider advertising on the Net, in an electronic mall, or with a search engine that shows your ad to people who type in certain keywords.

Word of mouth is a great advertisement. Let everyone know what you're doing. People like to help. They like to hear that someone is looking for a CD-ROM designer and be able to say they know someone who does exactly that. And before you know it, you've gotten a referral. Referrals are the best thing you can hope for when you're self-employed. They're like someone coming out and offering you a job without your ever having to apply for it. And they mean you've made it. You no longer have to convince people you know what you're doing because they're already telling other people that you're the right person for the job.

How to Price Your Services

Say you're a painter who specializes in fake finishes on interior walls. One night at a party, you meet a guy who has been looking for a painter and would love to give you the job. He wants to know how much you charge. You're just starting out and you really need the work, but you don't want to jeopardize it by tossing out a number that's too high. Then again, you don't want to price your services too low and appear to be an amateur who doesn't know better than to work for peanuts. You find yourself wishing you'd talked to some other painters about how much they charge BEFORE someone was asking for a number.

There are industry standards that you can use to help determine what you should charge. If you are selling a product, you can figure out what your costs are and add a profit margin onto that. If you are providing a service, such as designing, consulting, or copywriting, you can base your prices on what others in your field are charging. Just cold-call a few places that offer the same types of services you do and find out if they charge by the hour or by the day and what their fees are.

If you do find yourself in a situation where you're forced to come up with a number before you've done your research, your best bet is to aim slightly high and present your fee with confidence. If your prospective client starts to stutter and wheeze, you can offer to come down in price a bit. But if you appear confident about your fee, people will generally assume you're worth it. And while you may have to settle for some lower-paying jobs when you're first starting out, eventually you will be able to raise your rates.

Ten Great Things about Working at Home

1. You can set your own hours to fit the times when you work most efficiently, which can mean you'll work less overall.
2. There are no chatty officemates to distract you.
3. Commuting means walking from your bed to your desk.
4. Better coffee.
5. You can wear whatever you want—this can save you money on work clothes and on dry-cleaning expenses.
6. Your flexible work schedule lets you run errands at off-peak times—your time is your money, so saving time. . . .
7. You may be able to write off a portion of your rent on your taxes.
8. The time you'd spend commuting can be used for something else, plus you save money on transportation expenses.

9. No harsh fluorescent lighting, cubicles, or buildings without windows.
10. Since more and more people are working at home, there are better phone services, smaller computers, printers, and fax machines, and online services to help you create a great home office.

Ten Drawbacks to Working at Home

1. Occasional lack of motivation.
2. Distractions like dirty dishes, mail, and TV.
3. No one to share your gripes about work over the water cooler.
4. Working where you live means you live at work—sometimes you have to force yourself to "go home."
5. You get bothered by phone solicitors and leaf blowers.
6. No benefits like pension plans, profit sharing, health insurance, and free office supplies.
7. You sometimes wonder if anyone knows you're alive.
8. You get phone calls from people who think you're not really working since you work at home.
9. It's less exciting to spend a quiet evening at home when you've been there all day long.
10. You generally have to go out, market yourself, and find the work instead of having someone drop it in your IN box.

Keep Work and Play Separate

The main thing you can do to make your home office routine function smoothly is to set up your office in a place where you won't be doing anything else. In other words, don't use your kitchen table as your office, because you'll find yourself sitting at your desk while you eat your frozen fish entrée, and before you know it you'll be scribbling notes to yourself and making To Do lists long after your workday should officially end. On the flip side, you might find yourself in the middle of a food frenzy when you should really be working. If your workspace isn't clearly separated from the rest of your living space, you'll start to feel like you literally live in your office . . . because you do. It's nice to be able to finish your work, turn off the light, and retire to another part of your apartment where you don't have to think about work anymore.

You don't have to have a multiroomed apartment for this to work. You can throw a tablecloth over your desk at the end of the day so you don't have to look at it. This is especially useful if your office is sandwiched between your couch and your kitchen or set up in a corner of your bedroom.

Don't Get Distracted

When I first started working at home, I had to make all these little deals with myself to force me to work. There were always about a million other distractions calling out to me and it seemed like I could go for days without doing anything productive if left to my own devices. I started myself off on a modest plan that required me to do one work-related thing per day. This didn't seem like so much to ask—one pitch letter in the mail, one follow-up phone call, one small piece of prose. Then I was free to go on my merry way—to talk on the phone, go for a walk, hang out with friends who worked nights.

Once I got the one-a-day plan under my belt, I got a little tougher on myself. I decided it wasn't too much to ask to spend a half day working on things, especially since some of them didn't take very long. Then a surprising thing happened: I started to have more work to do. So I'd work a little longer, stay at my desk a little later.

> "On the days when your lawyer friends are taking week-long ski trips at high season and you're thinking about canceling your cable TV or even selling your TV to make ends meet, you've got to take a deep breath, remember what you're made of, and keep working because things will get better."
>
> —Jennifer, 29, self-employed for three years

Motivation (Self-Bribery) Techniques

1. *Promise yourself a reward for working a few more hours—a snack, a long phone call, a bath, an hour in front of the TV.*
2. *Remind yourself that if you don't do it, it's not going to get done.*
3. *Remind yourself what your goals are and how hard you've already worked to reach them.*
4. *Sit at your desk as though you're going to work, then pay your bills or read a magazine article that pertains to your work—once you've been at your desk a while, start working.*
5. *Go online and look for information you can use for your work.*
6. *Look at the classified ads and remind yourself of all the jobs you wouldn't want to have working for someone else.*
7. *Drink something with caffeine in it.*
8. *Turn on some music if it won't distract you too much.*

Eventually I didn't have to force myself to do anything because it had become a routine.

Admittedly, it can be hard to glue yourself to your desk chair on a beautiful day in the summer. Then you look outside the next day and it's just as beautiful. It seems hard to justify staying indoors and working when the sun seems to be beckoning you out for a bike ride. But think of it this way: If you worked for someone else, you'd be inside at your desk all day. So just make yourself part of the working world who has to look out the window and pine for the weekend. If you can be flexible with your hours, take advantage of it. But don't sacrifice building your business for the sake of a few hours in front of the TV or an all-day happy hour.

Take Some Time Off

After all the talk about how motivated and disciplined you need to be to make it in the business world, the last thing you may be considering is taking a breather. But do it anyway. The only thing that can threaten your future productivity is total burnout. You're young and you can take a pretty brutal work schedule, but just remember to stop yourself before you hurdle over the brink of mental breakdown.

This goes for the short term as well as the long term. There's no point is nailing yourself to your desk at eleven o'clock at night if all you're doing is coming up with ways to stay awake. This would be an excellent time to eat something, sleep a little, and recharge your batteries. And in the longer term, cut yourself some slack. Sure, there will be some weeks when you'll work seven days and nights to finish something or launch something off the ground. But if you work fourteen days in a row, take a day off in the middle of the week and don't feel bad about it. You can't go anywhere with a dead battery.

What If I'm Not Self-Employed?

Even if you're not working for yourself and never plan to, you should understand how self-employment works. The workplace is changing and you never know where you'll find yourself later. You may have a boss now, but you'll always be your own boss, first and foremost. You can also learn from the following to guarantee yourself a better experience in the business world.

- Get computer literate. You've probably worked with computers, and you can use this as a basis to learn a little more and really outshine the competition.
- Set up a workspace for yourself at home. You never know when your job might require you to telecommute. If you already have a computer, invest in a modem. Not only will it give you Internet access, but it will also allow you to send information back and forth to work. So some days you might even be able to avoid the office altogether.
- Learn how to manage your finances. This includes doing your taxes and keeping track of your spending. If, some day, you decide to branch out on your own, you'll already understand

the financial basics. They get more complicated when you're self-employed, but if you have a foundation, you'll be able to add to your bed of knowledge. There's plenty of instruction about finance in the second half of this book.

- Become a reporter. Learn how to do thorough research and get comfortable cold-calling people for information. The more you do it, the easier it will get. Information gathering is an important part of any job search or entrepreneurial venture. If you learn how to ask a few good questions, you'll be able to maximize the time you request of other people. And learning how to get information quickly at the library or online will help you go from panic to comfort in any situation with which you're not familiar.

8

ALTERNATIVES

Volunteer, Travel, Give Something to the World

If getting your first job looks like it will become a two-year odyssey into finding your inner self, you might think about taking a different tack. There are many alternatives to starting in a job right away. You can enrich yourself and gain some valuable experiences and skills by pursuing some less traditional paths.

Organizations like the Peace Corps and Teach for America will allow you to spend a couple years working to help other people and gain important training and skills in the process. Employers look favorably on these experiences because they show your commitment to a project and your broadened bed of experience. There's nothing wrong with postponing the more traditional job search for a bit, especially if there's an alternative you'd really like to pursue now.

One- to Two-Year Commitment

These volunteer opportunities are divided into two categories according to the type of work you'll be doing and the kinds of skills you'll gain from the experience. The first group includes the Peace Corps, AmeriCorps USA, and AmeriCorps VISTA. These are jobs where you're placed in a community, either domestically or internationally, and you work to create better situations and solve problems. The second group includes Teach for America, the Japanese Exchange and Teaching Program, and WorldTeach. They are focused on teaching here or in other countries and will help you develop a slightly different set of skills. But training and skills aside, all of these programs will provide you with an unforgettable, valuable opportunity for personal enrichment.

Volunteer Programs

Peace Corps

If you have visions of faraway places and a desire to see the immediate product of your labors, you should consider the Peace Corps—termed "The toughest job you'll ever love." You could be teaching dental hygiene and health care, teaching math to students, or working with wildlife and crops. It's not for the meek. You'll work and live in a foreign environment, and the workday doesn't end at five. Be prepared for total immersion.

Peace Corps assignments take you to parts of the world with unrivaled natural beauty and cultures you've never experienced—in more than ninety developing countries—but they're not a vacation. Assignments last for two years, plus an additional three months of training that you complete beforehand. Host countries need volunteers to teach a variety of subjects, as well as people to help with public health and agricultural and environmental development.

Peace Corps assignments include transportation to and from

the country where you'll serve plus a monthly allowance to cover food and housing, twenty-four vacation days a year, and possible deferment of student loans. Dental and medical care are also included. After your twenty-seven-month service, there is a $6,075 "readjustment allowance," which can fill in the gap while you're looking for a job when you return.

How To Apply. When applying, you'll be asked about preferences of countries. The more flexible you're willing to be, the better chances you'll have of being placed.

Give yourself a good year of lead time. You should begin the application process the year before you'd like to serve in the Peace Corps. According to the Peace Corps, the best time to apply is between September and March for the following year, since most training begins in the summer.

Call or write to:

PEACE CORPS
Room 8500
The Paul D. Coverdell Peace Corps Headquarters
1111 20th Street, NW
Washington, D.C. 20526
(800)424-8580
online: www.peacecorps.gov

AmeriCorps USA

AmeriCorps sends volunteers into selected communities to help with the nation's educational, public safety, and environmental problems. The goal is to produce lasting change. Most AmeriCorps USA members serve at existing or newly created local nonprofits, with some working at national or federal organizations. You could be working on local environmental cleanup, teaching a child to read, or working on a number of individual projects designed to help. Teach for America is an AmeriCorps program, as is AmeriCorps VISTA, discussed below.

All AmeriCorps members receive an allowance to cover living expenses, as well as health insurance. The programs also offer an education voucher for $4,725, which can be used to pay for past student loans or future educational expenses. You must serve a full year to receive it.

To get information on AmeriCorps USA programs or Ameri-Corps VISTA, contact:

**CORPORATION FOR NATIONAL AND
COMMUNITY SERVICE**
1201 New York Avenue, NW
Washington, D.C. 20525
Phone: (800)942-2677
Online: www.americorps.org

AmeriCorps VISTA

There's an age-old proverb that says if you give a man a fish, he'll eat for a day, but if you teach him to fish, he'll eat for a life-time. That proverb more than bears itself out in VISTA programs.

VISTA brings volunteers to impoverished communities with the goal of developing long-term solutions to problems that affect the people who live there. The idea is that by developing viable solutions that low-income people can implement themselves within their communities, they will be on the road to permanent change and better conditions.

During the one-year program, you'll have freedom to set up local programs and work with community members to implement them. You could be applying for government funding, designing a community resource center, or finding sponsors for community programs. Part of your role is to look for community volunteers and train them to be leaders, so that problem solving can happen from within the communities.

VISTA volunteers receive a monthly allowance designed to cover living expenses in the community while they're serving and either a stipend of $1,200 or a $4,725 education voucher at the end of a year. All travel and training is paid for by VISTA, as well as health insurance.

How to Apply. You can apply for either a local assignment, in the community where you live, or a national assignment, anywhere VISTA places volunteers. For a local assignment, look up the Corporation for National Service in your state for a list of approved VISTA sponsors that you can apply to directly. Your completed application will be reviewed and qualified applicants will be nominated to positions that match their skills. For a national assignment, contact:

AMERICORPS VISTA
1201 New York Avenue, NW
Washington, D.C. 20525
Phone: (212)606-5000
Online: www.americorps.org/vista

What Skills Will I Get?

If you're interested in ultimately pursuing a government job, Peace Corps or AmeriCorps service will give you preference over other applicants. But these experiences will serve you well for any career. Employers respect your commitment to spending one or two years volunteering. You'll come away with good problem-solving abilities as well as skill at overcoming communication barriers.

Most Peace Corps assignments will involve some degree of teaching and you'll learn to give clear explanations and take a leadership role in instructing people. You'll also come away with a greater understanding of global or regional issues and a broadened view of the world. You'll have a better sense of your own ability to take on challenges and find ways to handle them.

These volunteer opportunities will give you hands-on experience in dealing with issues and problems in the communities where you work. AmeriCorps programs will give you skill in originating projects and coming up with alternate solutions.

Teaching Programs

Teach for America

By far, one of the most gratifying experiences is to see a light-bulb come on for a child who's never had something explained that way before. Teach for America fills a double role of giving you the chance to see the impact you make firsthand, and providing good teachers for schools that need them. Your fresh approach can be the difference between a child's staying in school and losing interest.

Teach for America is a national organization that places skilled recent college graduates in urban and rural public schools to teach for two years. Teach for America also makes an effort to keep its teachers involved in community and education issues through retreats, discussions, and newsletters. You'll be paid the regular starting salary for teachers in the district in which you're placed, in the range of $22,000–40,000. Through a relationship with AmeriCorps, Teach for America offers deferment of student loans plus an education award of $4,725.

Competition is stiff for the 2,000 positions. Assignments range from the inner city to outlying rural areas. Before you start, you'll spend six weeks preparing, which includes introducing yourself to the community and the school where you'll teach.

How to Apply. Students from all majors are eligible, but math, science, and foreign language majors are especially needed. The application process includes a written application and interview, as well as a discussion group and sample teaching session. You also need to provide letters of reference.

Applications are accepted until early April for the following fall. Request an application at:

TEACH FOR AMERICA
315 West 36th Street
New York, NY 10018
Phone: (800)832-1230
Online: www.teachforamerica.org

JET—Japanese Exchange and Teaching Program

JET is sponsored by the Japanese government, the Ministry of Education in Home and Foreign Affairs. It's a year-long program of about thirty-five hours per week, starting in July each year. You need to choose between the two programs offered, and depending on your language skills, one might be a better match for you than the other.

The teaching program, called ALT (Assistant Language Teacher), places you in a school or on a board of education where you assist with English language classes, help train Japanese teachers, work to design and prepare materials to use in classrooms, and perform other duties related to English instruction. You don't need a prior knowledge of the Japanese language. Training is provided by the Ministry of Education.

The CIR (Coordinator for International Relations) program is slanted more toward helping with projects in local government offices that require editing and translation, as well as teaching English to government employees and helping with international exchange projects. You need to have a working knowledge of Japanese. Training is provided by the Council of Local Authorities for International Relations.

Housing is found for you by the institution that serves as your host and you're given a stipend of 3.6 million yen, which translates to approximately $31,000 per year, plus round-trip airfare.

How to Apply. To meet eligibility requirements, you must have a bachelor's degree, and be a U.S. citizen or legal resident.

You need to submit your application, which will ask for transcripts and letters of recommendation, by the December due date. If you're selected for an interview, you'll meet with someone at the embassy or consulate in your city early in the year. Once you're selected to participate, you'll need to provide a medical report, photos for your entry visa, and proof of graduation. For an application, call or write to:

JET
Embassy of Japan
2520 Massachusetts Avenue, NW

Washington, D.C. 20008
Phone: (202)238-6772
Online: www.us.emb-japan.go.jp/JET%202003/index.htm

WorldTeach

WorldTeach is a way to volunteer in countries that need your help, while having some time to explore and understand another culture. After completing a three- to four-week orientation, intensive language instruction, and teacher training, you'll teach for the summer, six months, or a full school year in a foreign country. Depending on your experience and the needs of the host country, you could be teaching in a primary or secondary school or in a university. WorldTeach has programs in China, Costa Rica, Ecuador, Namibia, Poland and the Marshall Islands. You'll live either in a dorm or an apartment, or with a host family.

This program gives you a chance to immerse yourself in a foreign culture and work closely with a group of five to seventy-five other volunteers. A great benefit of WorldTeach is that it follows the school schedule. You'll have weekends off as well as school vacations—ample time to travel.

To be eligible for a year-long program, you need to be a college graduate. You don't need foreign language or prior teaching experience, although you will be required to complete twenty-five hours of teaching English as a foreign language through World-Teach before you go.

WorldTeach charges fees of around $2,000 for summer programs and $5,000 for year-long programs. Scholarships are available. If you have student loans, you can defer repaying them while volunteering for WorldTeach.

How to Apply. The programs have rolling admissions, so you can apply any time before the deadline specified by your program, roughly six months before your program starts. You must complete three essays as part of the application, and include a resume, transcript, and letters of recommendation. An interview is part of the process. To get information on specific programs, write or call:

WORLDTEACH
Harvard Institute for International Development
79 John F. Kennedy Street
Cambridge, MA 02138
Phone: (800)4-TEACH-0
Online: www.worldteach.org

What Skills Will I Get?

These teaching programs will give you organizational skills and the ability to speak in front of groups and present material clearly. In the JET and WorldTeach programs, you'll gain an understanding of other cultures and learn how educational systems work in other countries. When teaching abroad, you'll deal with language barriers and find ways to overcome them. In the Teach for America program, you'll learn about community issues and educational needs here in this country.

These jobs also teach you to think on your feet and come up with creative solutions to problems. You'll learn to plan lessons, explain concepts, and take a leadership role. These skills will prepare you to continue in teaching or to work in business settings or jobs that require creative thinking.

Enrich Yourself Abroad

Do something else. Write some poems, see the world, climb mountains, trek through deserts, take a job that has nothing to do with your major—or your future. Think about traveling, working abroad, or even working as you travel. Consider volunteer opportunities and other programs that allow you to give something to the world around you.

If you're interested in working overseas, a good place to start is the International Employment Hotline. They have a newsletter that lists work opportunities and ways to get started on your job search abroad. Look online at www.internationaljobs.org/monthly.html for information. You might also consider applying to the programs listed below for overseas work experiences that are less than a year long. Think of these experiences as internships—places to learn, enrich yourself, and add skills and knowledge to your resume.

Council on International Educational Exchange

The Council on International Educational Exchange is a nonprofit educational organization designed to provide opportunities to work and study abroad. The experiences you have overseas will better prepare you for the working world here by enhancing your language skills, teaching you to cope with diverse situations, and giving you the knowledge of international cultures that could point your career search in a new direction.

CIEE's Work Abroad Program. CIEE programs range in length from three to six months and allow you to work in one of thirty-four countries. These aren't jobs like digging latrines—you could be picking grapes in the French wine country or serving sandwiches in a New Zealand café. CIEE provides you with a work permit, so you can work among the local citizens and learn about the culture from experiencing it firsthand. CIEE's housing office helps you locate jobs and put down roots in your new country, and an overseas contact gives help when needed.

How to Apply. Most countries have programs all year long, but some are more limited. You can choose many European countries, such as France, England, and Germany, or teaching programs in China or Thailand. Fees range depending on the country, but expect to pay $500 or more to enter the Work Abroad Program and as much as $1,500 for the teaching programs in Asia, as well as your own round-trip airline ticket and living expenses until your paychecks start the cash flowing.

You can write to CIEE or look at CIEE's Web site for more information and instructions on how to apply:

COUNCIL ON INTERNATIONAL EDUCATIONAL EXCHANGE
Work Abroad
633 Third Avenue
20th Floor

New York, NY 10017-6706
Phone: (800)40-STUDY
Online: www.ciee.org

CIEE's International Volunteer Projects. This is a way for you to volunteer on an environmental or community service project with an international team. These programs run in the summer for two to four weeks in communities in twenty-five countries in Europe, Asia, Africa, and North America. You have the benefit of choosing the project and country you'd like for your assignment. You also get the unique experience of working with people from other countries so you'll not only learn from the project you're working on, but from the people you're working with as well.

The volunteer efforts are organized by a national voluntary service organization, which is tied to volunteer organizations here, so there's an international exchange of volunteers between many countries.

While you're working abroad, you'll receive room and board from the host organization.

How to Apply. For all countries except Ghana and India, you pay a $300 fee for one two- to four-week project plus about $40 for insurance. Some projects require additional fees. You're responsible for paying your round-trip airfare and health insurance.

Any time after April, apply online for that year. The fee is refundable if you enroll in a program. After you fill out the application, you'll be placed in an assignment on a first-come, first-served basis between the end of April and the beginning of July. For more information or for special instructions for the Ghana and India programs, write to:

COUNCIL ON INTERNATIONAL EDUCATIONAL EXCHANGE
International Volunteer Projects
633 Third Avenue
20th Floor
New York, NY 10017-6706

Phone: (800)40-STUDY
Online: us.councilexchanges.org/opportunities/ivp/
index.html

Volunteers for Peace

VFP is a nonprofit organization in Vermont that places volunteers in international environmental work programs in thirty-five countries. VFP programs are unique in that you live and work with ten to twenty people in a cooperative situation, meaning you'll be dividing up your daily chores as well as your volunteer duties.

The international work camps are two- to three-week programs that are sponsored by an organization in a host country. Fees range from $200 to $400. While volunteering abroad, you'll get a chance to experience the social, cultural, and political climate of a foreign country while working on an environmental project. Generally these consist of restoration or agricultural projects designed to improve the conditions in a designated community.

How to Apply. Choose a program from the International Workcamp Directory (www.vfp.org/DirectoryIntro.htm#top) for the year you're applying and fill out an application in April or May. Contact Volunteers for Peace at:

VOLUNTEERS FOR PEACE
43 Tiffany Road
Belmont, VT 05730
Phone: (802)259-2759
Online: www.vfp.org

Getting Skills in School

The *most important thing* to consider when contemplating graduate school is whether you really want to go. Sounds obvious, but a lot of people enroll in graduate programs just to put off having to make the real decision about what to do after college. Graduate school, however, is a lot of work and not the best place to bide

"When I took the LSAT, I didn't really want to go to law school. But then I figured I might as well apply so I sent out a few applications. Then I got into one of the schools, and since I didn't have any other ideas about what to do after graduation, I went. Now I'm looking for jobs and I wish I had been more serious about being a lawyer when I was applying—so I could have studied harder for the test and applied to more schools because I think that would open more opportunities for jobs."
—Keith, 26, attorney

your time while you're coming up with a game plan.

The *second most important thing* to consider regarding graduate school is what you hope to get out of it. If you go into graduate school with your eyes wide open, you're not likely to be disillusioned when you're handed a diploma and expecting it to open doors. Some graduate degrees, like an M.B.A., will definitely get you a higher salary when you're done. Most applicants work for a couple years before beginning M.B.A. programs.

Other degrees, like a master's in most liberal arts subjects, offer little additional guarantee of a job or a big paycheck. If your chosen career doesn't require an advanced degree, you don't need to feel like a failure for simply choosing not to go to graduate school. But there are certainly reasons to consider such programs. One good case for pursuing a graduate degree is when you want to specialize in a subject area you didn't study in college. For example, if you want to go into an art curatorial field and you majored in math in college, you might consider going to grad school for a master's in art history. That way, when you apply for jobs, employers can see that you've taken a serious step in a direction that applies to the career you want to have.

Employers will respect your dedication to further study of a subject, so this could give you an edge over the competition. Advanced degrees in subjects like mechanical engineering, computer science, film, or teaching will give you technical knowledge that you can use on the job. There can be direct career applications of these degrees.

Another good reason to go to graduate school is if your career requires an extra degree. For example, you need an M.D. to be a doctor and a law degree to be an attorney. If you're pursuing careers that require advanced study, the question isn't whether to go, it's *when* to go. In many fields, however, even after completing advanced study of a subject, you'll still need to go out and gather some skills to make yourself hirable. You can choose to do this before you start graduate school, during school, or after you're done. So your main decision becomes when to go.

When to Go

One argument for starting graduate school right after college is that you're already in school mode. You're well versed in study techniques and your academic record may be your biggest accomplishment to date. Plus, if you apply to school right away, your professors will still remember you when you ask them for letters of recommendation. As long as you know what you hope to get out of grad school, there's no harm in starting early, especially if it will be a long course of study. If you're planning to get a Ph.D. or an M.D., you might want to get going sooner rather than later, just so you're not in school when you're 40.

On the other hand, going to graduate school is not just signing up for more undergrad classes with higher course numbers. It's a whole different animal. It's a lot of work and can get quite expensive. The main argument in favor of waiting before starting grad school is that you'll have time to pinpoint exactly what you want from the experience, if you don't know yet. If you wait, you might have a better idea of how you'll integrate grad school with your work experiences when you're shaping your career.

For some fields, the standard is to wait a few years. An M.B.A. degree is a good example of this. Most people in graduate business schools have worked a couple years and are following a directed program of study that they'll use when they go back to work. That doesn't mean you can't apply right out of college—it just means most people don't. You need to know what the standard is in your field because it might be harder to compete for business school admission when your fellow applicants have a few years' work experience under their belts and you have none. Again, this doesn't mean it can't be done—it just means you should know the lowdown when you start applying.

What to Study

Definitely give this some thought. Deciding on a graduate course of study has a much bigger impact on your career than picking a major in college. After you devote one, three, six, or more years to graduate study, you should plan on working in a related field. So undergo a selection of graduate programs carefully, considering the careers people have when they finish. Call up schools you're interested in and ask where their graduates work. See if you can get a few alumni referrals and call them up. Find out what they got out of the program and how hard or easy it was for them to find a job afterward. Also get your letters of recommendation lined up even if you're not planning on applying for a few years. You don't have to ask that the letters be written now, but do keep in touch with the professors you'll want to write letters for you later.

Consider different types of programs. If you want to make documentaries, you could get an advanced degree in film to learn how to complete your projects or you could study business to understand how to budget and fund them. Consider which program you'd like better and which would give you a better start to your career.

Then take your application process seriously, starting with the standardized tests and applications. Don't hesitate to reapply if you don't get into the school you want or to defer if you get accepted but aren't sure you're ready to go yet. The point is that you want graduate school to give you the best possible platform for launching your career. So choose a school, a program, and a course of study that will provide a good launching pad.

GETTING A LIFE

While you're busy getting your career life in order, it's only fair to indulge yourself in the rest of what life has to offer. Just because you're dealing with job issues doesn't mean you want to sit in a dark part of your parents' garage counting the penny collection you've had since you were nine. You can get your own place, be your own boss, take care of your finances, find some transportation, and live.

Getting a life requires participation but not much else in the way of supplies. You don't need binders and spreadsheets to track your spending. You won't need graphs of your checking account or a map of all the places you've driven your car during the past year. But as you put your life in order, do yourself a favor and get a file cabinet and a handful of manila folders. It's easy, it's quick, and, most important, it will allow you to create the illusion of being organized without very much effort. You see, having a file cabinet will give you a place, other than the floor or the trash, to put things like old bills, receipts, and copies of insurance policies.

You don't have to organize, collate, transcribe, or otherwise make sense of what goes into the folders. You just have to put all your car payment stubs, insurance information, receipts for gas, and bills for service and repairs into the folder brilliantly marked "Car." In no particular order, with no particular flair for neatness. Then, if or when you need them, you'll know where to look. You need not have an actual file cabinet to make this system work. If you'd prefer a stack of ten shoeboxes in your closet, that will work too.

Here are some ideas of folders you might like to have:

- Job—job search information, lists of contacts, benefits packages from work
- Car—insurance, repairs, payment coupons
- Apartment—copies of lease, renter's insurance, correspondence with landlord
- Health insurance—bills, copies of health plan provisions, any changes to plan
- Bank—statements, canceled checks
- Taxes—last year's return, anything you may need for next year's
- Investments—mutual fund prospectuses, statements, CD account information
- Retirement—information about 401(k)s, IRAs, other retirement accounts
- Utilities and phone bills—speaks for itself
- Credit cards—bills, information that comes with any new cards
- Frequent flier (if you're on a program like this)—mileage statements, travel coupons
- Major purchases—receipts, user manuals, warranty information
- School—student loan payment information, transcripts you may need later

And now, properly prepared with filing space to document your foray into life, you begin.

9

YOUR BUDGET

Do I Have to Clip Coupons?

A household budget sounds like something Carol Brady would use to make sure she still had enough corn dogs to feed her six kids by the end of the month. It conjures up an image of ladies with beehive hair in the supermarket line, tendering raggedy coupons to save seven cents on cat food. And it doesn't seem vaguely realistic that you should say no to a night on the town with friends because your budget won't permit it. That's almost as bad as saying your mommy said you couldn't go. The whole point of making it on your own is to be able to do what you want whenever you want. Only now, you're done with college and someone's actually paying you. Isn't the cash supposed to flow? Are you really supposed to start comparing cans in the market to see if the 36-ounce jar of mayonnaise is cheaper per ounce than the 24-ounce jar?

No. And yes. Yes, you definitely have to figure out a way to live within your means. But no, you don't have to carry a calculator down the condiment aisle in the market. Just buy the big jar and be done with it. Yes, you need to know what you spend so you can do one of two things: hold out for a job that allows you to continue your spending habits, or bring your spending habits in line with your somewhat-shy-of-whopping paycheck, such as it is. But no, you don't have to carry around a little notepad and write down every pack of gum you buy under the category of miscellaneous. In fact, why not get rid of the concept of the Carol Brady budget altogether? "Spending target" is a much more gratifying term. It sounds more like a goal than a restriction.

That way, when you turn down the big night out and tell your friends it interferes with your spending target, you'll be greeted with respect, like you're on to some challenging fiscal dart game.

Scoring Goals

Probably the best thing about having a spending target is it allows you to set goals for things you want to do or buy, and to save the money to meet your goals. If you decide you want to put a CD player in your car or start investing in mutual funds or go on a snowboarding weekend, you'll be able to work it into your finances instead of melting your credit card. And that way, living within your means becomes a way to do more of what you want to do, not less.

Another plus to hitting your spending target is that you won't go into debt. Staying out of debt and paying off any obligations you have now will save you thousands in interest that might as well go toward meeting your goals. So again, having a spending target is a way to meet your goals. There's a pattern here.

Finally, sticking to a spending target will give you a feeling of financial well-being that will contribute to your self-worth and overall sense of . . . okay, we don't need to go there. In short, you'll figure out where your money goes, see where you can cut some corners, keep your finances under control, and have more money to spend on the things you want.

So in order to begin targeting your spending, start by
making a list of big things
you'd like to buy. This may
sound contrary to the idea of
saving money, but the idea is
that if you have a list of things
you want, it will be easier to
give up on things that aren't
really necessary so you can
meet your goal. The other pos-

> *"I got this weekend job sweeping leaves off the tennis courts at a country club. It could not have been more mindless, but after about forty weekends, I'd saved a hundred bucks here, a hundred bucks there, and had enough to take a two-week trip."*
>
> —Megan, 24

sibility is that if you put everything, from new skis to boxing
gloves, on a list, you may later decide you don't want some of
them after all.

Playing by the Numbers

It seems like you can always find someone willing to toss out
mathematical equations to help you estimate how much of your
pay to use for various expenses. The numbers are good guidelines, but it's not worth making yourself crazy if your numbers
don't fit.

One rule of thumb applies to rent, with the guideline of spending no more than 40 percent of your take-home pay on the place
you hang your hat. Another goal is to spend 15 percent of your
take-home pay on everything related to your car. That includes
insurance, car payments, gas, parking, and tolls. You're also supposed to be able to comfortably save 5 percent of your take-home
pay each month.

It doesn't seem so bad to have 60 percent covering rent, car,
and savings because there's so much left over. The problem is,
these numbers can vary depending on what city you live in, what
your transportation needs are, and what else you have to accomplish within your spending target. But they're a good starting
place.

Throwing Darts at the Spending Target

Working up a spending target doesn't need to take an entire week-end. Every dollar you bring home has one of two destinies: It will be spent or saved. So all you need to do is figure out where the money for spending will go and where the rest will be saved. The money you spend will pay for necessities like rent, utilities, car pay-ments, insurance if you don't have it through work, clothes, and food. Then you'll spend money on incidentals, like laundry and dry cleaning, haircuts, stamps, car washes—things you pay for on a reg-ular basis but don't really count in your rent and utilities calcula-tions. Then there's money you spend just to have a life—on movies, dinners out, poker games, coffee.

To begin with, you need to know how much you'll be bringing home each month so you'll know how much you have to spend or save. The table below will give you a breakdown of your approx-imate monthly take-home pay, which will differ from state to state due to local taxes, at various annual incomes. This way, if you're out looking for jobs and apartments on the same day, you can make sure the numbers add up without carrying an abacus.

Here's about What You'll Take Home						
Annual Income	$20,000	$24,000	$30,000	$35,000	$40,000	$60,000
Tax as % of Income	15%	15%	15% on first $23,350, 28% on rest	15% on first $23,350, 28% on rest	15% on first $23,350, 28% on rest	15% on first $23,350, 28% on rest
Monthly Pre-Tax Pay	$1,667	$2,000	$2,500	$2,917	$3,334	$5,000
Monthly Take-Home Pay	$1,416	$1,700	$2,046	$2,346	$2,646	$3,834

These numbers are in the ballpark of what you'd take home if there was no withholding for health insurance plans through work or other withholdings such as a 401(k) contribution. So in all likelihood, your take-home pay will be a bit lower. Now that you know how much you have to work with, you can start allocating it to your necessary expenses, your discretionary ones, and your saving fund.

If you've been on your own for a little while, you may already have quite a long paper trail to help you estimate what your expenses are. If you're just beginning this journey into life after college, you may need to spend the next couple of months gathering small slips of paper to identify what you spend.

Start by gathering together a year's worth of credit card bills, your checkbook register, and a couple of utility bills to use as samples. You can either grab a pad of paper or enter all this information into your computer using a program like Quicken, Microsoft Money, Managing Your Money, or Simply Money, which allows you to assign categories to each check you write, each cash expense, and each charge on your credit card. Either way, the idea is to look at what you spend regularly as well as what you spend sporadically and come up with a monthly average.

Make a list of things you know you'll spend money on every month. Your list will include rent, which is a fixed expense. If you write checks at the market, add up a couple months' worth and compute your average for one month. Do the same with utility bills. Car payments and insurance payments are set in stone, so they're easy to calculate on a monthly basis. Even if you pay your car insurance twice a year, figure out what it costs you per month.

Slightly Brady

Below is a worksheet that you can use to jog your memory about how you spend money each month. It's divided up according to expenses you must pay for to survive, as in food and rent, and expenses that are discretionary in the sense that you don't need to

Necessary Expenses	Additional or Occasional Expenses
Rent	Cable TV
Car payment	Newspaper
Car insurance	Cab fare
Car registration	Magazines
Phone	Charitable donations
Cellular phone	Parking
Electricity bill	New glasses/contacts
Gas bill	Eating out
Bus/subway fare	Movies/theater/concerts
Gas for your car	Bottled water delivery
Groceries	Haircuts
Clothes for work	Cable modem/DSL
Health insurance	Renter's insurance
Emergency fund	Museum or club membership
Savings	Doctor/dentist
Student loan payment	Gym membership
Internet service	Dry cleaning
	Apartment cleaning
	Clothes
	Car maintenance
	Investments
	Friends' wedding/birthday gifts
	Credit card payment
	Travel/vacations

have all of them all the time, but you'll probably want some. And when you're trying to figure out how you can cut corners, you may give up some of the additional expenses because you won't be able to live without the necessary ones. Some of these things may be provided by your job, such as health insurance or a cellular phone. Only fill in the sections where you pay for the expenses yourself.

If you're going to use one of the above-mentioned personal finance programs on your computer, you'll have to enter about a year's worth of expenses by category, so that the program can give you your monthly spending averages. If you don't have a year's worth of bills and deposits handy, collect them as this year progresses, so you can use them for next year.

Running the Numbers

First calculate how much you already spend or plan to spend on the necessary expenses. Then figure out how much you spend on the rest. Add it up and divide by twelve. If your monthly total is less than or equal to your paycheck, you're in good shape. You've hit your basic spending target.

Now your goal is to stay within your target range by paying your necessary expenses and balancing your additional ones so you always end up in the black. If you want to do more of one thing one month, you'll have to do less of something else. If you want to join a gym, you may want to eat out less. If you want to subscribe to four newspapers, you may decide you don't need so many magazines.

The point is, anything's possible. It just requires trade-offs between the things you spend money on now and the things you'd like to spend money on in the future. For example, you might decide to change your health insurance deductible from $1,000 to $2,000 since you're young and healthy. Then you might use the money for a gym membership so you'll stay that way. Since you can't have everything, prioritize what's most important and get rid of expenses you can do without.

Self-Worth

If you're self-employed or work on a per-project or contract basis, you'll take a slightly different approach. You probably don't just receive one paycheck at the end of each month, so you need to know how much to earn for yourself. In essence, you'll be working backward, figuring out what your necessary, fixed expenses are and how much you're likely to spend on additional ones. That will be your earning target. So if you tally up the commissions or paystubs for the month and you've met your target, you'll know you'll be able to pay all your bills.

Cash Is Liquid

There must be some law of financial dynamics that proves that money can seep out through the cracks in your wallet and never be seen or heard from again. It's easy to spend cash and have no idea where it went.

If you like the idea of carrying around a little notebook and whipping it out each time you buy a scone to monitor what you spend cash on, knock yourself out. This method will certainly yield an accurate total. But a less painful way is to ask for receipts and stuff them in your wallet. Even if you buy a Coke at McDonald's, ask for a receipt. Just pretend it's for business. There are enough people who have to collect receipts everywhere they go that no one will look at you twice if you ask for a receipt. You just have to remember to do it.

When your wallet gets full, empty the receipts into an envelope and keep them until you've collected about a month's worth. Then divide them up. Most likely, they'll be receipts for food, coffee, drinks at a bar, magazines, parking, and cab, subway, or bus fare. Then see if certain patterns emerge. You may be spending $50 a week at the market and thinking you're saving money on restaurant meals, but when you look at your receipts, you may find that you're spending another $50 on snacks, drinks, and lunch at your desk while all those great sandwich supplies rot in your fridge at home. You'd be surprised.

The idea isn't to put yourself on some kind of austerity plan. You don't have to start walking through the snow in winter to avoid cab fare. The point is simply to identify where the money goes so you'll have some sense of control over your spending. You may notice a pattern, and you may decide there are some things you could do without. If you buy a large coffee every day on your way to work for $1.95, that's over $500 a year. You might decide to invest $30 in a coffeemaker and have your java at home a couple days a week. Your small, everyday habits can add up.

If the Numbers Don't Add Up

If you divided by twelve and the number on your calculator bears no resemblance to the one on your paycheck, you'll need to do some adjusting. If you thought you could afford a one-bedroom apartment but forgot to consider what food, lights, and heat would cost, you might reconsider and invest in a roommate. If a $399 car lease sounded manageable but you forgot about insurance, gas, maintenance, and bridge tolls, you might opt for a less expensive model.

Even the necessary expenses can be reduced. For example, your utilities can add up to quite a heap, especially if you live in a place that's freezing in the winter and boiling in the summer. If you can stand it, a fan uses less electricity than an air conditioner. And for keeping warm at night, it will cost you less to use a space heater in your room than to heat your whole apartment with central heating. Throwing an extra heavy blanket on the bed doesn't hurt either. Of course, if you live in a place where the heat just comes on (or not), you may have to find other ways to save.

The battle of the long-distance phone companies can work in your favor as well. Because AT&T, Sprint, and MCI are all trying to win your business, they'll offer you some sweet deals to win you over. If you can identify where most of your long-distance dollars go, like calls to your friend upstate or your parents across the country, you can get a long-distance plan that will make the most of your calling habits and save you money in the process.

Fixed Expenses Are Good Ones to Reduce

Your fixed expenses are the ones you'll have for the rest of your life, in one form or another. This makes them good candidates for cost cutting. Saving three bucks on a haircut you get four times a year isn't as important as buying energy-saving appliances that will save you money every time you use them.

You might also try to get some of your expenses covered by your employer if you find that a large percentage of what you spend is going toward work-related things. It's a good idea to ask your employer to take this into account and bump up your salary or take on part of the expense, such as paying for parking. For example, if you work in San Francisco and live in an outlying suburb, you may be making a hefty commute, paying for bridge crossing every day, plus paying a large tab at the parking garage in the building where you work. Try to get your salary to make up for some of these expenses. It doesn't hurt to ask.

Don't Be Too Proud to Clip

By clipping coupons, you can save money on groceries, dry cleaning, car washes, car maintenance, and apartment cleaning. Coupons are everywhere. They come to your apartment in envelopes addressed to Resident, they come on the back of grocery receipts, they come with the Sunday paper. Some supermarkets even offer paperless coupons in the form of discounts on red-tagged products in the store. Many dry cleaners offer substantial discounts that you can use every week. The more coupons you use, the more they send you.

If you save $10 a week on dry cleaning you'd have to pay for anyway, that's over $500 by the end of the year. Same with groceries. Many supermarkets offer double coupon value, so if you're buying the cereal you'd be buying anyway, you can save twice the money, which definitely adds up in the long run. If you save $8 a week at the market, that's another $400 a year. Since you're buying the groceries and getting your clothes cleaned anyway, there's no reason you can't save a few bucks in the process.

Another good way to save money at the market or drugstore is to buy the plain-wrap, generic brands. When it comes to things like canned crushed tomatoes and frozen spinach, the generic brand is virtually identical to the big names. Similarly, facial tissue and cotton balls rarely have any defining features that makes a name brand preferable. Unless you have an overriding preference about where you blow your nose, the generic brand will probably do the trick and save you money.

Inexpensive Enrichment

The extras in life don't come cheap, but fear not. There are ways to stretch your dollar here as well. If your job offers you certain extracurricular perks, take advantage of them. Perks can be in the form of bagels every other Friday morning or a gym in the building. Whatever they are, include them in your life.

Also think about volunteering. Museums, environmental groups, and charitable organizations can all use an extra hand. Many of these organizations sponsor events, so if you volunteer to be a ticket taker at a charity auction or serve drinks at a museum exhibit opening or escort a group of kids to a charity event at the circus, you can go along for the ride. Plus, it's a great way to meet people.

You can also pick up an entertainment coupon book that gives you discounts off admission to theaters, amusement parks, and movies. If you're in graduate school, take full advantage of your student I.D. for discounts when you go to movies and plays, when you make travel reservations, and when you subscribe to magazines and newspapers.

Also put yourself on mailing lists from bookstores that have au-
thor readings and book signings and cafés that have poetry nights
or live music. Pick up the local paper that lists clubs with live music
or bands. You may end up paying a cover charge, but far less than
you'd pay for a concert.

Of course, for truly cheap entertainment you could always stay
home and play Scrabble. But saving money doesn't have to turn
you into a hermit.

Signs You're Not Getting Out Enough

1. Your friends' answering machines regularly cut you off for
   leaving messages that are too long.
2. You and Rover/Fifi are on the same nap schedule.
3. You read all your junk mail.
4. You find yourself having a forty-five-minute conversation with
   a telemarketer who sounded cute and switching to a long-
   distance company you've never heard of.
5. You have a pizza topping rotation list.
6. You've learned to identify the sound of the mail carrier opening the boxes to put in your mail.
7. You're thinking about getting a pet hamster for late-night
   entertainment.
8. You don't answer the phone during a *Cheers* episode you've
   seen ten times already.
9. You've given names to your plants.
10. You don't remember what the outside of your building looks
    like.

Fitness—Your Target $ Rate

Exercise can be an expensive pursuit, especially if you like to do
more than one thing. Granted, if you're a runner, a pair of shoes
is all the equipment you need. But if you like to Rollerblade and
do a little yoga and maybe some cardio jazz, and you like to step

on a stair-climber and maybe take a boxing class, how can you do all this on a budget? First of all, shop around. If you are an alumnus of a college nearby, your alumni card might get you a cheap membership to the campus gym.

Many gyms will let you try out a class for free, so check out a few places. Find one you like, rather than picking the first one you see and hating it, then buying a mountain bike instead. When you've found a place you like, ask for a bargain. Most gyms have an initiation fee and a monthly plan. See if you can strike a deal— a lower monthly fee if you agree to be a member for two years, or a reduced initiation fee if you recruit a friend to join, two-for-one. Don't get wheeled and dealed into joining if you're not sure you like the place just because the sales rep tells you it has to be TODAY in order to get the great deal you're being offered. If you come back a few weeks later and look interested, they'll have a deal for you then as well.

Moonlighting

Try as you might, there's only so much mileage to be squeezed from your lowly paycheck. And there are still things you want to do, like take a scuba class, and things you have to do, like pay off your Visa bill. If you feel industrious, you can take on some part-time work to supplement your cash flow.

Sometimes it helps to think of your extra job as your trip fund or your ski boot fund. That way, instead of being used to pay your gas bill, your moonlighting money gets earmarked for something fun. Let your paycheck take care of your gas bill. Below are some options you might consider.

- *Tutoring*, either independently or through a company that offers tutoring services. This can be an opportunity to use your knowledge in subjects that you don't get to use on the job, like math, writing, or foreign language. Post notices at schools and call companies that offer SAT prep courses.
- *Teaching a class*. You could teach tennis to a group of kids over

the weekends, aerobics at a local gym, or a college essay-writing class to high-school students.

- *Doing temp work.* If you have a job that leaves your weekdays free, a temporary employment agency can get you work that fits your schedule. You're free to turn down an assignment if you don't want to work on a particular day.

- *Taking care of kids.* You can babysit, which is sometimes as easy as putting the kids to bed and spending an evening in front of the TV. Have friends who work in big offices circulate a flyer for you. Post signs at the gym, or if you live in a big building, put notices in common areas.

- *Walking dogs.* Depending on what time you have to be at work and where you live, you could earn money by rounding up the dogs in the neighborhood and taking them for a twice-daily spin around the block so their owners don't have to. Post ads in your neighborhood, especially on streets where people walk their dogs.

- *Waiting tables or bartending.* This can be a cash-producing complement to a day job if you don't mind working nights, plus it allows you to be on your feet, talking to people, thinking about different things than you think about all day long at work.

- *Working in retail.* This can also be a job with flexible hours, allowing you to work weekends if this is when you have free time. You'll probably be eligible for store discounts, so if you have a passion for backpacking and know you'll be spending a lot on equipment, a job in an outdoor adventure store might fit the bill.

- *Giving your opinions.* Call companies that do market research and offer to participate in a focus group where they ask you questions about why you like certain products or services. They pay cash and typically meet evenings.

- *Working the phones.* Sign up with a telemarketing company that pays you on commission for what you sell. You can solicit alumni donations for your alma mater, newspaper subscriptions, or investor services. Ads for these jobs are everywhere.

- *Freelance writing.* Write articles for magazines or a local newspaper. If you have a particular area of knowledge, let that work for you. Call and pitch ideas. Also inquire whether they hire copy editors on a freelance basis—many publications do.

Profit for Pack Rats

It's amazing how much stuff piles up. You move it from place to place on the chance that you may need it someday. And then you never do. Having a yard sale is a good way to accumulate some cash and get rid of useless baggage. This is especially timely if you're planning to move. Rather than cart your useless belongings to a new apartment, spend a Sunday morning on the sidewalk, collecting cash for the books you've already read and the kitchen utensils you'll never use.

You can take books to used bookstores and textbooks to the campus bookstore if the class is still being taught. If you want to thin out your CD collection, look for music stores that will trade your used ones for cash.

And don't forget about online auction sites. Your useless Mighty Morphin Power Rangers action figures may be someone else's kitschy collection. Or that digital keyboard that you swore you'd learn to play could find its way into the hands of an appreciative new owner who is willing to pay to take it off your dusty shelf. Check out www .ebay.com or www.auctions .yahoo.com.

> *"Writing is the most important skill you need in today's world. But potential employers don't want to read your senior thesis. I started doing film and book reviews for the local paper and eventually built a decent portfolio of material. The local papers are usually looking for a stringer who can cover small events. You can get paid $25–$75 per piece depending on the assignment. Plus the movies make a great date."*
>
> —Ben, 29

10

STUDENT LOANS:
INTO THE BLACK

The Time Has Come

O kay, six months and counting. That's how long they give you after graduation before you start repaying your student loans. Barely enough time to say, "Pour me a tall one," and already you have to worry about who's buying.

The average graduate owes $17,000; think of it as the price tag that comes with your hat and tassel. Hey, and you get to keep the tassel, so think of it as a very expensive hat rental. It was all worthwhile, remind yourself, because the education you bought will serve you well in the years to come. Unfortunately, this doesn't make it any more fun to face the loan officer. If you find yourself screaming for someone to cut you some slack, relax. Someone has.

Welcome to the joys of the grace period. Take advantage of it—you get no extra points for paying early. And there are all kinds of interest rates and repayment periods that you can choose to fit your income. The grace period is a good time to look at what you owe and who you owe so when you have to begin paying, you have a plan. Your plan might be to hop the next train to the border, but there are a few others you should consider.

Your first step should be figuring out who extended you the loan. Here are the likely possibilities:

- Your school
- Sallie Mae (the Student Loan Marketing Association)
- The U.S. Department of Education
- Banks

If you don't know who your lender is, it doesn't mean your lender doesn't know who you are. You can find out who lent you the money by calling the Federal Student Aid Information Center Hotline at (800)4FED-AID.

Then look at the interest rate on each loan. If one loan carries a higher rate than another, you've just prioritized your repayment schedule. You'll pay more on the expensive (high interest) one and the minimum on the lower-interest loans. If you owe money on credit cards, factor their interest rates into your priority schedule.

Most lenders will work with you to determine what repayment schedule fits your current and expected income. You could pay the same amount each month for the length of your repayment period, or you could pay a graduated amount that increases when your income does. If you have more than one loan, you should consider loan consolidation, which allows you to lump all your loans together and then choose a repayment schedule.

How Loan Consolidation Works

Both Sallie Mae and the Department of Education have loan con-solidation programs that allow you to combine your loans and pay them back at lower rates over a time period that fits your budget. Check Sallie Mae's Web site at www.salliemae.org/manage/index

.html. The Department of Education's loan consolidation Web address is www.studentaid.ed.gov/PORTALSWebApp/students/english/consolidation.jsp?tab=repaying.

Sallie Mae Plan

You're eligible for loan consolidation during the grace period before repayment or after you've already begun repayment. Your combined eligible loans need to total $7,500 or more. There are four basic repayment options you can choose from. Base your choice on your income level right now and your expected income in the next three to five years. Also take into account other debts you might have, such as credit cards, and how long it will take you to pay them off.

- The **Level Payment Plan** divides your total loan into equal payments for the term of the loan. This is the least expensive option in the long run.
- The **Max-2 Option** allows you to pay only interest for the first two years, which keeps your payment low, then fixed payments for the remainder. You'll pay more than the level plan, but you'll get a break when you may need it most, during the first two years.
- The **Max-4 Option** has you pay only interest during the first four years, slightly higher payments during years five and six, then your highest payments from year seven onward, the same amount per year. This costs the most in the long run, but can give you the lowest payments in the years when you need it.
- The **Income Contingent Plan** allows you to pay a portion of your income, 4 to 25 percent, as long as that covers the interest that accrues. Again, the less you pay, the longer it will take and the more interest you'll pay in the end.

Under all four of these repayment plans, you're eligible for two other options. Under a Direct Repayment Plan, Sallie Mae will reduce your interest rate for choosing to automatically debit your checking account each month. Under the Smart Rewards Program, your interest rate gets reduced 1 percent after you make the first forty-eight payments on time. Both of these incentives work in your favor because they shorten the time you'll spend repaying your loan and thereby save you money.

Department of Education Plan

Not wanting to stifle you, the Department of Education puts no minimum or maximum on the amount you can consolidate. Your repayment term can be up to twenty-five years and you can choose from the following programs:

- The **Standard Repayment Plan** divides your loan equally over ten years and has a fixed payment of at least $50 each month. You'll save the most in interest.
- The **Extended Repayment Plan** is one you might choose if you have substantial loans. This plan allows you to extend your repayment period from twelve to thirty years, and pay a lower fixed payment than if you paid it back in less time under the standard plan. You end up paying more interest the longer the repayment term you choose.
- The **Graduated Repayment Plan** gives you the lowest payments at first, with increases every two years. Your repayment term can be from twelve to thirty years and you'll pay more interest on the longer terms.
- The **Income Contingent Plan** allows you to pay based on your income level, rising (or falling) as your income changes. You have up to twenty-five years to repay the loan, accruing more interest with the longer term.

Like any other debt, the longer you take to repay your loan, the more you'll end up paying in interest by the time you're done.

How to Decide on a Plan

The repayment plan you'll choose will greatly depend on the amount you originally borrowed. This in turn affects your monthly payments under the various plans. If you owe less than $15,000 and your income permits it, you should try to pay the loan off as quickly as possible while accruing the least amount of interest. The standard or level payment plans allow you to do this.

On the other hand, if you have other debts to contend with, such as your credit cards, which typically carry much higher interest rates, you should take care of those first. Choosing a longer term will keep your payments low so you'll have more to put toward your cards.

Finally, if your loans are costing you so much each month that you'll need to live off your credit cards or contribute nothing to your savings account, you should choose a longer repayment term or graduated plan to lower your monthly bill. Even if that means you'll be paying more interest, it makes sense to keep your sanity, and the rest of your finances, intact.

The key isn't necessarily to pay less interest, it's to find the plan that fits your finances.

Why You Might Not Want to Consolidate

When you have several loans at different rates, you may get the best deal by consolidating. Or you may not. It will depend on what loans you have and what special subsidies or interest rates accompany them.

- If you have a subsidized loan, you may be able to get lower interest rates during certain periods, like the first few years. If you combine these with other loans, you might not get the break.
- If you have very-high-rate and very-low-rate loans, consolidation will go for a happy medium rate that could cost you more in the long run. By keeping your loans separate or leaving the high-rate loan out of your consolidation package, you can pay the high interest early and take a longer term for the lower-interest loans.
- If you're planning to go back to school, ask in advance if you'll be able to stop the interest from accruing on your original loans

while you're in school. If this is impossible under certain consolidation programs, you might choose to keep your loans separate.

When You Don't Have to Pay

Depending on your situation, you might be able to *defer* your loan or qualify for *forbearance*, which allows you to pay over a longer period or stop making payments for a specified period. If you're going back to school or you have special circumstances, such as financial hardship, ask about deferment and forbearance.

Your lenders want to be paid back, so they'll work hard to come up with repayment options that work for you.

11

CREDIT CARDS AND THE ART OF REPAYMENT

You Owe It to Yourself

"I'm stimulating the economy," I tell myself with pride. If it weren't for me, the nightly news reports would lament that consumer spending was down, way down. Gotta do my part to keep the economic pendulum swinging. And what better way than buying tons of stuff and putting it on Mr. Visa's tab. Nutty Uncle Visa. The guy will buy anything. And everybody likes him. He's never refused service at a bar and he'll sign off on a whole ski weekend in a heartbeat. All I have to do is ask. His word is that good. It's nice to have someone special like that in your life.

Every time you think you've tapped your limit, you're happily informed that you can spend a little more. Hey, it's on the house. Visa's buying. Unless you have a wealthy relative who really is named Visa (no, Vito doesn't count), you could hit your limit with very little effort. But never fear, you'll open your mailbox to find more invitations: Charge it on Visa or other wealthy members of the clan, Cousin MasterCard, Aunt Amex. The spending frenzy can continue thanks to these folks. Welcome to the debt spiral—enjoy your visit but don't stay too long.

They don't even call it debt—they call it credit. Like they're giving you something great. It is great because it allows you to spend all kinds of money you don't have. They have confidence in you and, well, they should. When they extend your credit limit to ten grand, doesn't it mean they're certain you'll make eight times that your first year out of school? Go ahead, spend, spend. You can pay it back later. And so what if it's 19 percent interest. That's only a paltry 1.5 percent a month. "What's that to you, moneybags?" they might as well say.

The Plastic Monster

Credit cards. They'll put them in your mailbox, they'll set up booths on campus. It's easy to get a credit card while you're in school because you don't have to prove you have enough income. Once you get one card, the doors of purchasing are open to you. Credit card companies are willing to believe either that you're on the dole from your parents (which is why they often ask about their incomes on the applications) or that you'll be able to make the minimum payment and pay a lot of interest before you're done.

Since the credit card companies probably won't rush in and offer debt management courses any time soon, you need to work out a debt control system for yourself.

Look at Fees and Grace Periods

For any card you have, it's important to know what they're charging you and when. If you pay your card balance in good faith each month, you can almost always get your annual fee removed. But what about the other little fees you find at the bottom of your bill each month?

The main culprit is a *late fee* that you'll be assessed if your pay-

> *"I got a credit card from an environmental group that had a green tree frog on it. It was fun using the card at first because everyone would ask me about it, and 10 percent of what I spent would go to the environmental group. Meanwhile it had one of the worst interest rates on the planet and I was starting to rack up debt. I had two other lower-rate cards in my wallet but I felt like I'd be letting down the endangered tree frog if I used another card."*
>
> —Ricky, 25

ment doesn't arrive by the due date. The problem is, the bill's due date can vary from month to month, within a few days. So you could go along thinking your bill is due on the eighth like it was last month, when it's really due on the fifth. Your next bill comes with a big $15 penalty. Always call and ask if these charges can be removed. Explain that you're a good customer and have been a cardholder for years. They'll usually remove the fee, "on a one-time basis."

Then there's the *grace period*, the amount of time you have before interest starts accruing. Some cards will set the interest meter the day you make a purchase, so even if you pay your bill in full each month, you'll still owe interest. Avoid these cards—why should you pay extra interest when you don't have to? The one exception is *cash advances*. When you use your credit card to get cash, interest starts accumulating on that day and you'll usually be charged a transaction fee as well.

Also be aware of when your *billing date* is for each card you have. If you charge something right after this month's billing date, you won't have to pay for it on your next bill—you'll be billed the following month. If you have more than one card, knowing your billing dates can help you get the most out of each card because you can juggle them and let your money earn interest in the bank in the meantime.

Teaser Rates

The upside of all this debt balancing is that as your credit record gets better and you've been able to show proof of repayment capability, you can get better loan rates. If you pay off your credit cards, you'll experience the pleasure of new offers streaming in from banks you've never heard of, several per week. They all want to be the one to receive your interest payments. While they are annoying, they may be worth a look, especially the ones that offer teaser rates as low as 4 or 5 percent annually.

One thing to be aware of is that teaser rates don't last forever. Read the fine print carefully and you'll find that regular rates, the high 18 percent ones, kick in after six months or so. This is okay if you'll have your balance paid off by then or if you can transfer it to another card with a low rate. There is no reason for loyalty to a card with high rates. Just make sure to read the terms.

Frequent Buyer/Flier/Diner Cards

There are just as many buyers' incentives out there as companies waiting for you to spend your hard-earned clams on them. Some are better than others. You can end up with free travel, long-distance calling minutes, free gasoline, money toward a car, or even cash back.

The main thing to keep in mind is how valuable the incentive they're offering is to you. It doesn't make sense to rush out and get a card that earns you long-distance dialing minutes if you never call outside your area code. But if you've gotten into the habit of charging and paying off your balance each month, these incentive cards can be a good deal. The reason you should pay these cards in full each month is because the free round-trip airfare is peanuts compared to the interest you'll rack up on the purchases it took to get you there.

Out of the Red . . .

Why should you pay more than the minimum balance? Here's a graphic example. Say you have $3,900 in credit card debt and make the monthly minimum payment—which credit cards typically calculate as 2 percent of the total amount you owe. It will take you *thirty-five years* to pay off that amount, assuming 18 percent annual interest. You'll also end up paying $10,097.40 in interest on that $3,900 for a total of $13,997. Enough to make you cut your cards or use them to tile your swimming pool? You could probably come up with a few hundred other uses for the ten grand in interest.

The amazing thing is, if you can scrape together a measly $10 a month extra and increase your payment, you'll save time and money. It will take you only six years to pay off the $3,900 and you'll only be paying $2,579 in interest for a grand total of $6,479. When you think in terms of bringing a bag lunch a couple days a month instead of going to the food court, it seems like little sacrifice. Don't forget that the $7,518 in interest you're saving is your money—and the difference between having it to use for rent or invest in a mutual fund is a mere ten bucks a month.

The worst thing about paying only the minimum balance is that you'll end up paying interest on the interest you racked up the month before—better to pay the card off and let your money *earn* interest in a savings account.

Paying an Extra $10 per Month Makes a Big Difference*		
Amount Charged on Card	$3,900	$3,900
Interest Rate	18%	18%
Amount Paid Each Month	Minimum balance, which is 2% of total amount owed	Minimum balance, which is 2% of total amount owed, plus an extra $10
How Long to Pay Off Card	35 Years	6 Years
Total Paid	$13,997	$6,479
Total Interest Paid	$10,097	$2,579

*Data provided by Bankcard Holders of America.

. . . And into the Black

Prioritize

- Make a list of what you owe, whether it's credit card debt, student loans, or IOUs to your parents.
- Pay off your most expensive loan first. If you owe money on two credit cards, one at 18.9 percent and another at 12.9 percent, make the minimum payment on the card with the lower rate and concentrate your resources on getting rid of the higher balance. This will save you money. Better yet, see if you can transfer your balance from the higher-interest card to the lower one and eliminate it completely.
- Avoid sending your monthly payment late. The late fee can tack on $15 or more per month and there's no sense in paying it when you can mark the due date on your calendar and pay on time.

Interest Rates and Annual Fees

- Check around and see if you're really getting the lowest interest rate. Often different banks have incentive programs, so switch your entire card balance to the card with the lowest rate. You can always switch again when the offer expires and regular rates kick in. While you're at it, ask if your existing credit card companies will lower your interest rate—often they will if you ask. To find out which credit card companies offer the lowest rates, call:

  Bankrate.com: (800)327-7717 (charges $5) or www. bankrate.com
  CardTrack: (800)344-7714 (charges $5) or www.cardweb.com/cardtrack

- Try to choose cards that do not charge annual fees. If that's not possible, call your credit card company and ask if they will remove the annual fee. Often they will, especially when you explain that you have two other credit cards that charge no fee

and you'd have no problem cutting theirs up and feeding it to
your pet pterodactyl. The one exception is your airline mileage
credit cards—they consider the free travel to be enough of a
perk so they usually won't remove the fee.

- Don't fall into the golden trap. Sure, it looks good to flash your
gold card on a date at Chateau Meatloaf, but the annual fees
aren't worth the extra metallic pizzazz.

Change Your Spending Habits

- Try to stop using your cards to charge more and just concentrate on paying them off. This will mean paying for what you
buy some other way, but sometimes that makes you more aware
of what you're spending. It's easy to keep charging things with
no concept of how much you've racked up until the end of the
month when the bill comes. But if you have to keep taking $40
out of the ATM, you might start to notice how your cash flows.
- Commit to paying for any new purchases the month you make
them. This means if you have a $1,500 balance on your card and
you spend $350, commit to paying for at least your new pur-
chases plus your minimum payment and the interest.
- On any card you have, if you pay the minimum payment plus
the interest for that month and don't spend anything extra,
you'll pay it down to zero in four years—no matter what balance you started with.

Break Your Patterns

- Cut down on the number of cards you have. There are advan-
tages to using only one card. First of all, it's easier to see exactly
how much you're spending when it's all on one bill. Use the
shock factor to persuade yourself not to spend as much. Also,
you may not get approved for other loans if you have too many
credit cards—even if you don't carry balances on all of them.
You don't want to jeopardize other lines of credit. If you decide
to finance grad school, for example, you don't want to look like
a bad credit risk.
- Figure out how much you can realistically commit to paying

each month to reduce your debt. Pay that before you figure out how much discretionary income you have left.

Ask for Help

- There are companies that can help you figure out how to pay off your debts most efficiently. The Consumer Credit Counseling Service (800)388-CCCS can help you devise a payment plan that fits your budget and satisfies your creditors. Check the CCCS Web site at www.cccsintl.org. You could also call the nonprofit group Myvesta at (800)698-3782 or look online at www.dca.org.
- If you're in school, find out what the alternatives are for borrowing money—if you can get a low-interest student loan that isn't due before you graduate, you can pay off your high-interest credit cards now. Then, start paying down the student loan.

The First Bank of Parental Devotion can serve as a last resort, but you should keep your credit record clean by paying them back in good faith. Also, be wary of parents who act shocked that you're not financially solvent—just because things might have been easier when they were your age. Remind them that all you're asking for is a loan. My parents' eyebrows went sky-high when I asked for a temporary loan for the first time at age 26.

In my mind, it made more sense to know I could pay my bills while I looked for a job and I didn't want to have the additional stress of wondering how I'd pay for my next Big Mac. So I asked for a temporary loan. My parents, in shock because this was the first time I suggested I needed serious financial help, figured things were a lot more dire than they were. In fact, it turned out to be a temporary loan, like I had said. Parents react in strange ways sometimes, so be forewarned.

Give Yourself Some Credit

In all likelihood, this is not the first nor the last time you'll be dealing with debts. As life gets more complicated, so do the methods of paying for it. Therefore, you may have a car loan. You may have a home loan. You may open a small business and borrow money for that. And none of this means you'll be under water— it just means you'll have to get pretty good at managing your debts, getting the lowest rates, and keeping your credit record clean.

A Final Word on Credit—Your Credit Report

Your credit report is important because everyone and anyone who thinks about lending you money, extending you credit, or even renting you an apartment gets to look at it. If it's unsightly, you may not get what you want. The only way your credit report will raise eyebrows is if you're delinquent about paying someone you owe. If you've kept your record clean, you have nothing to worry about. In any case, it's your right to see your credit report. Call one of the three credit-reporting agencies:

- Equifax: (800)685-1111; www.equifax.com
- Trans Union: (800)680-7289; www.transunion.com
- Experian: (888)397-3742; www.experian.com—one free credit report per year

12

FINDING A NEW NEST

Life with Mom and Dad—It's Not Going to Be Pretty

Coming home for the holidays was one thing. Limited exposure to relatives and you knew soon you'd be going back to college: the independent life. But now what? Much as you like your parents, they may not be what you had in mind when you pictured the ideal roommates. And depending on your job situation, that is, whether you have one yet, Janet and Phil might be looking a lot like the dorm buddies you never had.

Living at home can put you on the road to living on your own. It can give you time to scrape together the first and last months' rent and security deposit that you'll need for move-in costs. Again, it all comes down to money. If you don't have it or need to save it, you may find yourself eating Fruity Pebbles in your mom's breakfast nook.

Undeniably, it's hard for parents. They've been on their own for four years and have had to fend for themselves. Now that you're back, you'll notice them becoming dependent again. You're now a part of their home entertainment system. They'll want to know who just called, as soon as you hang up the phone. They'll want to know where you're going and who you're going with. And what time you'll be back. Then they'll want to know if you'll be home for dinner and they'll worry every time the phone rings after 7 P.M. if you're not back from work yet. You can't blame them. You have to admit you're pretty damn entertaining. But to maintain your sanity, you'll have to lay down some ground rules.

Living at home requires some immediate retraining of the parent-turned-roomie. You can't blame parents for being confused. When you last lived with them you were probably a teenager with a curfew and a knack for leaving laundry everywhere but the clothes bin. So now you've matured and gotten that vital dose of freedom. You may have to sit your parents down (more than once) and explain that you've been living on your own for four years and have done quite well. Remind them that they didn't (hopefully) call your college dorm to find out if you made it back from the party before 1 A.M. and there wasn't a monitor in the dining hall to make sure you ate all your vegetables. See, you turned out just fine.

As much as you love your parents, at times it will be frustrating. Keep reminding yourself that it's not forever. That way when your mom asks you where you're going, you'll be able to answer politely instead of screaming that it's none of her business. Counting to ten before you speak helps too. Remember, it's not for long . . .

Roommates "R" Us

There comes a time in your life when independence screams out to you like a track from a Nine Inch Nails CD. You've got the cash, you've got a few free Saturdays, and the time has arrived to look for apartments. But before you can buy the black-lacquered entertainment system and the cool fish tank, you need to start by answering the roommate question. To have or not to have?

One option, of course, is to live alone, though this costs more than sharing. The good news is you're guaranteed to get all your phone messages and you'll never come home to find the apartment a mess and your refrigerator cleaned out unless you left it that way yourself. Then again, you're responsible for all the bills: utilities, phone, cable TV, newspaper, and, most importantly, rent, that you'd otherwise share with a roommate.

Roommates come with their own pluses and pitfalls. While it's nice to have someone to share some of the basic living expenses, you also have to share your space. This may be nothing new if you had roommates during college—and a permanent Sony Playstation partner is never a bad thing.

Your apartment is more than just a place to accumulate bills and dirty clothes. Ideally, you'd like to enjoy the prospect of coming home. And whether you're coming home to roommates you knew beforehand or someone who advertises a room to rent, maintaining your sanity should always be Priority One. So if your potential roommate won't have a conversation between seven and nine o'clock because this is "quiet time," you may reconsider this domestic love match. Then again, it might be the ideal situation. Maybe you could even suggest that "quiet time" last until midnight.

Finding a Roommate

If you've just moved to a new city and don't know anyone you can live with or if none of your friends happen to be looking for roommates at the moment, you might consider rooms for rent. Try to get access to the housing office at the nearest university since their listings will attract people roughly your age. You can post notices there as well, if you're looking for a roommate, apartment, or both. Deciding on a potential roommate match has more to do with gut response than anything else. If you walk in the door to find your potential roommate cooking boiled cabbage and watching the weather channel, your gut response may be to run— even though the apartment is freshly painted and you'd get to have the big room.

There's nothing worse than a roommate who makes you feel

like you never left Mom and Dad's house. You don't want to hear, "So what time did you get in last night? Must have been pretty late," over your morning Corn Flakes. Nor do you want to come home after a long workday to find your roommate has turned your pad into the ultimate love shack, with incense burning in one corner and a candlelit ritual happening in another. Unless you're into that sort of thing.

There are roommate matching services that can make partnering up less of a gamble. They're listed in the phone book under "Roommate Referral Services," or something similar to that. There are also tons of roommate matching services online. If you already have an apartment and are looking for someone to share it with, you shouldn't have to pay a fee to be listed with a service. Typically, matching services charge the person who's looking for an apartment to share.

Shopping for a Pad

Finding Your Neighborhood

The first thing you should do is walk or drive around and eyeball areas where you might like to live. The neighborhood of choice can be based on different factors, depending on the city. You may want to choose a place near a freeway or subway so you can get to work easily. This is definitely something to consider if you live in a cold climate and have to walk twelve blocks to the subway every time you want to go anywhere. You may choose a neighborhood based on the entertainment factor: coffeehouses and movie theaters within walking distance. You may want to be near a beach, park, shopping mall, restaurant row, or business district.

Other concerns may be the safety of the neighborhood, the availability of parking if you have a car, or a building with a security gate or a doorman. Do all the buildings in the neighborhood have bars on the windows except yours? Is permit parking available in areas where parking is otherwise restricted?

Yes, But Can You Live There?

Not all cities are created alike. The heavy rains in the Pacific Northwest may inspire blithe creative verse in some of us and outright irritability in others. How do you find your haven? First you should think about what is important to you. Consider whether you want to be in a metropolitan area with access to museums and mainstream theater or whether you want hiking trails in your backyard. Do you want to work in a field that necessitates city living or can you work from home no matter where home happens to be? For help in finding the best city for your lifestyle and interests, check out the CNNMoney Web site at www.money.cnn.com/best/bplive, where you can select criteria that are important to you and find information about cities that match.

Finding a Vacancy

Once you've located the area you like, ask around. Find out how much people pay for rent and how often apartments open up. In some areas, like those where rent control laws apply, apartments may not open up very frequently. In that case, you'll want to find out the modus operandi: Do people go door to door, putting their names on managers' waiting lists? Do they go through apartment property management companies? Or do they have to know someone or have mob connections to get a place within this century?

If you're going to look at classified ads for vacancies, try the smaller neighborhood papers before the big city editions. The smaller papers will list apartments in the specific area where you're looking and will often have more listings. Let friends know you're looking. You'd be surprised how often you'll hear, "Oh, someone just moved into my building. I wish I'd known you were looking." Let everyone know.

A good source of apartment listings is often the housing office at a college or university nearby. Some students move as often as every semester so apartments around campuses frequently have vacancies and campus housing boards change listings regularly.

If there's a particular building or neighborhood you especially like, try to talk to the manager or super even if there isn't a vacancy sign. If you develop a rapport with a manager, you could be the one called when there's a vacancy.

One of the best things you can do is just walk the neighborhood. You'll be amazed at how many more "For Rent" signs you see on foot than when you're whizzing by in a car or bus. On foot, you can be more thorough since you'll have to pass by each building and might notice small details.

You can look for apartments online at www.rent.net or www.aptsforrent.com. Both sites give you vacancies by city and type of housing you want. Be aware that in some cities, like New York, the apartments get snapped up quickly.

When to Consider Help

There are also companies around town whose sole job is to match renters with landlords. These brokers or Realtors try to find vacant apartments that meet your specifications. The upside is that they'll know about apartments that aren't listed in the classified ads. The downside is that you have to pay for their services, sometimes a month's rent.

Find out the norm in the city you live in. In New York, for example, it's tough to find an apartment without a broker, but in Los Angeles, "For Rent" signs abound. If you use a broker, ask for apartments that cost a hundred dollars less than what you're willing to spend. If you say you can only spend six hundred, the broker will assume you'll spend seven hundred, possibly eight, for the right apartment.

You could also enlist the help of a property management company to help you in your search. The advantage to this tactic is that the companies typ-

> *"I told the broker my roommate and I could spend $1,500—everything she showed us was $1,600 or $1,700. We finally ended up taking a place that cost $1,680 and felt like we were getting a great deal."*
>
> —Todd, 29

ically manage many buildings so if there isn't a vacancy in one, there might be one in another.

When to Look

Apartments can be found year-round, but certain times of the month may yield more choices. Since many new leases begin on the first of the month, you're likely to find people moving out if you look toward the end of the month. On one hand, more people will be looking right alongside you, but on the other, there will probably be more vacancies. By the month's end landlords are eager to fill units that haven't been rented.

Sometimes it works to look "off season," right after the first of the month. If it's down to the wire and it looks like the landlord will have to wait another whole month to find a tenant, you might be able to wheel and deal a little, knocking off a month's rent or lowering the overall rent in exchange for moving in right away. Don't be afraid to ask for a deal.

Stay organized as you look, keeping all the information you collect in a notebook. Don't worry about developing any anal-retentive habits you won't be able to shake later on. In the notebook, keep a list of apartments you've visited, along with the managers' phone numbers, and whether the manager lives in the building or is a phone call away. Make note of things like the apartment size, rent, move-in costs, and date of availability. These are all things you can ask over the phone without ever seeing your potential digs. Then set up times to look at the apartments you like.

Bring an Unbiased Observer

If you think your judgment might be clouded by the pool table the last tenant left behind and the groovy bathroom skylight, bring a friend, parent, or other impartial observer with you to check the place out and ask the hard questions. *They* have nothing to lose from quizzing the manager, whereas you might feel like you do— like if you ask too many questions or turn on all the faucets and start flushing the toilet, the manager will think you're a problem

---

Here Are Some Things to Find Out

- *How long after a problem is reported is it fixed?*
- *Can you go ahead and hire someone to fix a leaky toilet and deduct the cost from your rent?*
- *How long a lease must you sign?*
- *When is rent due each month and is there a grace period?*
- *Are any extensive (loud) repairs planned for the building?*
- *Does the apartment come with a refrigerator? You'd be surprised how many do not and if you're going to have to plunk down six hundred bucks for a big appliance, you should know that going in.*
- *Are there thermostats in the apartment or is there central heating for the whole building?*
- *Is there a manager or superintendent on the premises?*
- *Is there a washer/dryer on the premises? If not, how far will you have to go each time you want to wash your clothes?*
- *If you want to paint the apartment blue (or any other hue) to match your upholstery, is this okay?*
- *Are pets allowed?*
- *Is storage space available if you need it?*
- *Can you sublet your apartment?*

---

tenant in the making and rent the apartment to someone else.

Don't force yourself to consult a mental checklist when the manager is breathing down your neck and looking at the clock every two minutes. Just ask the questions written in your handy notebook, run down the basics, and move along.

Inspector Clouseau

If all these issues check out to your satisfaction, you're ready to conduct a top-to-bottom inspection of the place. This doesn't require white gloves or a fingerprint kit, though you might want to bring along a friend to create a disturbance and distract the manager when you take out your hammer to see if the walls are too thin. Also keep these things in mind:

- Make sure the rooms are big enough to fit your furniture. If you have a ten-foot couch and the only wall that isn't broken by a doorway or sliding glass door is nine feet wide, you're going to have a problem.
- Check noise levels. Those great hardwood floors look stunning until you realize your upstairs neighbor has them too. Carpet is quieter, though hardwood may be easier to clean. On the noise issue, check the bedroom windows to see if they face out onto a busy street that might keep you from getting enough z's.
- Sniff around for any strange smells permeating the halls that could indicate poor ventilation or neighbors with a penchant for cooking oxtail and beet soup.
- Look at the walls, floors, and ceilings. If the ceilings are stained, make sure the leak has been fixed—repainting is useless unless the leak has stopped. If the walls are waterlogged, it could be a sign of bad plumbing, plus your art collection will go sliding to the floor. The doors should come all the way down to the floors, preventing any visitors from crawling in.
- Check to see if the windows are painted shut—often they are, which makes it hard to install an air conditioner or inhale any real air when you need to.
- Bathrooms have great potential for gross discoveries. Not only will you be able to sense the hygienic habits of the person who lived there before you, but you'll discover whether you'll be cleaning mildew off the ceiling if there are no vents or windows.
- Turn on the shower and check the water pressure. Then flush the toilet and see if the shower will scald you when your neighbor does the same.
- If you're going to install an air conditioner, make sure there's a place for it—a large enough window with a ledge.
- Move to the kitchen, the other potential area for disaster. Open drawers to see if they're on their runners. Open cabinets and check for strange smells.
- Look for outlets: you'd be surprised how many kitchens have electrical outlets in places that don't make for easy plugging in of the toaster.

- Look under the sink for leaks.
- If the apartment comes with a dishwasher or garbage disposal, make sure they work. Same with the oven.
- Look for fire extinguishers in the hallways or smoke detectors within 15 feet of the bedrooms.

When to Visit Your Potential Nest

If you go during the day, chances are few of your future fellow tenants will be around. You won't be able to get a sense of how loud the apartment gets in the evening when your neighbor to the left is grinding onions in his Cuisinart, the one below you is trying to quiet a screaming baby, and your neighbor above is working out on her stair-climber. Granted, you'll never find a noise-free apartment, but at least you'll be able to find out if your walls are excessively thin or your neighbors are excessively loud.

If you're going to be parking on the street, check out the parking situation at the time it's most likely to be crowded. You might have no problem parking during the day only to find nothing within blocks in the evening when all your neighbors are home from work.

This doesn't mean you should limit your apartment viewing to evenings only. If you plan on working at home or you need a little morning sunlight to wrench yourself out of bed in the morning, you'll want to see how bright the apartment gets during the day. And if you're thinking about moving

> *"My last apartment had the things I considered important at the time: hardwood floors, bay windows, and a clawfoot bathtub. It turned out there was a dribble of water pressure in that tub and no heat. I mean none. I shivered through one of the coldest winters ever in front of a space heater. There was a fireplace, but it had been so long since it was cleaned that the one time I lit a fire, smoke backed up into the room and I had to leave the door open all night. Had I asked about the fireplace or checked the water pressure? Of course not. I was too busy planning how my couch would look under the window."*
>
> —Karen, 28

to an apartment that has no air conditioner, you might want to check the temperature on a hot day to make sure you won't be sitting in your underwear in front of a fan all summer long. Of course, if you're apartment hunting in the winter, you may not be able to witness this firsthand, but you can always ask the neighbors. Hopefully they won't lie.

You also want to keep in mind the traffic patterns in the area. If the building is on a street with bus stops, you'll probably hear buses at all hours. If it's near a freeway or subway stop, this could be an issue too. Apartments with windows that open onto alleyways may pick up noises from trash trucks. You may be a heavy sleeper and noise may not make a difference to you, but if it's a concern, find out how much noise there's likely to be.

So You've Found a Place You Like, What Next?

Okay, your furniture will fit and your toilet will flush. You like the view and the superintendent promises to fix any problems within a day, plus throw in a fresh coat of paint. Now what? You'll probably fill out an application, which will ask about where you work, where you bank, where you've lived over the past five years, and a few other tidbits that will allow the landlord to run a credit check. Sometimes there will be a fee for the credit check, generally about $25 to $50. You may need to supply references that will vouch for you as an upstanding human being, so have some handy.

Now is where the real fun begins. Depending on where you live, your next step may be as easy as writing a check and being handed a key. Then again, it could also become a process of flattering the landlord, making promises about all the improvements you'll make on the place, and bringing your roommates over for inspection. If you're looking for space in a co-op, you'll be grilled by the co-op board.

In some cities, especially those where rent control laws have made apartments cheap, you may be doing battle with fifty other people who want the same apartment. People get crafty, coming with the first month's rent in cash, offering to recarpet the place, giving the landlord a "finder's fee," which is basically an illegal cash thank-you for renting them the apartment. I've heard stories about people "borrowing" friends who look upstanding to come and meet the manager because they're worried their grunge rocker roommates won't make the cut.

Some apartment owners have special guidelines for their tenants, like they should be nonsmoking or vegetarian. One friend of mine lied and pretended to be an egg-free, milk-free vegetarian to get a rent-controlled place in Berkeley. He was always running from one friend's apartment to the next, trying to grill a hamburger. Be persistent and try any tactics you can think of and you *will* get a place.

Sometimes the landlord will ask for other deposits and fees, but don't pay anything else until your application has been approved. Often the landlord will ask for a guarantor, like your parents, who promises to pay the rent if you don't do it. If everything looks good and you can move in on the first of the month, the landlord will want a deposit, typically equivalent to first plus last months' rent and a security deposit, generally about half a month's rent. Only pay this if you're dead set on taking the place.

When You're Ready to Sign at the X

Read your lease entirely before you sign it. This may sound obvious, but leases can be long and tedious and just signing at the X is tempting. If something in the lease is unclear, ask about it. Make note of the length—not the piece of paper, but the amount of time you'll live in the apartment. Usually leases are for six months or a year. The good news is the rent is locked in and can't be raised until the lease comes up for renewal. The bad news is, if you want to move before then, you may not be able to. (See below on breaking a lease.) Some leases are month to month, which means thirty days' notice is all that's required from you or the landlord to move you out. The landlord needs to have a reason, like failure to pay rent.

Your lease will indicate how much the rent is and who can live in the apartment. It lists building rules, such as whether you can have pets or barbecues on your balcony.

Your lease will explain how your security deposit will be used, whether for rent if you fail to pay or for hiring a repairman if you put your foot through a closet door. Sometimes the security deposit will cover increases in the rent between the time you move in and move out. In other words, if you paid first and last months' rent at the beginning and the rent goes up $20, your last month's rent will be short. The $20 can come out of the security deposit if it's specified in the lease. Your lease should tell you when you'll get the security deposit back. Ask that your security deposit be kept in an interest-bearing account until you move out—this is required in some states. Call your city hall to find out the rental housing laws in your city.

Also ask whether there are any sleeper clauses in your lease, things like extra charges for use of the pool or gym or surcharges for central air conditioning that will be on all summer. Avoid sleeper clauses that say your rent can be raised before the lease is up.

The lease should state when rent is due each month and whether there's a grace period. There may be a penalty for paying late or you could risk eviction, so you should know these things in advance. Look to see how much notice you need to give when you want to move out. Finally, remember that you hold the power of the pen. You can cross out parts of your lease if the landlord agrees. For example, if your lease holds you responsible for fixing toilet backups, you might revise it to read, "After the first two months," to cover yourself if the toilet never worked in the first place.

Out of the Old, into the New

You have a few options when it comes to getting your stuff from one place to another: Do it yourself with the help of some friends, rent a truck and get some friends to help you load or unload, or hire movers. Trucks cost between $25 and $50 per day to rent, plus

25 to 50 cents a mile, and movers charge between $65 and $100 per hour. If you have renter's insurance already, find out if it covers damage to your belongings during the moving process.

Moving In

Now that you have a place to live, you'd like people to be able to find you. Most of your bills have change-of-address forms on them somewhere, lest you go more than a day without them knowing where you are. But for the list of places below, call or write with your change of address, or use change-of-address postcards from the post office. Then look forward to living in bliss for a few weeks until the junk mail companies find you.

- Your bank
- Doctors and dentists
- Catalogs
- Magazines and newspapers
- Credit cards
- Health insurance, car insurance, auto club
- Book or music clubs
- Voter registration
- Friends and relatives
- Utilities—let them know where to send the final bill from your old address and when to establish service at your new one
- Alumni associations
- Former landlord—so you can get your security deposit back and any unforwarded mail

If You Ended Up with a Lemon

Hard as you tried to keep all the rules of apartment hunting in mind when you sought out the ultimate nest, you ended up with a dud. It can happen. Rather than living in the lap of luxury, you ended up riding the rump of rent control. So you're saving some money, which is always nice. Then again, the worn-out carpet isn't getting replaced unless you do it yourself and the dishwasher will be a storage facility because it's long since finished serving its original purpose. There are certain things you may be stuck with, but in any rental situation you do have rights as a tenant and some recourse if your ceiling falls on your head. Call the chamber of commerce (listed in the phone book) in your city to find out your tenant's rights. Buildings must meet codes and standards. If yours doesn't, you can file a complaint.

You don't want to spend the first month freezing your buns off and running the heat at full blast to no effect, only to receive a bill for a couple hundred dollars from the gas company at the end of the month. Some apartments are so poorly insulated that one little gas heater on High in the corner of the room will yield only a modicum of heat. You'd be better off turning it off and buying a couple of space heaters to heat individual rooms.

Ask your landlord if you can fix some of the problems yourself in exchange for a break on your rent. Often they'll agree because you're taking the responsibility for hiring plumbers and electricians off of them.

The most important thing you should do is take some photos of the apartment when you move in, highlighting any problem areas like stained carpet or the rusty oven that doesn't work. (You'll see why later, on pages 202–3, when we talk about security deposits.) Keep copies of any correspondence between you and the landlord about problems you want fixed. If the apartment is in severe disarray, you might consider having the manager or landlord sign a sort of counterlease, detailing what isn't working or what needs cleaning so you won't be held responsible later.

My roommate and I had one of those apartments where the toilet stopped flushing after the first month. I called my landlord and she came over with a string of silver beads from Mardi Gras. She rigged up a makeshift toilet flusher that required us to lift off the tank cover each time we wanted to flush. If we wanted a plumber, it was going to cost us. We finally reported a bunch of code vio-

---

Decorating on Pennies

You don't have to spend an arm, a leg, and two thousand bucks to make your new place fit for guests. Here are some ways to fill your space without emptying your wallet:

1. *Buy furniture from a store that offers a discount—sometimes as much as 25 percent—if you open a charge: get the credit card, buy what you need, then cut the card.*
2. *Go to flea markets and yard sales.*
3. *Place a couple of ladders a few feet apart against the wall and put wooden shelves across them to make a bookcase.*
4. *Resort to cinder blocks and milk crates.*
5. *Look in your parents' garage or your friend's parents' garage for stored furniture you can borrow.*
6. *Find out if the person moving out before you wants to unload anything instead of moving it.*
7. *Move in with roommates who already have stuff.*
8. *Make a desk by finding an old door and laying it across two small file cabinets.*
9. *Go to Ikea.*
10. *Eschew all things material, eat on the floor, buy a couple of beanbag chairs, and call yourself a minimalist.*

---

lations to the Codes and Inspections Unit and they came and wrote up a nineteen-page report of things that weren't up to code. We finally moved out because we couldn't take it anymore, but the landlord was required to fix everything.

You and Your Roommates

Paying the Bills

If you live alone, bill paying doesn't have too many permutations. They come in the mail, and you pay them, preferably near the time they're due. When you have roommates, on the other hand, bills and responsibilities can be divided a number of different ways. Maybe you've been able to identify which of you is more meticulous when it comes to remembering due dates, keeping a supply of stamps on hand, and having a bank account with money in it. That person might choose Bill Payer over Shower Mildew Monitor when it comes to divvying up household titles.

The Extras

Besides bill-paying responsibilities, you also have to divide up other duties like cleaning, shopping for groceries, and taking out the trash. This may seem obvious to the point of stupidity, but it's worth at least establishing some basic "You do this and I'll do that" deals so you don't feel like you're doing everything and your apartment doesn't turn into a garbage dump.

You should resolve certain issues at the outset, such as whether to get cable TV, a daily newspaper, or other apartment extras. The last thing you want is a situation in which your roommate doesn't want to subscribe to newspapers or magazines but will read them "if they're there." In other words, it's fine if you pay for them. Try to strike some common ground. If you're both using them, you should split the cost. This goes for other shared things like kitchen sponges, toilet paper, paper towels, dishwashing detergent, lightbulbs, and anything else you'll both be using. If you have a roommate who'd rather use the bathroom at work than pay for toilet paper at home, there may be nothing you can do, but at least make an effort to divide the expenses.

Check into various options when figuring out how many phone lines and answering machines to get. Instead of getting separate phone lines and answering machines, it's typically cheaper to get one phone line with a message center, offered by most phone companies. And remember that it costs less to buy a phone than to rent one.

Also figure out how you'll deal with groceries. You might each want to have a shelf in the refrigerator and one in the cupboard. That way you can shop separately and you won't get uptight if your roommate eats like a horse, because you'll only be paying for your own groceries.

> *"I came home late one night after a long day at work and flipped on the living room light. All I could see sticking out from under a blanket on the couch was a tuft of white hair. My roommate invited her grandmother to spend the night and somehow forgot to tell me. This would have possibly been bearable if she hadn't just invited her parents to come and stay with us for two weeks. The next day, I closed down the hotel and asked her to move out. Then I found out her sister was planning to come and visit for a month."*
>
> —Jen, 25

On that note, beware of bulk. Bulk shopping seems like a money saver's dream. It is. Right up until the point when you get hungry and open your cupboards to find only a gallon jug of BBQ sauce and a twelve-can pack of Corn Niblets. Don't go bulk crazy. If your apartment only has two cupboards in the kitchen, you should remind yourself of this several times while cruising the bulk-food aisles. While a sixteen-pack of toilet paper may be convenient, you don't want to have it as a living room sculpture.

Another thing to keep in mind when shopping is your lifestyle, based around your job requirements. If you're working mean hours and might not see your apartment before 10:30 each night, you probably shouldn't stock up on lots of perishable stuff that seems healthy. True, the magazine articles tell you to stuff your face with carrots and celery to stay thin as a twig, but if you're going to end up stuffing them in the garbage, don't buy them.

Other Ground Rules

One obvious perk to moving out of your parents' house is that you'll have your freedom. You can invite friends, boyfriends, girl-friends, anyone you want, to come hang out with you in your new place. But so can your roommate. Just a word to the wise: Work out some kind of understanding about these things in advance. You don't want to come home to find your dinner waiting in the hall while your roommate entertains a date.

Tell your roommate, in advance, what bugs you. There's no sense cringing each time you go into the bathroom and see the

toothpaste cap off when you could simply mention to your roommate that you're anal about such things.

Covering Yourself

Now that you've got the cool pad with the multi-tiered entertainment system and a few drought-resistant plants, you'd like to keep
it that way. You want to make sure a bad leaky overhead pipe or a
conniving burglar doesn't wipe you out in one fell swoop. The
answer is renter's insurance, something that costs far less than any
other insurance you'll get. In the event of disaster, renter's insurance will help you replace your worldly goods, right down to your
Snoopy alarm clock. Here's what renter's insurance covers:

- Losses from theft or vandalism
- Destruction from fire or smoke
- Losses due to windstorm, lightning, or explosion
- Water damage from plumbing
- Earthquake damage, if you purchase a special add-on

You'll also be covered against lawsuits that come from someone getting hurt in your apartment or using your stuff. Individual
policies may have differing degrees of coverage for this, so you
should find out the specifics when you sign up. Also find out
whether your policy covers theft by a roommate—just in case.

Where to Get a Renter's Policy

Any insurance agent that sells homeowner's insurance can write
a renter's policy. You can find an agent in the phone book and have
a policy written over the phone. Your policy will cover either *actual
cost* or *replacement cost*. It's important to know the distinction
between the two.

Actual-cost insurance pays you what you initially spent on the
item that was destroyed. The problem here is that you'll most likely
have to spend far more to replace that item. That's why it makes

more sense to get insured for replacement cost. This will cover the cost of replacing the damaged or destroyed item with a new one.

What Will It Cost?

The cost of your policy will be based on your estimate of how much everything in your apartment is worth. To do this, take an inventory of everything you have, from your oak bedframe right down to your gym socks. Make a list of the biggest, most expensive items and what they cost when you bought them. Take some photos around your apartment and keep them with your list.

There are a few ways you can lower your policy costs:

- Shop around. Not all companies charge the same for the same coverage.
- Ask if your car insurance company also has homeowner's and renter's policies. Sometimes you can get a discount if you have more than one policy with a company.
- Ask if you can get a discount for living in a relatively safe area or in a building with gated entry, bars on the windows, or an alarm.

What Your Policy Covers

Your policy covers all your furniture, clothes, electronic equipment, dishes—in short, everything in your apartment. There are a few extra things to keep in mind:

- If you have expensive jewelry, worth more than $1,000, or a computer worth more than $5,000, you'll need to buy a separate category of insurance to cover them.
- Your bike is covered, even if it's stolen when it's parked outside the 7-Eleven down the block.
- Your roommates may or may not be covered. If you and two roommates buy a policy together and then one roommate moves out, the new roommate isn't automatically covered. Call your insurance agent to revise your policy.
- Rented items that are stolen or damaged while in your apart-

ment are generally covered, but ask your insurance agent to make sure.

- Anything below your deductible is your responsibility. Generally renter's policies have relatively low deductibles—$250 to $500—and the insurance doesn't pay for any losses until you've met your deductible.

Filing a Claim

If you need to file a claim, start by writing down everything that happened. For example, if there was a fire, write down the date and approximate time it occurred. Also write down what was destroyed. If you have pictures of the items you need to have replaced, have these handy. Call your insurance agent and ask for claims forms. Fill them out as completely as you can, assessing all the damage. The insurance company will often send someone over to check out the damage. Then the company will process your claim and mail you a check.

Hopefully, you'll never file a claim. If ten years down the line you end up resenting all the money you paid for insurance that you never needed, you'll be in good shape.

When You're Ready to Move Out—Breaking a Lease

When you see a swanky one-bedroom at a bargain basement price, just down the block from the pad you just rented, what can you do? Should you try to have one loud party too many and see if your landlord will force you out of your lease? That's one option, but one that probably won't work. First, read your lease and look for a termination clause that will tell if there's a procedure you must follow.

You could choose to just give your notice, but you would most likely lose your last month's rent and security deposit. Or you could approach the landlord in a reasonable, friendly voice and ask if you could locate a good replacement tenant in exchange for being let

Helpful Hints

1. The market is the worst place to buy shampoo and other bathroom items. Go to a large drugstore chain or team up with a friend and get an eight-pack of soap at the Price Club or Costco.

2. Get Teflon or no-stick pots and pans. This seemingly innocuous purchase will save you hundreds in Brillo Pad expenses, not to mention the wear and tear on your fingertips. Dishwasher or no, you don't want to spend any more time cleaning than you have to.

3. You don't really have to register things you buy. They make it sound like if you don't send in the product registration card that comes with everything from computers to sunglasses, your new toaster will explode or something. But you can feel justified in using your time more effectively because all the registration cards do is put you on mailing lists.

4. Don't pay full price. It doesn't always work, but often you can get the electronics store or the appliance store to take a little cash off the top of your purchase just by asking.

5. When shopping for work clothes, pay attention to washing instructions. It may sound stupid, but there's a big difference between dry cleaning and laundering costs. Getting cotton shirts that can be laundered will save you cash.

6. Do your own home repairs. For example, if your garbage disposal jams but the motor's still whirring, try a home fix solution before calling for repair. Under the sink on the disposal unit is a Reset button. If it's out, push it in. Then use a broom handle in the sink to turn the blades. If that doesn't work, call the plumber.

7. Righty tighty, lefty loosey.

8. White toothpaste is a good substitute for Spackle. Be sure not to get the blue gel or the landlord might be onto your scheme of filling nail holes to ensure that you get your security deposit back.

9. Ordering the return address labels from the coupon section in

the newspaper is a cheap way to save you time and writer's cramp when you pay bills.

10. *Don't plug your space heater into an extension cord or put light-bulbs into lamps that exceed the maximum allowable wattage.*

---

out of your lease early. Always give the landlord plenty of notice—this will increase your

chances of successfully breaking your lease.

Another option is to sublet. In other words, you stay on the lease, but someone else moves in to cover the months you have left. They pay the rent but they have no guarantee of getting the apartment when your lease is up. This will only work if you can find someone who wants a short-term place to stay with no strings. And it can save you money and aggravation if your landlord will let you do it.

You Shouldn't Get Reamed for Something You Didn't Do

Some landlords think of a security deposit as money they get to keep unless you make a big fuss and take them to small claims court. Most tenants don't go this far to recover a few hundred beans. So the landlords keep the money, even if it didn't cost three hundred bucks to spackle a few holes left from thumbtacks. Or to clean a carpet stain that was there when you moved in.

The best way to ensure that you get your deposit back is to know your tenant's rights. It's your money. Money you could use for a winter coat or a fax machine or a night in a ritzy hotel—or, most likely, the security deposit on your *next* apartment. Why should the landlord keep it when it's rightfully yours? If there are a few scuff marks on the walls, your landlord shouldn't be claim-ing the whole apartment needed to be repainted.

If the apartment was not the portrait of cleanliness when you moved in, you hopefully took a minute to snap a few photos to prove that you left it in better shape when you moved out.

13

YOUR WHEELS

Caveat Emptorium

When I told a guy I worked with that I'd just bought a car, he asked me all the questions that supposedly any intelligent car shopper would be able to answer about her purchase. Not me. "Is it simple interest?" "Wouldn't you get a bigger tax deduction if you leased a car?" "Why did you put $4,000 into a depreciating asset when you could have made much better use of the money by investing it?" "Why did you use your old car as a trade-in at the dealer's lot when you could have gotten more by selling it to a private party?"

Why? Like I had a good reason. "I don't know, because I'm an idiot?" was the best response I had.

When you go to the car dealership, you don't realize that you've just made your grand entrance onto the stage of car buying. Everything from that point on is an elaborate performance designed to let Honest Abe (or Abby) the car salesperson win your confidence and sell you a car at the most inflated price in the history of auto buying. You get to play the part of the customer who doesn't know a gasket from a gas tank. Honest Abe gets to throw out one-liners based on a bond of trust he's built with you until you all but make him your next of kin.

The Script

According to a friend of mine who used to sell cars, Honest Abe wasn't born yesterday and he didn't come up with those great lines on the spot. Some car dealers are actually given a script to follow that tells them exactly how to hook their prey. Scenes like these are all well planned:

- *You're shown what your car payment will be and you say, "But that's too high."*

  Abe then says, "I don't blame you one bit. But everyone you see driving one of these cars is paying $399 a month. How about this: I'll lower the payment by two bucks a month. On 48 payments, that's a hundred-dollar discount." Then, when you're still not convinced, Abe goes on. "Now I'm stumped. How close to $399 can you come?" Honest Abe lowers the price two dollars at a time, then one dollar at a time until you acquiesce.

- *Abe gets you to come into the office and offers to get you coffee or look at your trade-in—anything to keep you there longer. The longer you're there, the more likely you'll want to buy a car so you're not just wasting your time.*

- *Honest Abe will ask you questions to which you can answer "yes," to get you in the right frame of mind to leave with a car. "If the numbers come out right, you'd like to drive home today, right? You want the XYZ stereo, right? And we agreed on XYZ amount for your trade-in, right?"*

- *Abe says things he knows will make you irate, like quoting an insanely low value for your trade-in, then going through a process of calming you down until he wins your trust.*

  Surely not every car dealer will do this to you. And you can avoid being suckered by getting informed before you call a dealer or walk onto the lot.

Getting the Basic Numbers

The first thing you need to do is decide exactly which model car you want to buy. Know which features come standard and which are optional. You can do this easily by asking the dealer for a brochure and comparing the features on the different models of the car you want. Then you can compare apples to apples when you call various dealers and negotiate prices—you don't want to be negotiating for the LX model with one dealer and the cheaper S model with another. Then you'll want to find out exactly how much the dealer paid for the car you want to buy.

One way to do this is to look up the wholesale prices of cars and their accessories in the Blue Book, officially known as the *National Automobile Dealers Association (NADA) Handbook*, available at bookstores and libraries or at www.NADAGuides.com. Depending on the availability and the demand for the car you want, you should offer the dealer about 5–7 percent over invoice. The dealer will act like this price is a severe injustice to the car-buying world, but stick to your guns.

Negotiating from Home

Another good method is to sit yourself down in the comfort of your living room on a Sunday morning and start calling around. Get a list of the dealerships in your city and tell them exactly which car you want. Ask the dealer to fax (you'll have to get access to a fax machine if you don't have one) you the factory invoice or the window sticker on the car. That way you'll be sure the car you're negotiating for on the phone is the one you'll see when you go to the dealership in person. Dealers may not like to negotiate over the phone because they figure if they can get you to come in, they're that much closer to selling a car. But insist—say you don't have time to come down.

Then ask the dealer to make a note on the fax telling you how much over factory invoice you'll have to pay for the car. Some dealers may give you a hard time, but if you can get four or five faxes, you'll be in good shape. If the salesperson you're dealing with won't help you on the price, ask for a fleet manager or department manager, both of whom can make deals on the price (salespeople typically can't).

Then get a little gutsy. Call a dealer back and say, "You weren't really the lowest, but you're the closest to my neighborhood and I'd really like to give you the business. Can you come down a hundred dollars?" Remember that it's a buyer's market. All the dealerships have an identical product and only one will be able to sell to you. That means you should be able to get yourself a good deal. If you're leasing (more on benefits of buying vs. leasing later), you'll typically negotiate a higher purchase price than if you're buying. But don't forget that if you lease a car, you can still negotiate the price and the interest rate.

Online Info

You can also use an online search engine to find sites with the lowdown on cars and their prices. A good place to start is *Edmund's Automobile Buyers Guides* at www.edmunds.com, which has car reviews, factory invoice prices, and buyer's tips. Look for the dealer invoice, holdbacks, or profits the dealer gets when the car is sold, and other incentives and costs. You can also get information about the car you're interested in by typing the name of the car manufacturer, such as Ford or Mazda, into a search engine and looking at their Web pages. For car reviews, try the sites of auto magazines, such as: *Popular Mechanics* at www.popularmechanics.com or *Car and Driver* at www.caranddriver.com. You can also read a publication called *Shopping for a Safer Car*, from the Insurance Institute for Highway Safety on its Web site at www.hwysafety.org/vehicle_ratings/sfsc.htm.

You also may consider buying online. CarsDirect (www.carsdirect.com) or Autobytel (www.autobytel.com) allow car buyers to shop directly on their Web sites. After you submit your request, a dealer will call you with a price. You're under no obligation to buy and the service is free. You can also use these Web sites to help you with your comparison shopping. Find out the exact invoice price of the car and any options you want before shopping in person.

About That Ad

When you see that enticing ad in the paper that describes the red Miata fully loaded at a low, low price, should you trust it? Sure. If you see an ad for the car you want, go to the dealer in the morning and try to get that car. Not a car like it but without the alloy wheels and cruise control or one that costs a thousand bucks more. Usually there's only one like the car described in the ad, and once it's sold, there are no more deals to be found on the lot. If you stay, you could end up getting talked into something you have no desire to buy.

Honest Abe figures that once you've driven out there, you won't want to leave in your old beater. That's when you'll be shown cars LIKE the one in the ad, coincidentally at a higher price. If that's the case, you should take your checkbook and the CDs you were going to play on the drive home and move off the red carpet. Give your old car a big kiss on the dashboard because it's going to have to make it another mile or two.

If you call a dealer on the phone and don't get a copy of the invoice or sticker, you could be in for a surprise when you come on down. The dealer might tell you the car you want is collecting dust on the showroom floor and that it can be yours for a great price. This is known as low-balling. When you drive out to see the car you'll be told that the dealer already sold that one. Or "Oh, THAT car? I thought you were talking about another car. The price on THAT car is going to be a little higher." A little. Again, the dealer figures now that you've driven out there, you're determined to buy a car before you go home. Not so.

Keep Your Cool

Honest Abe will flatter you, tell you how smart you are for choosing this car. He'll explain this is the difference between you and all the other bumblers who've bought cars before you. But, unfortunately, it's going to cost you. If Abe has the car you want on the lot, tell him you like that price, but that actually, you have a better one. Toss out your NADA plus 5–7 percent and give Abe a blank look, like you don't know where that number came from. You'll hear the standard "that's far too low, we have to make a profit, be fair" garble. That's when it's time to put on your look of distaste and start to walk away. He'll go lower, but not low enough. Threaten to walk again. Abe will start talking about your trade-in, the accessories you want—anything to get you excited about buying the car—hoping to get you to settle on a higher price.

This is when you suddenly remember that the dealer six counties away was willing to give you the price you wanted. Maybe you'll take a little drive. Honest Abe will start talking about how lucky you are that it's the end of the month and they have to make room for new cars. Maybe it's possible to get your price after all.

In order to avoid being taken for the ride of a lifetime, go to Abe's showroom with the following in mind:

- Never feel sorry for the dealer. I know it seems like Abe's depending on your car sale to keep food on the table for another month, but pity shouldn't factor into your bargaining session.
- Don't negotiate based on monthly payments. There are many ways to make payments low and keep overall cost high. You'll get the best deal by negotiating on the purchase price.
- Get a better deal at an out-of-the-way showroom first. Better yet, get a few. You'll bargain better if you already know you have an ace in the hole. Show the salesman you're prepared to walk away if necessary. Get up and do it just to get his attention—before you cross the threshold of the office, he'll be back with a better offer.

- Don't let the money you're getting on your trade-in substitute for getting a good price on your new car. Research its value beforehand.
- Find out what the car costs the dealer before walking onto the lot and taking "your baby" for a test drive.
- Ask how much any add-ons will cost and bargain down the price until the salesperson is begging you to take the damn stereo for nothing. Everything is negotiable.
- Remember that dealers like to tack on miscellaneous charges that they somehow forgot to tell you about when you negotiated the price. Ask about any charges you don't recognize.
- Don't rely on the dealer to get you a good deal.

Your Trade-In

When you're in the market for a new car, your old car (if you have one) starts to become the enemy. You almost feel like the dealer is doing you a favor by taking it off your hands. This makes it hard to negotiate for a great price. But if you can instill a little attitude adjustment and view the car like a dear departed relative, you won't dream of taking less money for it than it's worth. The NADA handbook lists used car prices according to year, so you can research the value of your trade-in. If you've kept it in good shape and maybe put in a great stereo or an alarm, bump up your car's value to a few hundred over Blue Book.

You'll probably get the most for your car by selling it yourself. It's a hassle. You have to deal with people driving out

> *"I was so sick of my old, hand-me-down car, the one the dog threw up in when we took a family trip when I was nine. In my head, I'd decided it was worth about 30 cents but I told the dealer I thought $500 sounded like a fair price. He couldn't get out of the office fast enough to avoid letting me see his big grin. He pretended to argue with the manager about the price and then came back and said he'd gotten me my price. I hadn't even checked the Blue Book. If I had, I'd have known the car was worth a lot more than 500 bucks."*
> —Mauricio, 28

from the canyons and beyond, telling you how rundown your car looks and offering you absurdly low prices for it. But after letting a few people test drive your baby, someone will offer you a decent price. Another option is to sell it to a dealer who sells your make and model of car. Take your used Volkswagen to a VW dealer and they'll give you a better price than a Honda dealer would. If you want to trade your VW in at the dealer where you're buying your new Acura, get a price from the VW dealer and present it to the Acura dealer and try to get a match. A competing offer is a great weapon. Get prices from a few dealers and let them battle each other, not you.

If the dealer has "good news" and says you can have what you're asking for on the trade, you could probably get more for it. Make up for it by bargaining lower for the price of the car. If the dealer won't go lower, revisit the price for your trade-in until the numbers add up. And don't wrangle the price down only to be told about some other cost, such as dealer's prep, which is essentially the cost of getting the car to the lot. Since when did that become your job?

Who Loans You, Baby?

There are two ways to pay for your car if you're buying: either you pay in cash or you finance. If you pay in cash, you won't pay any interest. You'll just pay the cost of the car, plus tax, license, and registration. If you don't happen to have a giant wad of cash laying around, you'll come up with a small down payment and finance the rest (or you'll lease—discussed later). You can get your financing from a credit union, your own bank, or the car dealer. Each has its merits. Banks and credit unions generally offer lower rates than the dealers. If you can get a loan preapproved by a bank or credit union, take it to the showroom and don't accept dealer financing unless they can top it. When you're right out of school, credit may be hard to come by, so as a last resort, dealer financing is better than none.

If you don't have a year-long track record of income, banks may

> "I had a hard time getting a car loan the year after graduation because I only had half a year's worth of income as the grand total on my tax return. The banks looked at that paltry sum and decided I wasn't a good credit risk. I ended up paying a higher interest rate by getting dealer financing, but at least I got the car."
> —Sarah, 24

be hesitant to offer you a car loan. In that case, it may not be worth the hassle of endless window-shopping for loans when the dealer can approve you on the spot. You're at an advantage because car dealers want to sell you a car. This means they'll help you get approved for a loan—even if you don't have a sterling credit record. Again, try banks or credit unions first because you'll get a better rate.

If you don't get approved, you're entitled to know why. You can get a free copy of your credit report from Experian by calling (888)397-3742.

Big Numbers and Those That Get Crunched

The most important thing to remember when working the numbers is that car dealers do this every day, which means they're better at the car game than you are. One ploy to watch out for from car dealers: they'll get you to focus on your monthly payments rather than the overall cost of the car. The numbers are smaller and more manageable—hundreds, not thousands. Once they've got you looking at the monthly sum, they'll try to get you to go a little higher. If you say you can afford to pay $250 a month, they'll try to push you to $299. And if you balk at that, they can stretch the term out. In other words, instead of paying $299 for 36 months, you can pay $250 for 60 months. You walk away thinking you got the best deal ever and the dealer just made an extra $4,000. Bring your own calculator and figure out exactly what you're being offered.

Here's a basic chart that will show you exactly what the same car will cost you at different interest rates and over terms of dif-

If You Borrow Ten Thousand			
Interest Rate	36 Months	48 Months	60 Months
8%	$314 per month $11,304 total	$245 per month $11,760 total	$203 per month $12,180 total
9%	$318 per month $11,448 total	$249 per month $11,952 total	$208 per month $12,480 total
10%	$323 per month $11,628 total	$254 per month $12,192 total	$213 per month $12,780 total
11%	$327 per month $11,772 total	$259 per month $12,432 total	$218 per month $13,080 total

ferent lengths. As you can see, a higher interest rate doesn't raise your total as much as a longer term. Then again, the longer term significantly lowers your monthly payment cost, so sometimes it's better to pay more overall so that your monthly payments won't break the bank.

In Whose Interest?

It's important to understand the kind of interest you're paying. Isn't all interest just interest? Yes. But depending on whether your car loan is calculated using simple interest or interest on a pre-computed basis, it may have different implications.

Suppose you take out a five-year car loan because stretching out your payments over sixty months brings them down to a level you can afford. But say three years down the line your income goes up—you've gotten a promotion or your start-up business is turning a nice profit. So you think about paying off your car loan so you don't waste any more money in interest payments. You call the bank that made your car loan and find out that, of the $5,500 you still owe on your car, only $400 is the interest portion. Because they've calculated your loan on a *precomputed* basis, you paid most of the interest in the first two years. Precomputed loans (also called the Rule of 78 because they base it on a twelve-month loan and $12 + 11 + 10 + \ldots = 78$) make you pay more interest at the beginning and less at the end. Doesn't make much sense to pay it off.

News flash. If your car loan had been calculated using the simple interest method, you'd have paid more principal and less interest. Therefore you'd owe more interest after the same three years and would save more than $1,600 by paying off your car early. So depending on what you think you might do, look into getting the interest that's in your best interest. The *simple interest* method calculates the total amount of interest you'll pay on the amount you borrow and divides it by the number of months of your loan. So every month, you pay the same amount in interest and the same amount of principal. This is a good way to go if you think you might want to pay back your car loan early.

Also watch out for a *front-end installment loan*, which makes you pay interest on the entire amount you've borrowed each month. Again, you'll be paying far more than you'd pay on a simple interest loan. Finally, make sure you get a *fixed-rate loan*, because variable rates could mean you'll pay low interest at the beginning of the loan period but risk paying higher rates later.

How It Works When You're Leasing

In a lease, you're only paying for the percentage of the total price that you'll use during the lease term, called the *depreciation*. Here is how it's calculated: At the time you lease the car, it has a certain selling price or *capitalized cost*, say, $27,000. At the end of the lease term, typically three years, it has what's called a *residual value*, which is what it's worth at that time, say, $12,000. Your lease payments are based on the difference between the two. This means that over the three-year term, you'll be financing the $15,000 difference between selling price and residual value.

To find out the car's residual value, check your library for the Automotive Lease Guide. Many dealers will offer a subsidized lease price, something they're able to do because they're getting cash back from the car maker as an incentive to lease more cars. You can take your trusty calculator and find out if you're getting a great deal by figuring out what the lease payment normally is and comparing it to the subsidized payment. Here's how:

Find out the money rate on the lease, which is essentially the interest rate you'll be paying. To determine what your monthly interest payments will be, add the selling price and the residual value (27,000 + 12,000 from above = 39,000) and multiply that by the money rate. Add that to your monthly payments, which you calculate by subtracting the residual value from the selling price and dividing it by the number of months in the lease. Using the above example, divide $15,000 by 36 months to get 416 and add the interest, which is $146. If the dealer is offering you less than $562, you're getting a subsidized price.

Another way for dealers to lower your lease payment is to estimate high on the residual value, so you're paying less for the depreciation that you'll use. Inflating the residual value is fine if it will lower your payments. It's only a negative if you plan to buy the car at the end of your lease because you'll owe the inflated residual, also called a *balloon payment*.

You can lower your payments yourself by putting some money down at the beginning of the lease term. Like a down payment of a car loan, this will mean you owe less, so you'll pay less per month.

If you want to lease a car, start by calling some banks in your area. Ask for their leasing departments and find out what money rate they use. If they won't tell you exactly, try to get a ballpark figure. Then you'll know the rate you should be getting—which can be a far cry from what the dealer initially offers. Ask the dealer to compare the number you got from the bank with the numbers from the dealer's financing company.

The Buy or Lease Debate

Depending on your driving habits, it may make more sense to buy. Or it may make more sense to lease. How do you know which is better for you? Don't rely on the dealer to tell you. That would be like asking a water salesman if the bottled water really tastes better than tap.

When deciding what you should do, ask yourself the following questions:

- How long will you keep the car?
- Does your career have the possibility of relocating to a city where you won't need a car?
- Do you have money for a down payment or do you need available cash for something else?
- Do you drive more than 20,000 miles per year?
- Are you hard on cars?
- Do you use your car for business purposes, other than getting to and from work?

What It All Means

If you plan to keep your car five years or more, it probably makes sense to buy because you'll own it after five years. For the remainder of the time you have it, you won't have monthly payments. Lease terms are generally three years, sometimes two. Leasing is like renting a car and returning it when the lease is up. You owe nothing, but you own nothing. A lease will give you lower monthly payments, but as long as you have a car, you'll have a payment.

More than monthly payments, consider your future. For example, if you're working for a small newspaper and foresee yourself moving to New York to work for a magazine next year, you may not want to get tied up in a three-year lease. Or you may live in a place where you need a car and will keep it awhile. You might decide to buy one because after three to five years, you'll have one less monthly expense. If you know you can commit to a three-year lease and need a snappy car for work, you may choose to lease one because your dollars will lease more snaz than they could buy.

Lease payments are typically lower than the payments you'd owe if you bought the same car. This means that leasing could cost you less. Or, conversely, it could mean you'll be able to get a nicer car by leasing than by buying. Leasing will also save you the sales tax you'd pay on a car purchase. Under a lease, you pay tax on your payments, but far less than if you'd bought the car.

Know How Far You'll Drive, How Gently, and How Long

Leases allow you to drive anywhere from 10,000 to 15,000 miles per year. For each mile over your limit, you must pay extra, about 12 to 15 cents per mile. Not good if you work for a messenger service and average 100 miles per day. But for most people, the mileage limitations are reasonable.

When you lease a car, watch out for wording in your lease agreement that penalizes you for excess wear and tear. Find out what this means: worn-out shocks or rips in the upholstery, chips in the paint or worn floor mats? If you're going to be charged for it, make sure you know what it is. Also, check the car's warranty and make sure it lasts the length of the lease.

Find out if there is a penalty for turning the car in early. You should know in advance whether the lease carries a penalty for an early exit, and what that penalty will be. You don't want to get stuck with all your remaining lease payments if you decide to move to a city where you won't be needing a car.

Mind the Gap

Your lease should cover something called gap insurance, which covers you if your car is lost or stolen before the lease is up. Your regular car insurance will generally reimburse you for the car's market value, but if this is less than the amount due on the lease, your gap insurance will fill in the abyss. Its cost can be negotiated with the dealer. Some might throw it in at no charge, but if not, don't pay more than a few hundred, total.

Buy at the End of a Lease: Yours or Someone Else's

You can lease your car and opt to buy it at the end of your lease term. Financing the car from the beginning is a more economical option than leasing and buying the car at the end of the lease, but buying after a lease will be less expensive than starting over and financing a new car. You also have the term of your lease to see if you like the car enough to buy it. Its price is the residual value or balloon payment calculated at the beginning of the lease. This price can be financed just like a new car. Most car dealers that advertise their leased cars will tell you what the residual value will be in their ad.

The general rule is: Lease a new car, buy a used one. Leasing a used car doesn't make much sense because your lease payments will be about the same as the payments on a new car lease. One thing to remember, if you're planning on getting financing on a used car, is that the interest rate will be two to three percent higher than the rate for a new car.

The Extras

You may be able to get a better price on extras like car alarms and stereos from an independent retailer. Dealers have choices, but they may not have the exact six-CD changer with detachable face plate you had in mind. So you may prefer to buy these things separately. The drawback is that the dealer may void any electrical warranty on the car if they didn't install your stereo.

The other thing to consider when comparing prices at the dealer versus an independent retailer is that the retailer's price doesn't include installation, while the dealer's price does. So that $500 stereo becomes $750 when you tack on installation and it requires an extra trip to an installation facility if the retailer doesn't offer this service. When compared to the dealer's offer of $800, you may decide to go for the factory model and not risk voiding your electrical warranty. But if the dealer doesn't have the stereo you want, either try to use this as a bargaining chip to get the dealer to lower the price of the car or make the decision to get the stereo elsewhere. The same goes for alarms, window tinting, phones, and floor mats.

The following is a list of extras that you should be aware of when negotiating the price of the car. Under the guise of "For only seven extra dollars a month, you can have . . ." the dealer will try to get you to tack on extras that you may or may not really need. Often the best way to get the price down is to coax the dealer to

sell you these add-ons at close to cost, so the price comes down
but the dealer still makes a profit on the car. Here are some extra
items that will add to the price of your car:

- CD player/stereo
- Floor mats
- Window tinting
- Alarm
- Lo-Jack alarm
- Custom wheels
- Pinstripes
- Maintenance agreements
- Phone
- Leather interior
- Air conditioning

Don't Get Walked On

You'll hear about warranty plans. "As far as I'm concerned,
that's the only way to buy a car," Honest Abby, the head of financing will tell you. You don't want to appear naive. You don't want
to be the first person to buy a car the wrong way. Suddenly your
monthly payments are twenty-five dollars higher. Then there's the
car alarm. "I don't know why anyone would spend this kind of
money on a car without protecting it from theft," Abby says. Add
another fifteen to the payments. And then there's window tinting.

Unless you are a floor mat, you should be able to get through
the car-buying experience without someone walking all over you.
Don't fall for cool-sounding add-ons that you really don't need, and
don't pay more than you should for the ones you do need. Things
like paint protector are just an extra waxy coating that dealers will
use to wax philosophical about extending the life of your paint. You
don't need rust protector or fabric protector. If you really want
your car interior sprayed, a can of Scotchguard works great. Your
car will come with a warranty, so only consider buying an extended
one if you plan to keep your car after the manufacturer's warranty
expires. It's an extra that you don't really need, buy if you err on

the side of caution and want the warranty, negotiate its price as well.

Sleep on It

You want a night to sleep on the idea. Haste makes waste, and all that. Don't let the dealer grab your hand and push you into signing all the paperwork. They'll tell you, "You can still change your mind, but it's easier to get everything signed and ready to go." Easier for them maybe, but it pushes you one step closer to buying a car you're not sure you want. Impulse buying is fun in that instant gratification sort of way, but it's not a great way to spend thousands of dollars.

If you're not sure you want it, walk away and think about it. You may be able to give the dealer a nonrefundable deposit to keep the car on the lot until you've had time to think and sleep a little. This good faith offer can save you the hassle of endless paperwork and give you the peace of mind that the car won't be gone the next day if you decide you want it.

First-Timers

What do you do if you're fresh out of school, not a dime to your name, and no credit history except the phone bill you paid almost all of the time? Most dealers have first-time buyer programs that have qualifications you must meet, such as having a job in a field related to your major or a letter from your employer. If you're still in the middle of your job search or you majored in philosophy and haven't been hired as a professional thinker, you may have to head home . . . to your parents. Parents can be cosigners on car loans if none of your other financing plans work out.

Buying Used

With so many cars being leased nowadays, it's a buyers market when it comes to used car deals. You'll get the best price if you look for ads in the paper or another publication that lists used cars. The only drawback to buying from a private party is that you'll have no recourse if you end up with a lemon. You can stack the odds in your favor, however, by taking a car you're interested in to a mechanic.

If the owner has taken the car to one mechanic for years, you can get a good sense of the car's history. If you're worried that the mechanic may be biased toward the owner, you may feel more comfortable going to the mechanic you've trusted for years. Either way, it's worth the fifty to a hundred bucks the mechanic will charge to look it over thoroughly. If the mechanic says a lot of repairs will be needed and you still want the car, get a repair estimate and use it to work down the asking price.

Where Else to Look

When you want to buy used but don't want to drag yourself to the front yard of every Ma and Pa in town, you can turn to the dealers in your area. Go to the dealer that sells the kind of car you want to buy. In other words, buy a used Honda from a Honda dealer, a used Jeep from a Jeep/Eagle dealer. The genius behind this rule of thumb is simple. When a dealer takes back their car at the end of a lease or as a trade-in, they check it thoroughly. They check it for safety and they'll have a better idea of how the car should run than a dealer who sells another type of car. When you buy from a dealer, ask if the manufacturer's warranty has expired. If so, you'll probably want to purchase an extended warranty from the dealer.

Then there are the used car lots, armpits of the car-buying world. They're not all bad, but you never really know what you're getting. They buy fleet cars, like taxis and police cars, and they buy dealers' rejects, cars that didn't make it past inspection. Used car lots will check the brakes and the tires, but not much else. Often they don't have full maintenance facilities and will only make cosmetic repairs so the car looks good enough to sell. Buyer be wary.

When you're ready to buy used, arm yourself with information just as you would for a new car purchase and keep the following things in mind:

- Ask for service receipts and the warranty booklet for evidence the car has been kept up.
- Check to see that the tires are evenly worn, a sign they're properly aligned. If the car has low miles and very worn-out tires, the odometer may have been turned back.
- Check under the hood for signs of leaks and odd smells. Look on the ground where the car is parked for leaks.
- Look for signs that the car has been in an accident, such as uneven paint, rust, or wavy areas on the body where work may have been done.
- Check to see if the engine turns over promptly and that the car stays running, even if it started cold. When driving, the car should drive smoothly without rumbling.
- Make sure the brakes work if you stop abruptly and be sure there's no steering wheel shake if you brake at high speed.
- Drive up hills and check to make sure the engine has enough power. If the transmission is manual, look for smooth shifting. If it's automatic, make sure the car goes into gear when it's supposed to.

When You Need a Brake or an Oil Change

The dealer may have promised your car would be worry-free, but you'll still have to contend with its upkeep. This includes maintenance for regular wear and tear like oil changes every 3,000 miles, tune-ups, and brake pads as they're needed. If you have your car for a while or buy a used one that needs some work, you may need more extensive repairs. You can do certain things yourself, like replacing a headlight, but you'll need to find a good mechanic for more complicated repairs.

Go to the area of town where dealerships, tire stores, and repair shops tend to congregate. It's not necessary that the service department at the dealership change your oil. Oil changes, brake pad replacements, or tire rotations are not hard sciences and can be done cheaply at gas stations that have service departments or independent shops that specialize in tune-ups and oil changes. You can always go to the dealer's service department, but you may pay more. The dealer's service department is where you should go for the periodic checkups that are specified in your manual. It's also the place to fix something that's still under warranty.

> "I bought this used clunker, the kind they practically outlawed when gas prices went up. None of the gauges worked, or at least that's what I thought. It turned out the gas gauge, which read empty, was the only one that did work. I ran out of gas on the second day I owned the car."
>
> —Jamie, 28

When picking a place to go for basic repairs, look for evidence that others have been there before you. Look at the cars that are currently at the shop and make sure they're being moved along. You don't want to go to a place that's full of cars if they're the same cars just sitting every day. Look at the types of cars being serviced and see if they're like yours. If you paid a mint for your car, you don't want to take it to a place that services jalopies.

For something like getting your tires rotated, pick a national company that sells and rotates tires, like Goodyear. For transmission work, use Aamco. For brakes, Midas.

When it comes to parts, let the repair shop supply them. The price you'll get is fair because it has to be by law. Labor costs can be harder to estimate, but the price you'll be charged for an air filter is about the same as what you'd get at an auto parts shop. Bringing an oil filter and a case of oil to a gas station for an oil and lube would be like bringing ham and eggs to a restaurant and asking the chef to make you an omelet.

Like everything, you can sometimes haggle a bit on car repair costs, especially when they're estimating how long it might take to fix your car—pure labor costs. It doesn't always work, but it doesn't hurt to ask. If an independent service station presents you with a list of unfamiliar parts and services your car will need for repair, you can call the dealership that sells your car to find out what they are and how much the dealership would charge for them. This will give you a sense of whether the service station is aboveboard in their pricing or whether you're getting ripped off.

Help on the Road

Before you go for the big insurance plan, go for the little one that will bail you out when you need it most—on the road. The Automobile Association of America has offices around the country and can be found in the phone book for your area. For less than fifty bucks a year, Triple A will jump-start your battery, unlock your doors, tow you to a local service station, and a lot more. You'll get a card with numbers to dial in an emergency and an AAA truck will show up to help you within minutes.

If you use it once a year, it's well worth the cost. Plus you'll get peace of mind, which is invaluable. The auto club can also be a great source of free road maps, travel books, and services like getting new license plates on a used car or changing the address on your car registration. Their lines are usually shorter than the ones at the DMV.

14

INSURING THE BEAST ON WHEELS

Don't Drive Yourself Crazy

There are almost as many companies willing to insure your car "for less" as there are infomercials about the road to healthy gums. Just flip on the TV any weekday morning and you'll see. These insurance companies must think that if you have nothing better to do on a weekday morning than watch *I Love Lucy* reruns, your life must be in serious disarray, so perhaps your car isn't insured. Something like that.

In any case, how should you weed through the masses and find a company to suit your needs? First you have to figure out what you need. Base this on your driving record, the amount you can afford, and the amount of coverage you want. Make sure you don't pay for things that you don't need, such as towing service, which may be covered by your automobile club policy.

By law in most states, you're required to have bodily injury and personal property liability insurance. If you lease or finance your car, you'll also be required by the lender to purchase comprehensive and collision, usually with a $500 deductible on each. If you're financing your car, the bank wants to make sure it gets its money even if something happens to your car. If you lease, the bank wants the car back undamaged at the end of the lease or the replacement value from your insurance company.

Following are the basic types of coverage you can get to cover different levels of damage and expense:

- *Bodily injury liability.* This covers you when you injure someone while driving, either a pedestrian, someone in your car, or someone in another car. Your policy will give you options for coverage, with a certain amount the company will pay to each person and a total paid for each accident. This includes legal expense, up to the policy limits. It's mandatory in most states and generally required on leased cars, making them a bit more expensive to insure.

- *Property damage liability.* This refers to hitting another car, parking meter, stop sign, building, or any other property you might damage while driving. Like bodily injury liability, your coverage specifies a certain amount paid per occurrence, including legal expense if you're sued. Damage to your own property, however, is not covered. It's required in most states.

- *Medical payments.* Adding this type of coverage to your policy will pay for any medical expenses incurred by you or anyone in your car, no matter who's at fault in an accident. If you have a high insurance deductible, medical payment insurance can ensure that you're covered in a car accident even if you haven't met your deductible. It's optional in most states. However, in states with no-fault insurance, it's mandatory to have a form of medical payments known as *personal injury protection*.

- *Comprehensive.* If your car is broken into, vandalized, or damaged by fire or storm, this coverage pays for repair or replacement costs, once you've met your deductible. It's optional on cars you own and mandatory on leased and financed cars.

- *Collision.* This covers replacement or repair costs for your car that result from an accident, whether you hit another car or a lamppost. Like comprehensive, you'll have a deductible to meet before your insurance pays. Under some policies, you can buy an uninsured motorist deductible waiver, which means you won't have to pay your deductible if an uninsured driver is at fault. Like comprehensive, it's mandatory on leased and financed cars.

- *Uninsured motorist.* You can also purchase insurance to cover damage to your car caused by uninsured or underinsured drivers, including hit-and-run drivers. You'll have a policy limit that states how much will be paid to each person in your car and how much per accident. This includes damages incurred while you're in someone else's car or when you're a pedestrian. It's mandatory in many states, but optional in others.
- *Rental car expense/loss of use.* This optional coverage reimburses you for the cost of a rental car when your car is damaged in an accident. Depending on your policy, you'll have a different limit on how much you can spend and how many rental days are included.

Lowering Your Costs

There are some ways to lower your insurance costs and it's worth taking advantage of them if they apply to you. Shop around. Call up various insurance companies for an estimate. They'll ask what kind of car you have, how many miles you drive per year, whether you have air bags or a car alarm. Then they'll send you a printed report showing how much it will cost to insure your car at various deductibles. Depending on which deductible you choose and how much potential liability you'll have, your policy cost will vary. Choosing a high deductible and low bodily injury and property damage liability will reduce your annual insurance costs.

Car insurance costs can vary greatly depending on where you live and what kind of car you own. Insurance tends to be higher in cities than in rural areas. Some cars are considered easier to break into, so their comprehensive coverage costs more. If your new set of wheels is considered a sports car, your insurance will be higher. Similarly, if your car is expensive to repair, you'll pay more. If you have an old car that isn't worth a lot, you could save money by dropping the comprehensive and collision portions of your policy. If your car is worth little more than the deductible, don't waste your money on this kind of insurance.

Some companies will give you a discount for antilock brakes, automatic seat belts, and/or air bags. Ask about these discounts and others for being a good driver or good student. Some companies also offer discounts if you've had no tickets or accidents in three years.

If you know you'll only be driving a limited number of miles per year—if your job requires you to be out of town two weeks out of every month, for example—find out if the insurance company will give you a discount for low mileage.

Here are some other things you can do to lower your insurance costs:

- Pay in lump sums twice a year instead of in installments.
- Install an alarm.
- Take a driver's training course.
- Get a car with automatic seat belts.

Pack Your Trunk

Hopefully you bought the brightest, sturdiest, best car in the history of driving. Potholes won't scare you and you'll scoff when it rains because your wiper blades are so sharp. But just in case some little thing should happen to go wrong, even just once, be prepared.

Pack yourself up a little safety kit and toss it in your trunk, hopefully never to be seen or heard from again. Here's what to include:

- Flares
- Ten bucks or a blank check
- Jumper cables

- A copy of your AAA card, in case you misplace the real one
- Chains, and gloves to wear when putting them on (only if you live someplace where it snows)
- A blanket
- A flashlight
- A jack for your spare tire
- An instant tire repair kit
- A disposable camera, in case you need to document damage from an accident

You can be creative here too. If you think you'll want to have a Powerbar while you're waiting for Triple A to show up when your battery is dead, stock your kit with some of those as well.

15

TO YOUR HEALTH

Murphy's Law and Life on the Wild Side

Living dangerously has its merits. You're an adventurer, living in the now, not to be bothered by the trivia of health care for the masses. You picture yourself in a MacGyver feat of bravado, shimmying up the side of a building on a frayed rope, no net. Or you fancy yourself another Dr. Spock, making medical history in your bathroom using ordinary toothpaste to disinfect a bite from a rabid dog. Reporters flock to interview you, the one with a finger on the pulse of new medicine: If you don't worry about it, it won't happen. At least not to you. That is, until it does.

It's not that you thought you were flu-proof. And when you set out for the first time on Rollerblades wearing a thong, you had to admit there could be some damage. You just figured you'd wait until the guys in Washington got the whole health insurance system overhauled before you signed up. Hey, it could be any day now.

Well just in case it isn't, you need to cover your butt, and not only when Rollerblading. The main reason is Murphy and his Law, which is to be revered: The day you let your policy lapse will be the day you catch the Tasmanian flu—or the day you're forced to down a quart of Epsom salts because you didn't know English Stilton and sauerkraut would make you break out in hives. Ah, the joys of home remedies. You could see a doctor, the logical step. But you'd hate to do that, oh uninsured one, because you'd be footing the bill yourself. So instead you go home with a book of old wives' tales and spend the night with your chest wrapped in cooked onions and your feet in a bucket of baking soda. It's your choice. The ironic truth is that if you'd had health insurance, none of this would have happened. Murphy planned it that way.

In Case of Emergencies . . .

Many people our age either don't have insurance or they're afraid to go to the doctor because they perceive the system to be too complicated. It's always later that we hear about certain health plans or certain drugstore chains that offer discounts on prescription medicines. It's easy to get lost in the shuffle. But you don't want to take the wrong job just because it promises health benefits, especially when they consist of an HMO co-pay with no doctors or hospitals you like. Then again, getting full major coverage with a dental and vision plan can be valuable. It all depends.

Making Sense from Madness: Types of Coverage

Here's the basic scenario: Either you call an insurance agent or a few providers yourself or your employer hands you a packet describing the types of coverage on their plan. The temptation is to check the boxes, sign on the line, and be done with it. Good impulse, but make sure you know what you're getting.

Indemnity Insurance

This is the way people have traditionally been insured, but the trend is changing. Under this type of plan, you pick which doctor you'll see, whenever you want. You can choose anyone from your family physician to a neck and back specialist, and your insurance company pays on a *fee for service* basis, which means the doctor gets paid for the services provided. But the cost to you in monthly premiums is pretty near exorbitant, so this is no longer as popular.

The decreasing popularity of indemnity plans doesn't necessarily mean you have to say good-bye to your old family doctor. Let's say you've decided to go with a different type of coverage, such as an HMO or PPO (discussed below), but you're particularly partial to a doctor who isn't on that plan. You can pay out of your pocket for visits to that doctor and use your insurance policy for everything else. It may cost you a bit more, but you'll get the doctor you're comfortable with and lower overall health insurance costs.

Group Plans

These are plans that are sponsored, that is, paid for in part or in full, by your employer. If the company you work for doesn't cover the entire cost of the plan, typically the rest is taken out of each paycheck automatically. In some cases, you'll get some money back for choosing certain types of plans, an incentive for signing up for a plan that costs your company less money. Depending on the size of the company, you may be offered a choice between types of plans or your company may have selected one plan for everyone.

Generally, you have to meet basic criteria to get on your company's health plan, ranging from working a specified number of hours per week, generally thirty, to working for the company a certain number of months. When you start a new job, you generally have to wait thirty to ninety days before you can sign up for the company's health plan. If you're not a new employee and you want to switch plans, you have to wait until the next open enrollment period, usually once a year or every six months.

Group plans, which are typically HMOs or PPOs, allow you some choices, but not as many as indemnity plans. This doesn't mean you won't find a doctor you like under a group plan—in fact, your family doctor may be on the list of providers. It just means some of the choices—which doctors you can see, when you can see them, and how much you'll pay—have already been made for you.

HMO versus PPO—First of All, What Are They?

HMOs and PPOs are versions of what's called managed care insurance and they're no longer considered the wave of the future—they're the wave of today. The idea is that a *panel* of doctors and hospitals is created (sometimes called a *network*) to reduce the cost of health care for you and the insurance companies. The doctors and hospitals offer discounted fees in exchange for being listed on the panel, where they gain access to patients who sign up for the plan. The patients have incentive to use the doctors on the panel because the discounts are passed on to them. Again, you can still see a doctor who isn't listed on the panel, and your insurance will contribute to the cost of the visit, but you'll pay more out of pocket than if you see a doctor on the panel. Both types of plans have restrictions, HMOs more than PPOs. But then, PPOs cost more.

PPO Is Not a Typo

Preferred provider organizations give you a list of doctors from which to choose. The doctors in a PPO have agreed to discount their fees in order to be listed on the panel. This means that when you get the bill, it has been reduced by a certain percentage, usually around 20 percent, and you pay the rest, until you've met your deductible, at which point your insurance pays. Deductibles are usually $500, $1,000, or $2,000 per year. Choosing a lower deductible will raise your insurance payments, and vice versa.

As a rule, PPOs have extensive lists of doctors, increasing the chance that a doctor you already know and like is on the list. In this way, PPOs are like indemnity insurance because you have few restrictions on which doctors you can see and when you can see them.

How PPOs Work

When you need to see a doctor, say for stomach pains, you consult the list of doctors available under your PPO. You make an appointment with a gastroenterologist or a general practitioner or whatever doctor you want, as long as that doctor is on the list. You go to the doctor, flash your PPO insurance card, and later you get a bill. Your bill will show a discount given by the doctor who is a PPO member, so you'll pay less than the full fee.

When you are a PPO member, you're responsible for paying the bills you get until you've reached your deductible for that year. Say you have a $500 deductible and your bill is for $1,000. You're responsible for paying $500, to meet your deductible, and the insurance company pays almost all the rest. PPOs generally follow a policy of paying 80 percent of your health-care costs once you've met your deductible.

PPOs—The Pros and Cons

PPOs cost more than HMOs. You pay your monthly payments and you have to meet your deductible before the insurance company pays anything. You can raise your deductible to lower your monthly costs, but then you've decreased the chance you'll meet your deductible. This means you'll be paying for every visit out of your own pocket, save the fee discount the doctor gives you for using the PPO.

On the pro side, you have a wide choice of doctors and you can see a specialist any time you want, the main difference between a PPO and an HMO. PPOs are available to you on an individual basis or through a group plan.

HMO Doesn't Stand for
Hungry Man's Omelet

Ask about HMOs and you'll hear that your doctor is a gatekeeper, like someone who guards great medical secrets that only those in the land of Narnia are privy to. You'll also be told you have to pick a primary care physician. Sometimes when you ask about these things you get more information than you really want to know. Or rather, you get lots of information, some of which is important, the rest of which just buries all the important stuff so you can barely find it. Here are the basics.

The initials stand for health maintenance organization and they are used by a large percentage of Americans. An HMO is a type of insurance plan that provides comprehensive health care to its patients for a prepaid, fixed cost. The concept is that if the doctors and hospitals have a responsibility to control the cost of the care they provide, they'll only provide necessary and appropriate care. Because these costs are controlled, the result is that HMO insurance is the least expensive coverage available.

How HMOs Work

If your employer offers you membership in an HMO, you'll start by picking a doctor/primary care physician/gatekeeper from a list provided by the HMO. This makes an HMO more restrictive than a PPO. You can ask around for recommendations or close your eyes and point to a name. This will be your gatekeeper.

When you need to go to the doctor, say for the same stomach pains, you call the gatekeeper/primary care physician (PCP) and make an appointment. Your visit will cost you anywhere from five to thirty-five bucks because HMOs typically require a *co-pay* to the doctor for each visit. This means you pay a little bit each time you go to the doctor, but the HMO picks up the rest. Then the PCP, who is a general physician, will examine you. If it looks like your stomach pains are from stress or lactose intolerance or something else that the primary care doctor can diagnose, you'll be treated and sent on your way. The whole gatekeeper concept revolves around saving needless dollars from being spent on needless specialists, when your PCP can take care of the problem.

On the other hand, if your PCP thinks there's cause for concern, you'll be sent to a specialist. But you can't just go ahead and make an appointment with the specialist without seeing your PCP first because the specialist works behind the gate. Your visit to the specialist will also have a co-pay.

Like anything, you have to determine your needs and see if the HMO you're considering meets your needs. If you wear disposable contact lenses that add up to a mint by the end of the year, you'd probably like an HMO with a vision plan.

HMOs—The Pros and Cons

The main criticism people have about HMOs is that they're too limiting; they don't want to be restricted to choosing from a list of doctors they can see. People also worry that PCPs are too busy and overscheduled and that they don't give you as much attention as you'd like. Another concern is that patients don't get the care they need because HMOs cut back on services to save money, which eventually sacrifices quality. However, there are national quality guidelines and state-by-state oversight to keep tabs on all HMOs, so you needn't be overly worried when choosing a basic health plan. Every HMO has to go through an extensive application and qualification procedure to get licensed by the state. Then there are reviews to make sure the HMOs continue to meet state standards.

All that aside, HMOs and their participants are growing in number. Employers like them because they cost less, so it's more and more likely that you'll find one in your group health insurance packet at work. They also cost less for you, another reason to consider them.

How to Choose an HMO

You can take some of the guesswork out of the process by choosing an HMO that has been accredited by the National Committee for Quality Assurance, a national accrediting group in

Washington, D.C. The NCQA publishes a database called Quality Compass that has the results of its annual quality assessments. Look at their Web site, www.ncqa.org, or call their customer service department, (888)275-7585.

You can separate the wheat from the chaff by choosing an NCQA-accredited HMO that's affiliated with a hospital that's accredited by the Joint Commission on Accreditation of Healthcare Organizations and has a large number of board-certified doctors. It's a safe bet to choose a primary care physician who is board certified, which requires additional years of training and a tough exam, and the HMO should give you this information. You can also look up individual doctors' credentials in *The American Medical Directory* at the library.

Another important factor is what the laws in your state allow the HMO to do for you. In some states, an OB/GYN can be a primary care physician. So for women, this is a big plus because if your OB/GYN is your assigned primary care physician, you can schedule appointments directly without having to go through another gatekeeper. And it will cost you less than you currently pay.

Similarly, if you have a doctor you like, you can find out if he or she is part of an HMO and sign up with that plan. That way, you'll be sure to have a primary care doctor you like and you could save considerable money without having to change doctors.

Short-Term Individual Policies

During the short term, while you're looking for a job and trying to keep your life together, the idea of going out and finding health insurance may seem like an extra burden. But there are some temporary solutions that will tide you over until you either find a job with health-care benefits or enroll in a health plan yourself.

If you were on your parents' insurance policy, you might consider staying on it, paying for your portion, until you find a job that has benefits. But if you had health insurance through school and you know it's just a matter of time before you get hired or start the job you've been hired for, you probably want to leave your parents out of the equation. That doesn't mean, however, that you should go uninsured.

Many insurance providers offer short-term insurance policies to cover you from the time you graduate until you find a job, or for the time in between jobs. These temporary policies are inexpensive, about $75 to $100 a month, but they have high deductibles. The idea is that you're covered in case of catastrophe, but this isn't a long-term solution. Policies are written for three to six months.

Individual plans vary. Generally, they exclude preexisting health conditions and some have other requirements, such as paying in full up front with no refund if you discontinue the insurance early. Some companies will write subsequent policies, others will write only one. Bankers Life & Casualty at (800)621-3724 or www .bankerslife.com writes policies for people in all states except New York. John Alden at (800)435-7969 or www.nstarmc.com writes policies for people in any state.

Determining Your Needs

Not everyone has the same health insurance needs. At our age, we have different needs than our parents do, so we can't always follow their lead. There's no rule that will tell you an HMO or PPO or other plan is the only way to go. It depends on how often you go to the doctor, whether you regularly take prescription medication, whether you are in a high-risk profession.

If you are an athlete, for example, and need to see podiatrists and orthopedists regularly to treat injuries, you'd probably want a PPO plan with a low deductible. That way, you'd have a greater choice of specialists and wouldn't have to go to a primary care physician every time you wanted to see a knee specialist. As for the deductible, you'd want to pay as little as possible yourself before your coverage kicked in. If you're prone to getting the flu several times a year and need to see a doctor each time and buy prescriptions, you may not be as concerned about seeing a specialist, so the doctor from an HMO might be just fine. And the co-pay plan that an HMO provides will ensure that you're not spending an arm and a leg at the pharmacy.

Perform a similar assessment of yourself, asking yourself the following questions:

- On average, how often do you see a doctor per year?
- What kind of doctor do you see, a general doctor or a specialist?
- Do you usually go to the doctor for basic checkups or specific illnesses or injuries?
- What are you used to, going to a private physician or a doctor under a plan like Kaiser Permanente, the largest HMO in the country?

COBRA—It Can Bite

By law, a company with more than nineteen employees is required to offer you health insurance after you quit, leave, or get fired from your job, unless you're fired for gross misconduct. The Consolidated Omnibus Budget Reconciliation Act, or COBRA, was designed to let you continue the same coverage for up to eighteen months after you leave your job. But there's a catch: you pay for it yourself. So if your former health plan allowed for your employer to pay half of the insurance payments and take the other half from your paycheck, now you'll be paying both halves.

COBRA is a mixed blessing. On one hand, it keeps you covered while you're looking for your next job or your next insurance plan. On the other hand, it is the most expensive way to buy insurance. So the best way to make use of COBRA provisions is to think of it as temporary. Don't wait until the end of eighteen months to find a new plan. If you're looking for a new job, COBRA is fine to tide you over for a few months, until you find the next job and your new policy kicks in. If you're going to be looking for new insurance, say under an individual plan, take advantage of COBRA while you're looking, then cancel it when your new policy begins.

If you think of COBRA as a temporary solution, you can get the most out of it. You'll remain covered in case any medical emergency should arise, but you won't break the bank paying the whole cost for eighteen months.

How to Get Your Own Policy

Even if you work for a large company that provides great health benefits, you should still understand how to get your own policy. There may well be a time in your life when you'll need to sign up for one. You may work full time for an employer now and always plan to, but you may not be offered health insurance, or any benefits for that matter, as part of your work arrangement. Many companies, from law firms to newspapers, are using employees who are full-time contractors. They report to work every day and are taxed like employees, meaning the employer pays part of FICA and social security taxes, but they're not offered any benefits.

Then there's the other segment of the working population known as freelancers, independent contractors, and small business owners. In any of these cases, there's no one employer to provide health insurance for you, so you must do it yourself. Whether you choose an HMO or a PPO, you'll be buying an individual plan.

You have a choice between using an insurance agent and calling insurers directly. If your parents have an insurance agent, or if someone else can give you a referral, don't hesitate to call. You can also look in the Yellow Pages for an insurance agent who deals with health care and the agent will find a policy for you based on your preferences. You're not charged for this service since insurance agents get their fees from the insurance companies.

If you opt to call an HMO, PPO, or other insurer directly, look for their ads in the newspaper or use the Yellow Pages. A better option is to ask your doctor if he or she is on an HMO or PPO panel. That way, you can join an insurance plan and continue to see the doctor you like.

The Cost of Your Policy

The things that affect the cost of your policy are all things you can control, unless you have a preexisting medical condition. Here's what you can do:

- Raise your deductible to lower your monthly payments.
- Join an HMO instead of a PPO or indemnity plan to lower your monthly payments and your per-visit cost.
- Maintain a healthy lifestyle, that is, don't smoke and get some exercise, and you might get a break.

If you have a preexisting health condition, some policies will charge you higher rates while others will contain a provision that excludes that condition from treatment with full coverage. But by law, you cannot be refused insurance because of a preexisting condition.

Read the Fine Print

When you're deciding between policies and especially once you've chosen one, take a minute to read the policy provisions carefully. One thing you don't want to miss out on is a service your insurance provides for little or no cost. You can often get discounts at certain pharmacies in your neighborhood and some plans allow you one physical per year at a discounted price. But you have to read the plan carefully and make note of anything new you get in the mail or receive from the human resources department at work.

Vision and Dental

Some policies include visits to the dentist and eye doctor. If this is the case with the plan offered by your employer, consider yourself lucky. Otherwise, it probably doesn't make much sense to pay extra for these provisions since adding them to your policy is pretty expensive.

This doesn't mean you should wear the same pair of glasses you've had since freshman year of college if you're starting to see double. Nor does it mean you should let your teeth rot. It simply means you should pay for these visits yourself when you need them.

Things to Keep in Mind

More and more, insurance companies are requiring doctors to itemize their bills. When yours comes, look at every lab fee, exam fee, and equipment charge to see if they seem correct, even if your insurance company is picking up part of the tab. For example, if you get your bill and notice you're being charged for an initial exam and an intermediate exam on the same day, call and question it. People make mistakes—if you were only examined one time by one person, you shouldn't pay twice.

Also remember that there's more than one way to join a group plan. One way is through membership in a group that offers health insurance to its members. For example, unions and guilds that receive dues from their members generally offer excellent insurance plans as a benefit.

You can also save a lot of money by asking your doctor to prescribe the generic form of any prescription drug you need.

Staying Healthy

Of course, it always helps to stack the deck in your favor. Signing up for health insurance shouldn't be an invitation to eat triple-cream brie until you force your cholesterol to record levels, or to go skating on thin ice. This is a time in life when work takes up so many hours a day that it's hard to do much else. But if you can manage to eat right at least part of the time and exercise about the same, you'll come out way ahead of the game when it comes to staying well. Getting enough sleep helps too.

The office is not exactly a beacon for healthy habits. Think about your new lifestyle. Gone are the days of hikes or squash games between classes. Your college lifestyle of walking everywhere from class to the bookstore to the pub down the block has been replaced by a post-college lifestyle consisting mostly of sitting. Sure, you might walk to lunch or from your office to the bathroom twice a day, but there's only one word that describes the world of office work: sedentary.

This just means you'll have to make more of an effort. Whether it's walking to work twice a week instead of taking the subway or strolling during your lunch hour twice a week and eating at your desk, do something. Fortunately exercise is a million-dollar business. You'll find no shortage of gyms, studios, shoes, sweats, and Lycra to help you get into an exercise routine.

There are other new habits you'll develop that won't be so hot for your health, namely ordering from restaurants or grabbing fast food. It's not like you're going to be cooking balanced low-sodium meals for yourself wedged in beside the water cooler in the kitchenette, but you can fight the urge to eat a whole double-cheese and pepperoni pizza every night and maybe opt for a salad every so often.

You also need to take care of your teeth. Brushing and flossing are great, but if you're stressed out and grinding your teeth, you may end up with other problems down the line. Unless you have problems with your teeth, a biannual cleaning and checkup will be all you'll need. Here's to your health.

16

DOLLARS AND SENSE

Your Checking Account—The Financial Way Station

I t seems likely that the moon exerts some kind of gravitational pull on people's checking accounts. That's the only explanation for monthly movement so much like the ocean. The paycheck flows in, the rent check flows out. The ten bucks a friend borrowed flows in, the ATM withdrawal flows out. Seemingly no matter how much you put in, there's a spending tide to pull the cash right out to sea.

The nice thing is, once you find a bank with policies, monthly minimums, and fees you can live with, you can get on with the business of earning and spending and stop shopping around. Banks aren't like investments that need to be watched. Unless you have too much time on your hands, you're probably not going to go around opening and closing your checking account every time you see a bank advertising some new special deal or interest rate a quarter of a percentage point higher than what you're getting.

Your checking account will give you a way to pay your bills and a place to put your paycheck. Unless you prefer to pay for things on the barter system or by exchanging beads, you'll be writing some checks. Checking accounts are hardly an unfamiliar concept and banks make it easy to open an account, leaving the minor details like monthly charges for you to find out by reading "the literature."

Know Yourself

Start by figuring out what you want from your bank, bearing in mind that your checking account, savings account, loan source, and investment adviser need not be in the same place. In fact, you'll probably get the best deals by going to the best place for each of these things, rather than trying to find a bank of all trades.

Ask yourself a few questions:

- How much are you willing to let sit untouched in your account to earn interest or to avoid a monthly charge for going below your minimum balance?
- Do you regularly bounce checks?
- Do you regularly balance your checkbook?
- Do you use the ATM to get cash?
- How many checks do you write per month?
- Do you use a debit card or ATM card for groceries or gas?
- Do you already have other bank accounts?

Location, Location, Location

If you've just moved from your college town to a new city, there's a good chance your old bank doesn't have a branch there. Even if it does, you'll probably want to close your old account and open a new one because even if the name of the bank is the same, all transactions will go through your old branch and your new branch will take a hands-off, it's-not-our-branch attitude if it takes a week for a check to clear. So whether you keep your same bank or find a new one, you'll need to open an account.

On the other hand, location isn't everything. You don't want a bank branch too far from where you live, but there are perils of picking one just because it's near. While it's tempting to pick a bank that's two blocks away, you should make sure that bank is really a better choice than the one that's four blocks away—or ten. The extra distance won't make a big difference in your life but all kinds of other things, from charges for each check you write to monthly maintenance fees, might make a huge difference.

Check Bouncers

If you have trouble remembering to balance your checkbook and find yourself bouncing an occasional check, the first thing you should do is try to control yourself and reverse these habits. Like it took a genius to tell you that. If this isn't possible, you should definitely choose a bank that offers you overdraft protection, either in the form of a credit card tied to your account or a savings account at the same bank. Overdraft protection is basically a line of credit that you can tap into if you go below zero in your checking account. You pay the money back like any loan, only with high interest. If you keep a savings account at the same bank, money can be transferred into your checking account to cover any overdrafts. Either way, this is a far better plan than the alternative.

Bouncing checks is an expensive proposition. Besides risking ruining your credit by writing bad checks, you'll also have to pay hefty fees at your bank—upward of twenty-five bucks—plus the ten or so dollars the other person gets charged for trying to cash your bad check. Friends might be understanding about this, but businesses are less forgiving. If you bounced the check that was supposed to pay your Visa bill, you'll have the privilege of receiving angry notices threatening to revoke your line of credit. It doesn't take much to get blacklisted.

Busy Check Writers

Some bank accounts have limits on the number of checks you can write per month. Banks will sometimes offer to drop the monthly service charge if you only write a fixed number of checks per month. Some people don't write that many checks. If you use your ATM card or a debit card to take money from your account and pay for things, you may be writing only a few checks per month. In this case, a monthly limit won't cramp your cash flow. But if you rely on ample check writing, make sure you won't be charged for it.

ATM Users

If you rely on the ATM for deposits and withdrawals, choose a bank that has a lot of branches for convenient access. One advantage to this is that you'll always be able to find a branch wherever you are in the city and you won't be charged each time you use another bank's ATM. But if you travel a lot for business, it won't make a difference how many branches there are in your hometown because you'll rarely find your bank out of state. So you'll be paying to use the ATMs in other cities and no one will care how big your bank is at home.

All ATMs are part of a network of other ATMs that can be accessed if your card is compatible. Your ATM card will typically have one or more names on the back, such as STAR, PLUS, MAC, CIRRUS, or IN-

> "Bank charges for MAC card use and the fact that I had a low balance always messed up my checkbook. So with every deposit, I began marking in my checkbook $20 less than actually deposited. So my $800 salary check was marked down in my checkbook as $780. I never had to worry about the bank nickel and diming me on charges after that, plus in a year, I reconciled the account and had a nice chunk of change left over to use for vacation."
>
> —Ben, 29

TERLINK, which tell you which other banks' machines will accept your card. Some banks don't charge you anything for using other banks' ATM machines, but typically, you can expect your bank to charge about $2.50 for using another bank's ATM. Sometimes you'll even be charged by the bank whose ATM you're using as well. This can add up, so before you open an account, find out what your bank charges.

Interest Rates Aren't Everything

If you start calling around, looking into interest-bearing accounts that offer check-writing privileges, you can quickly get overwhelmed. This fund offers you great interest rates, but you can only write seven checks a month. That one offers you great rates but you have no ATM access. And yet another one offers you decent rates but you have to keep a $1,000 minimum balance to avoid monthly fees. Suddenly something simple like depositing your paycheck and writing your rent check has become a study in high finance. It shouldn't be.

Again, the best thing you can do is prioritize. Remind yourself what you want your checking account to do for you. If all you need is a place to deposit your checks and a way to pay your bills, you probably don't need to shop all over town for interest rates that will earn you a whole dollar a month on your $1,000 balance. Sometimes, choosing the bank whose interest rates are half a point higher can backfire if you more than make up for your gain in increased fees.

Then again, if you want to earn interest on your checking account (discussed in the next chapter), you might choose a money market checking account and only use it to write big checks like rent. That way the big chunks of money will earn interest until your rent is due. This will allow you to stay within the checks-per-month minimum and earn a little in the process.

If you want your bank to do more for you, like give you a debit card, handle your savings, and extend you a car loan, you'll want to shop around more thoroughly.

Choosing a Bank

Any bank you choose should be FDIC-insured. This means the Federal Deposit Insurance Corporation will cover your deposits if the bank goes belly up. It's worth it to know the FDIC is worrying about keeping your money safe so you can worry about other things.

Once you've figured out what you need from a bank, you can shop around by phone for a bank that has the features you want. Ask about how the bank handles the issues that are important to you. Use the following list for reference:

- Monthly fees
- Charges if you write more than a certain number of checks
- Interest rates
- Minimum balances
- Overdraft protection
- Credit cards or debit cards tied to your account
- ATM availability and fees for using machines at other banks

Opening a New Account

When you've found a bank you like, go down in person with your driver's license and another form of ID. A credit card or passport will do. The application will ask for a social security number, name, and address. You can open the account either with cash or with a check from the account you closed at your previous bank.

Maintaining the Delicate Balance

If you find that you have trouble keeping your checkbook balanced, you're definitely not alone. Just look at how much trouble the government has balancing its budget and you won't feel so bad. However, do as they say they'll do, not as they actually do, and you'll find yourself in the black, writing paper checks, not rubber ones.

ATMs are the checkbook balancer's nemesis. It's not such a big deal to record the check you're writing at the supermarket because your checkbook is already there, open in front of you. But at the ATM machine, your checkbook is nowhere to be found. So it's pretty easy to slide the card in, get your cash, and go on your way, stuffing the receipt in your back pocket or into the caverns of your purse. Then you call the bank's 800 number to find out your balance and learn that you've spent $400 more than you thought. The ATM withdrawals add up, and if you use your ATM to buy groceries and other things, you can deplete your account without writing any checks at all. So you'll have to have a system.

Eight Easy Steps to Keep Your Checkbook Balanced

1. *Write the total amount of money that's in your account at the top of the ledger that comes with your box of checks.*

2. *Each time you write a check, write the amount of the check in the ledger, along with the check number and the recipient of the check.*

3. *Subtract the amount of the check from the total in your account. Keep the running total in the far right-hand column.*

4. *For each ATM withdrawal you make, subtract that amount from the total as well.*

5. *For each deposit you make, enter the amount in your ledger and add that to your running total on the right.*

6. *If your account earns interest, add that to the total at the end of each month.*

7. *If you're assessed additional fees from your bank for ATM use, new checks, or monthly maintenance fee, subtract them.*

8. *Compare your bank monthly statement with your ledger to make sure your checks have been cashed, your deposits have been credited, and your ledger's balance roughly matches your bank statement.*

How to Be Anal about Checkbook Balancing

You can stuff all your ATM receipts into your wallet and balance your checkbook one night a week in front of the TV if that's easiest. Or, you can keep them in another special place and bring them to work with you where you've got your Quicken program all set up at your desk. Whatever works. Remember that if you have automatic check withdrawal to pay certain bills or if you earn interest on your account, you have to subtract or add accordingly.

Basically, you have to know yourself. If you absolutely loathe the thought of keeping track of all this stuff on paper, you can try to keep a mental tally. Look at your ATM receipt each time you visit the machine and make sure you have money in your account that will cover the big checks you most recently wrote. To use this technique, it's best to keep a cushion of cash in your account, so you're okay if you've forgotten a check or two. In other words, if you plan to live in oblivion where your checking account balance is concerned, keep enough in your account so you don't run out of money. The problem with having more in your account than you need is that your money would be better invested in a savings account or CD where it could earn more interest. Lost interest is the price you pay for living in oblivion.

Electronic Banking

You can take advantage of other services your bank offers such as electronic banking. As quickly as you can instruct your computer to electronically transfer the money to the phone company, it is gone from your account and your bill is paid. Definitely faster. However, depending on what kind of bill you're paying, it may not always make economic sense to bank via your computer at home. When you tell your computer to write your rent check, for example, the funds leave your account and the check is written. But if the landlord doesn't cash the check right away, the money's still gone from your account and you earn no interest on it.

> *"My purse was stolen so I put a block on the checks that were in it, just to be safe. Later, I found out the bank started refusing to pay other checks I'd written for rent and my credit card payment. It turns out they'd put a red flag on my account and weren't honoring any checks where the signature didn't exactly match the one on file. They were supposedly doing me a favor—meanwhile they were killing my reputation with the people I'd written checks to. I ended up having to close the account and open a new one."*   —Michelle, 23

Then again, if your checking account doesn't earn interest anyway, it won't make a difference to you. Plus, you won't be fooled when you look at your balance because every check written will already be subtracted, unlike regular checking accounts in which it might appear that you have money because someone hasn't yet cashed your check.

Another service you can take advantage of, if your employer will accommodate you, is direct paycheck deposit into your account. This can be a time saver as well as a temptation fighter. If you never have the paycheck in your hand, you may be less likely to spend it right away.

Things to Keep in Mind

- Your checking account is not the place for high-stakes investing. There are all kinds of interest-bearing accounts, such as money markets, that give you check-writing privileges, but most have stringent requirements for minimum balances you need to keep in the account. If you don't want to maintain a daily minimum, it's probably easiest to keep the amount you'll need to cover checks and ATM withdrawals in your checking account and put anything extra in a savings account, money market, or CD (discussed in the next chapter).
- If you have an erratic signature that looks different on each check you sign, tell the bank when you're opening your account so they can keep several versions of your signature on file.
- If you deposit a check in an amount greater than what's in your

account, the bank will probably put a hold on the money, refusing to honor any checks you write from your new funds until the check clears. Not only is this annoying, it isn't really fair. It's your money. If you deposit it, you should be able to spend it. So don't give in when the bank tells you there's going to be a two- to ten-day hold on your check. Take your check into the bank and ask that the funds be made available that day. If your account is in good standing, it shouldn't be a problem.

But don't count on such an easy path if you make your deposit through the ATM. In that case, your deposits are received by bank employees, antsy for their lunch break, who don't even look before pushing the button that generates a "We're placing a two-day hold . . ." letter.

- If you deposit cash at the ATM, sign across the sealed flap to ensure that it doesn't get opened (and emptied) somewhere along the way into your account.
- Don't feel like you have to find one bank to suit all your needs. You may find a bank nearby that is perfect for your checking account needs and that's all. If they have what you want in a checking account, don't worry if their savings accounts don't have the highest rates. You can go elsewhere for your other needs.
- A lot of banks will offer you extra incentives like free safety deposit boxes, free traveler's checks, or automatic overdraft protection if you open savings accounts with them too. The extra perks aren't a substitute for the higher interest rates you might be able to get at another bank.

17

A PENNY SAVED

Cash Flow: It Flows All Right, but Generally in One Direction

In my two-some-odd decades on this planet, I have won some, lost some, and failed to be considered for still others. But I do know at least one simple fact of life: Spending money is more fun and instantly gratifying than saving money. Find me anyone in their twenties (or anyone at all, for that matter) who disagrees and we'll have a hands-down new government financial adviser who can balance our sorry budget once and for all. Exactly. It goes against the heart and soul of commerce in America.

But living hand-to-mouth has its drawbacks. There's nothing worse than spending your last dime on rent and then having to decline when your friends tell you they're going on a road trip to Las Vegas. Not only can't you gamble, but you can't even go. Few things are as humiliating and panic-inducing as receiving angry bank notices about bounced checks after you've thrown caution to the wind and written a check for groceries, just hoping your paycheck will make it into your account before the supermarket comes to collect.

You need to have a cushion—some money in your account to take up the slack in case things don't match up perfectly at the end of the month. Little things can crop up—things like needing a new car battery or wanting to buy a new suit for work. If you have a little stash of cash, the unexpected hassles in life won't stress you out as much and the things you want won't be so out of reach. And the further along you get in your career, the better off you'll be financially, and saving will become easier. So getting in the habit now is a good thing to do.

Now that you've made the commitment to finding a career you like, you don't want lack of savings to keep you tied to a bad work situation. By saving until you have a cushion of two to three months' living expenses, you'll be giving yourself the financial freedom to leave a job you hate and spend all your time searching for a better one. This little job-search nest egg will give you peace of mind any time the company you work for talks about downsizing because you won't be left in the lurch. And if you're self-employed, you'll be able to cover the times when someone tells you the check's in the mail and it doesn't arrive for a month.

Saving the Big Bucks

You also need to save for the bigger things. If you plan to buy a computer next year and can start saving now, you'll have a good running start when it comes time to pay the bill. This way, you can avoid putting the whole thing on your credit card and racking up debt and high interest payments. As a rule, it's good to get in the habit of *saving something every month*, even if it's only coins in a piggy bank. Eventually, you'll be able to save more.

I have a friend who puts her loose pennies, nickels, and dimes into a jar until it fills up. About once a year, she rolls the change, takes it to the bank, and puts it in her coin account. Last time she rolled her change, she had $70 just in dimes. It's been five years since college and she's saved over $1,000. Now she's looking at mutual funds so she can watch her coins grow some more. When you're talking about saving, pennies count too.

If you can put yourself on a more rigorous savings plan, you should. Even if you're making $70,000 after slaving away in law school, you should go out for some nice dinners, blow off some steam, and then commit to saving what you don't need every month. It's tempting to spend the money when you have it, so if you need to have every other paycheck deposited directly into your savings account, do it. You'll be less likely to spend it once it's in the savings account than if it goes into your checking account first and you transfer some amount later.

Then there's that other category of saving known as saving for retirement. If you don't even start on this project until you hit the big three-oh, you'll still be in fine shape when you're ready to join the cardigan and golf shoe set. But some of us might start earlier than that. So I include a word here on retirement savings because it's something we all have to do, no matter what age we begin.

Your Money Picture

Every dollar you earn will have a place in your money picture. The dollars you need to pay your bills each month will go into your checking account—they'll earn little interest, if any, and will not hang around in your account for long.

Anything you earn beyond what you need for living expenses will go into some form of savings. Ideally, you'll have three months' worth of living expenses in a place that earns you some interest but keeps your money liquid (available) in case you need it. Your choices include bank savings accounts, money market deposit accounts, money market mutual funds, and CDs, all of which will be discussed in this and the next chapter.

Once you have your three-month emergency stockpile, you should put remaining savings in two places: a retirement account and non-retirement investments that will earn you a better return than the above-mentioned savings vehicles. For both retirement and regular investments, you'll typically be choosing from stocks, bonds, and mutual funds—all discussed later.

Work on contributing to each tier as your income permits, with the idea of allocating 10 percent of your income to the top two tiers each year. Your money picture should look something like this:

Your Money Picture

Longer-term investments: invested in a combination of stocks, bonds, or mutual funds

Retirement savings: placed in one or more of the following: Roth IRAs, SEP-IRAs, 401(k)s, 403(b)s, Keoghs, and invested in a combination of stocks, bonds, or mutual funds

Three-months' living expenses: an emergency stash saved in a bank savings account, money market account, money market mutual fund, or CD

Basic checking account: the amount you need to cover basic living expenses each month

---

How to Save

The easiest way to save money is to have a place for it—whether that's a bank account, change jar, or mutual fund—that you can contribute to each month. And every month, even when you feel tapped out buying gifts for the holidays or pinched because taxes are due, deposit something, even if it's $20. It will add up. Think of your savings account as a bill you pay every month, just like your electricity.

If you aren't scraping enough out of each monthly paycheck, you can try some other tactics. One is a kind of denial/reward program where, for example, you consciously decide to eat lunch at your desk two days a week instead of going out and split the savings between extra discretionary income and savings. Or you could deny yourself something else you normally do. In both of the above instances, part of the money you're saving gets allocated to extra spending money. That's because if you're making some sacrifices by taking on extra work or denying yourself something, you should get a little something back. Otherwise, you'll have a big fat savings account but you'll be cranky and bitter, so what's the point?

Where to Save

Regular Savings Accounts

All banks offer savings accounts that pay interest on the money you deposit. There are no minimum balances, but you can't write checks from a savings account. You can, however, usually get an ATM card that will allow you to take money from your account. Savings accounts are a good place for money you might need soon, but not yet. You don't want that money sitting in your checking account earning zip in interest when it could at least earn 2 percent or more in a savings account.

Interest is calculated one of three ways: on the money in your account from the day it's deposited until the day it's withdrawn; on the average daily amount in your account for the month; or on the lowest monthly balance. Of the three, the lowest daily balance method pays the least interest so try to avoid banks that use this method.

Savings accounts may also offer you perks like lower interest rates when you apply for a loan, free traveler's checks, or a no-fee credit card. Savings accounts are not the place for big investing. They're more like a good parking place for cash that's on its way somewhere else—either to your checking account or to your CD, mutual fund, or other investment where it will grow.

Money Market Accounts

A money market deposit account is a type of savings account that earns interest. Money market accounts differ from regular savings accounts in that they have more restrictions in return for yielding higher interest, and you can usually write a limited number of checks from them. Don't confuse them with money market mutual funds, which are a different type of investment—one in which your money is invested in short-term securities, yielding an interest rate that changes daily.

The advantage to money market accounts is that you can access your money whenever you want and the interest rate is usually higher than a regular savings account. You can invest in a money market account through a bank. On the downside, these accounts require a minimum initial investment, typically from $1,000 to $2,500, and their interest rates are lower than CD rates. You also have to maintain a minimum balance, as much as $1,000. Check to see if the money market account you're interested in is FDIC-insured, since many are not.

CDs

Since when did compact discs become a way to save money, you may be wondering. No, not those kind of CDs. Certificates of deposit are interest-bearing savings accounts that require you to keep your money in the bank for a specific term ranging from three or six months to several years. The longer the term, the higher the interest rate. Also, the more you put in, the higher the rate you'll get. A CD generally requires a minimum deposit, $500 or more, and will earn a higher interest rate than a money market or regular savings account.

CDs are good because you know what the return on your money will be. The interest rate is locked in and won't change until the CD rolls over, meaning it starts a new term. At the rollover time, you can either take your money out and put it into a different type of account, or you can leave it in the CD at the new interest rate. All banks offer CDs at various rates of return. If you have some money that you can afford to leave locked up for the term offered by the bank, a CD is a better place for it than your savings account because you'll earn more interest.

You can also purchase CDs at a brokerage, which won't charge you a penalty if you take your money out early (more on brokerages in the next chapter). Brokerages buy CDs from banks and sell them to clients—sometimes they offer higher yields than banks do.

Most major newspapers list the highest bank interest rates one day a week. Look at the business section of the newspaper to find out what day they're listed or read *Barron's*, the financial weekly, which also lists interest rates at banks and other savings institutions. You can look at CD rates online at www.bankrate.com, a service provided by Bankrate Monitor.

Credit Unions

Credit unions are like banks in that you can save money in them and they pay interest, generally higher interest than banks do. They also extend lines of credit and make consumer loans to their members. Again, their rates are better than those you'll get through a bank. Most are insured by the National Credit Union Administration. They differ from banks because they're sponsored by an organization. For example, the company you work for may offer you membership in a credit union—the interest rates will typically be better than a regular savings account, so if you're not worried about the company going belly-up, you should feel safe putting your money there.

A credit union sponsored by your company gives you the convenience of getting money when you need it, but credit unions typically don't give you ATM service.

Saving for Retirement

The credo of our generation goes something like this: I'm in my 20s. I've barely begun working. And honestly, in all sanity, I'm supposed to be thinking about retirement? Give me just a small break. On the horizon as far as I can see, I'm not going anywhere.

Intuitively, it seems to make little if any difference whether you start saving now or five years from now. Yet it's just this short-run mentality that merits a second thought. There may be relatively painless ways to save some money without having to picture yourself slathering turnaround cream on your face when you're 60.

The main reason for thinking about retirement is the aging behemoth known as social security. To hear the boomers tell it, social security is barely going to see them through their first bottle of Geritol, let alone last long enough to be much of a safety net for us. So like many other things, paving the way to retirement is something we're going to have to do ourselves. Consider contributing to your company's 410(k) or opening an individual retirement account (IRA).

401(k) Plans

If you work for a company, you may be offered participation in a 401(k) plan, which is basically a retirement account set up by your employer. A 401(k) plan allows you to designate a portion of your monthly income to be put away for retirement, before you pay taxes on it. There's a penalty for withdrawing the money before you reach retirement at age 59 1/2, but you can often borrow from your 401(k) and repay it without a penalty. When you start a new job, you usually have to *vest*, or wait a certain period, until you can contribute to your company's 401(k). In the meantime, you can contribute to an IRA, which is discussed below.

Some companies have a matching program, which means they'll give you a designated amount for every dollar you deposit. This is one of the few sources of free money that is upstanding and legal, there for the taking. So if you can deposit even the smallest fraction of your paycheck each month, take advantage of your 401(k). There is a limit to the amount you can deposit, approximately 9 percent of your paycheck, pre-tax.

A 401(k) doesn't earn money in and of itself. It's an account that holds onto your money until you retire. But within that account, you can choose how the money will be invested—so it's quite different from a bank account where you earn an interest rate decided by the bank, whether you like it or not. You can ask that your 401(k) money be invested in your choice of stocks, bonds, CDs, mutual funds, or other investments (discussed in the next chapter). Sometimes your company will offer you specific investments; other times, you have more discretion.

Once the money is in your retirement account, you can make it grow, tax-deferred, until you take it out. That means if you buy stock with the 401(k) money and sell it at a profit, you won't owe taxes on your profit until you withdraw the money at retirement. Sometimes your employer will offer you investment options. If your employer is matching your deposits *and* you choose high-growth investments, you can earn a substantial return by the time you reach retirement. And it doesn't need to put much of a dent in your lifestyle now—the money gets taken out before you get paid, so you'll hardly miss it.

403(b)

Depending on your job, your employer may offer a different kind of retirement savings plan called a 403(b). It's similar to a 401(k), but it is only for employees of nonprofit institutions and schools. So if you work for a university, hospital, charitable foundation, or other organization that doesn't operate for profit, you'll be offered a 403(b) plan instead of a 401(k).

Who's IRA?

An IRA is simply an individual account, much like a 401(k), in which you can save money for retirement. You can take it out before then, but you'll owe a 10 percent penalty. Like a 401(k), an IRA won't earn interest by itself—you need to invest what's in it. Then, any interest or capital gain (profit from buying low and selling high) the money in your IRA earns is not taxed until you take it out at retirement. So they can be a pretty good deal. You can set up an IRA at the bank where you have your savings or checking account or at an office of a self-service discount brokerage like Charles Schwab, Fidelity or Quick & Reilly (see next chapter for 800 numbers).

If you work for a company that has no retirement plan or if you're self-employed—including anyone who works as a freelancer or independent contractor—you can contribute $3,000 per year to an IRA and it's tax-deductible. That means you get to deduct $3,000 from your total income before you calculate your taxes on it. So you'll owe less in taxes *and* the money in your IRA can grow tax-deferred, meaning you don't pay taxes on your profits until you take the money out at retirement. If you're contributing to your company's 401(k), you can still contribute to an IRA, but it probably won't be tax-deductible, depending on your income. If your company offers a matching program, it makes sense to contribute the maximum amount to your 401(k) before you contribute to an IRA.

You can open an IRA through a bank, brokerage, or mutual fund—every financial entity handles IRAs. But some give you more investment choices than others. For example, brokerages typically offer you the most freedom to buy and sell the investments of your choice within your IRA account. If you want someone else to take care of your investing, you might open an IRA account at a mutual fund. If you want to participate more, you might choose a brokerage.

When considering investing in an IRA, you might want to opt for a Roth IRA. A Roth is a twist on the basic IRA that allows you to make a $3,000 annual after-tax contribution. Why would you want to do this when the regular old IRA allows you to invest pre-tax dollars? Because you are young. The Roth allows your money to grow until retirement, at which point you can withdraw it, plus any interest or capital gain it has earned, without paying any taxes whatsoever. When you are young and your retirement savings is likely to accrue a lot of interest and grow substantially, it makes sense to pay a little tax now to avoid a big tax later.

If you're self-employed, you can make a yearly contribution to a Keogh or a SEP-IRA (simplified employee pension). The difference is that Keoghs are for self-employed people who have employees working for them. If you work part time at a company for three years, you can also open a SEP-IRA account. These types of retirement accounts allow you to contribute a percentage of your annual income, about 15 percent or

> *"No sooner had I bought some stock with the money in my IRA than it went down a few points. But I don't care because I'm not going to touch the money for so long. By the time I take it out, I'm sure it will have gone back up."* —David, 26

$30,000 (whichever is lower), up to a set limit. The contributions are similarly tax-deferred. You have until the tax filing date in mid-April to make your contribution for the previous year.

Why This Is a Big Deal

This is an illustration of how your money can grow in an IRA, but the same is true of money you invest in a Keogh, SEP, 401(k), or 403(b). Plus, if you have a 401(k) and you leave your job, you'll have to roll the money into an IRA, so it's likely that you'll have one at some time or another.

Here's how it all works: If the government thinks you made $3,000 less income, you owe less in taxes. You get to keep the $3,000—you just don't get to use it for a while. Then you can choose how you'll invest the money. Since you're young and you're not going to see the money for a while, you can afford to choose higher-risk, higher-return investments. You can buy stock, purchase mutual fund shares, or choose other investments you like. You can also sell your investments, but all the money stays in your IRA account. Normally, if you bought stock and sold it at a profit, you'd owe taxes on the gain. But if the investing is done within your IRA, you don't pay any tax until you take the money out—at age 59½.

The Power of Compounding

The results of investing in your retirement account are surprising when you consider the power of compounding, which essentially means you're earning money on the money you've earned, year after year. Suppose that $3,000 put in today and left for thirty years (assuming you start saving when you're 29, but start earlier if you can) earns a fixed return the first year. Then, the second year, the interest earns interest. And so on, and so on. Kind of like that old shampoo commercial—Gee, Your Hair Smells Terrific, where you were supposed to tell two friends, then they'd tell two friends. . . . You get the idea.

The result of all this saving and compounding is that if you commit to putting $3,000 into an IRA each year for thirty years, you'll have far more than the $90,000 total that you've put in. The compounding effect will leave you with over half a million dollars (see chart below), if you're earning roughly 10 percent each year, the historical average return from the stock market. By contrast, if you put the $3,000 into a regular bank account instead of shielding it in an IRA, you'd have to pay taxes on both the $3,000 and any interest it earned each year.

It makes sense to start saving early. Consider two other cases, shown in the chart below, where you put $3,000 into an IRA each year for twenty-five years: in the first case, you start when you're 29 years old, stop when you're 54, and let the money compound until retirement. In the second case, you start when you're 34 and stop when you're 59. In both cases, you've put the same amount into your IRA—$75,000—over 25 years. But by starting when you're 29, you'll have almost $200,000 more in your IRA when you turn 59 than if you start when you're 34. That's the compounding effect.

So does that mean you wait until you're 54 to take that trip to Europe instead of going now? No. But, it does make sense to think about saving something now, whether it's $3,000 a year or $300. Today's $300 is a smarter investment than $300 saved at age 54. Inflation, you know.

The Rule of 72

The Rule of 72 is a bit of mathematical wizardry to determine how long it will take to double your money. You only need a cou-

Age When You Start	Age When You Stop	Annual Contribution	Interest Rate	Total Saved (tax-deferred)
29.5	59.5	$3,000 for 30 years	10%	**$542,830**
29.5	54.5	$3,000 for 25 years	10%	**$522,683**
34.5	59.5	$3,000 for 25 years	10%	**$324,545**

ple basic pieces of data: the amount you're investing and the interest rate. Say you have $3,000 to invest—your basic IRA contribution for the year. And say you can get a 10 percent return.

Divide your interest rate into 72. Ten percent goes in 7.2 times, meaning your money will double every 7.2 years. So after 7.2 years, your $3,000 will be worth $6,000. Say you plan to leave it to earn 10 percent from the time you turn 25 until you turn 60. Your money will double every 7.2 years, approximately five times, leaving you with $85,000 when you turn 60.

You can apply this rule to any investment as long as you know the interest rate will stay constant over a long period. The higher the rate, the fewer years it will take your money to double and the more money you'll have in the end.

How important is the rate of return? Would it really make a big difference to earn a 5 percent return on your money instead of 10? Use the rule of 72 to find out. At a 5 percent return, it would take 14.4 years for your money to double. Between the ages of 25 and 60, your money would double almost two and a half times, leaving you with about $16,500 at age 60. A big difference.

That Cash-Flow Problem

But what does all this stuff about saving mean if you have no (and I mean zero) extra money at the end of each month? It probably means you don't save anything for the time being. Plain and simple. And don't torture yourself about it. Why make yourself feel like you're some kind of failure just because your one-promotion-above-entry-level salary at an advertising agency doesn't afford you the same disposable income as your friend who's a lawyer at a large firm?

Sometimes there's no justice in the amount of money we'll get paid for jobs that require comparable amounts of education. Don't think I didn't cringe when my degree was getting me only sneers from employers as I slaved in a restaurant. Meanwhile other friends were slaving in investment banks and getting paid the big bucks.

There was little I could do to make any sense of the wage dise-quilibrium, but I did do myself one favor: I didn't torment myself over it (well, yes I did, but looking back, it wasn't necessary).

And I didn't do what one of my roommates insisted on doing: saving "for her future" on a shoestring budget by eating hot dogs every night and never going out with friends. She honestly believed that an oversupply of Oscar Meyer could pave the way for her to buy a house. I honestly believed she was insane.

Self-Torture Is Someone Else's Game

A helpful philosophy on these matters is this: It's bad enough that you're slogging away each day for little pay and a carrot of a pro-motion somewhere in the myopically distant future. When you come home after a long day, do you really want to stare into a pot of pork-n-beans on top of it? I mean, how miserable do you want to be? Allow yourself the small pleasures in life, because the few dollars you're saving are not going to spell "down payment" any time soon. Of course this doesn't mean you should fly off to Mazatl'an at high season just because you can't get good shellfish at your local market. Clearly, living within your means requires a little sacrifice of the good life, and clipping coupons and buying the generic brand of canned tomatoes never hurt anyone. But think of all of this as temporary. You don't have to sit home with the blinds down all through your 20s just to save money. You'll be in a bitch of a mood by the time you hit 30.

Saving money just means saving something instead of saving nothing. When you put it that way, it's not so hard.

A Final Note: Don't Borrow Money in Order to Save It

There's one major exception to the philosophy of incorporating the good life into your low-budget one: paying your debts. There's no such thing as saving when you're carrying a huge debt over your head, especially if you owe it on credit cards. The rates you're paying to stay in debt are far higher than the rate of return you'd get by investing the money. So there's no sense in having $2,000 earning 4.5 percent in a savings account when you owe $2,000 on your credit card at 17 percent. If you pay off the card, it's equivalent to a 12.5 percent gain. A no-brainer. That's pretty hard to beat in any investment.

18

INVESTMENT PROWESS FOR THE NON-FINANCIER

Investing—A Money Multiplier

When you go to cocktail parties, do you find yourself saying things like, "I like soy futures" or "I took my profits in the fourth quarter, before the market turned"? If so, you probably don't need this chapter. Contrary to popular perception, what follows is not the skinny on currency trades or the biotech wonder stocks of tomorrow or "the word on the street." Just so you know.

But if you find yourself using the business section to line your gerbil cage rather than reading it, there's some useful information for you here. You don't have to become a market guru to know where to put your money or to have semi-intelligent things to say in mixed company. The sad reality is that the age has passed when coin collecting and lemonade stands made you the financial whiz kid on your block. Now it's time to collect mutual fund portfolios and hope for stock splits and pay attention to what the Fed does.

The idea behind investing now is not to discover the next

Microsoft, make a million bucks, and retire when you're 35. The idea is to put you more "in the know" when everyone in town is talking about the Dow being off a few points.

Inflation—The Hungry Beast

Seems like you've been hearing about inflation for as long as you can remember, doesn't it? That's because the concept is as old as the hills and it's not going anywhere soon. The basic scenario is this: every year, the same things cost a little more. Milk goes from $1 to $1.25. Does that mean it's better milk? No, it just costs more. So say you have a dollar and you want it to buy you milk in three years and you put the dollar under your pillow. Three years go by and you take your dollar to the store. Milk costs more and your dollar doesn't cover it. That's inflation.

If you want to be able to buy the milk, you need your dollar to grow at the same rate as inflation. And preferably a little more. That's what investing is all about. You want to beat inflation, pay your taxes, and still come out ahead.

How to Read the Business Page

The Financial Tables

In a business newspaper like the *Wall Street Journal*, you can find the most comprehensive stock, commodity, and mutual fund tables on a daily basis. The tables show prices and recent changes in value for whatever you're looking up. They also show prices on government-issued bonds. Any daily newspaper's business section will also have financial tables, listing the major markets every day except Monday since the markets are closed weekends. The Sunday listing is a weekly roundup of how everything fared.

If you're looking up a specific stock—which is a piece of a company sold to the public—you need to know its symbol and the market where it trades. Symbols are usually abbreviations of company names. The main American stock exchanges are the New York

Stock Exchange (NYSE), the American Stock Exchange (AMEX), and the National Association of Securities Dealers Automated Quotations (NASDAQ).

The tables have headings at the top of each page, some of which might be the following:

- **High**—the highest price from the previous day
- **Low**—the lowest price from the previous day
- **Last**—the price of the stock at the week's close
- **Change**—the amount gained or lost since the close of the previous week
- **52-Week High/Low**—the highest and lowest price of the past 52 weeks
- **Dividend**—the amount paid annually to shareholders
- **Year to Date % Change**—how much the price has changed (+ or –) since the first of the year or since the stock was initially issued if the issue date was less than a year ago
- **P/E**—the ratio of price to earnings; so if P/E is 20, it means the price per share is 20 times greater than the company's earnings per share
- **# of Shares Traded**—tells you how many shares were bought and sold the previous day

Da Bulls and Da Bears

Wall Street talk incorporates these animals into the stock market game to indicate how people feel about the market. In a *bull market*, people are feeling good about stocks and their likelihood to go up in price. In a bull market, lots of trading occurs and prices rise. In a *bear market*, people are pessimistic about the market either because prices have been falling or because of other factors like interest rates. Either way, the bears expect prices to go down, and in a bear market, they do.

The Fed and the Prime Rate

The prime rate is the lowest interest rate, determined by the Fed (the Federal Reserve Board), at which banks can borrow from the

Fed. They turn around and lend this money to you, so the lower the prime rate, the better your borrowing rate. Sometimes a bank will advertise that its lending rates are 1 percent above prime. That means they're pretty low. The Fed lowers the prime rate to stimulate borrowing from banks when it wants consumers to borrow more and increase consumer spending. The Fed raises the prime rate to encourage saving and investing, when it wants consumer spending to go down.

What's the Dow?

Up until now the only Dow you may have been concerned about was the one that made a bathroom cleaner with Scrubbing Bubbles. But there's another one. The Dow Jones Industrial Average is a selection of thirty big, industrial companies that have been around for a long time, such as General Electric and Coca-Cola, and it measures how their prices change each day. People care about the Dow because they use it as a barometer for the health and well-being of the market in general. So if the Dow is off (down), it's an indicator that the rest of the market has probably gone down too. But this doesn't have to be the case—the Dow can go one way and the broader market can go the other.

Options

There was a time, before the explosion of the big dot-com bubble, when all anyone could talk about was options. Options, it seemed at the time, were better than gold. People were willing to forgo salaries in exchange for stock options and the promise of future riches. What's the big deal?

Options give the person who has them the opportunity, that is, the option, to buy shares of stock at a later date. The option conversion price is the amount you pay, per share, to turn each option into a share of stock. In other words, if you have 1,000 options at $.15, you are eligible to buy 1,000 shares of a company's stock for $.15, a total cost to you of $150. If the stock's price on, say, the NASDAQ is $11 per share, you're buying it at quite a steal. That's $10.85 profit per share for you. That's why dot-commers loved options so much. They generally were given at low conversion prices and tech stocks were flying high. Big profits.

Now the dust has settled. Does that mean options are worthless? Certainly it means some of them are. For example, if you have options that you need to pay $2 to convert to stock and the shares are trading at $.50, your options are said to be "underwater," meaning you'd be crazy to convert them. In that case, they are just pieces of paper. But they can still be an excellent add-on to your regular salary if the company that you work for is in good financial shape. So don't discount their value entirely. Just keep them in perspective.

P/E and Other Financial Gymnastics

Why, you may wonder, is the P/E something to get all excited about? For one thing, you can use it to analyze the price of a stock and determine if you think the price accurately reflects the stock's value. On the other hand, the P/E can only tell you so much. Here's how it all works.

The P stands for price per share and the E stands for current earnings per share (over the past one year). The ratio is a way of using a company's earnings as a measure of its value and comparing that value to its price. Some people have philosophies about never buying stocks with P/Es that are too high, say, over 20—in other words, they say if the price is more than 20 times the earnings, the stock is overvalued. The logical interpretation of this is that the stock price will go down.

The problem with such cut-and-dried thinking is that the P/E relies on earnings over the past year to connote value. What about expected future earnings? A company may have just tapped into the pulse of tomorrow but this isn't reflected yet in earnings. So if the price and the P/E go up does that mean it's a bad buy? Not if earnings go up too.

The point is that the P/E is a good measure of the stock's value today, but be aware that earnings per share can be manipulated using different forms of accounting, so it doesn't always tell you what you think it does. So while it's a good rule of thumb, it's not the be-all and end-all of a company's future value or the value of its stock.

What Do You Want to Buy?

Taking Stock

When a company sells stock, it's selling a piece of the company to the public in the form of shares. Stocks are also known as equities. When you hear about stocks being inflation fighters it's because stocks have traditionally outpaced inflation and grown at an average rate of 10 percent a year. If you're interested in a specific company's stock, you can call the company and ask for annual reports and financial statements called 10Ks and 10Qs.

Not all stocks are the same. Here are the basic categories:

- **Blue-chip stocks**—issued by big, tried-and-true companies that have been around for a long time. They're generally considered least risky when it comes to stocks.
- **Penny stocks**— stocks that cost under a dollar per share, generally issued by little-known companies. They're generally considered more risky, but if a stock that costs $1 goes up to $2, you've just doubled your money.

The companies that issue these stocks can do so in the following two forms:

- **Common stock**—shares of a company sold to the public, more risky than preferred stock, but with more growth potential.
- **Preferred stock**—a higher class of stock than common, meaning it's less volatile, and often pays dividends, which are like a quarterly interest payment.

How Stocks Are Sold

Stocks are sold in "lots." You can buy a round lot, which is a hundred shares or a multiple of a hundred. Or you can buy an odd lot, which is a bunch of shares that isn't a multiple of a hundred. What's the difference? Only the price. If you can buy a round lot, you can generally get the stock for an eighth of a point less per share. This is a relatively trivial amount when you're not talking thousands of shares, so don't worry about odd-lot purchases. They sound worse than they are.

Bonds Are an IOU

A bond is a way for the local or national government or a privately owned company to take out a loan. You, the bondholder, get promise of repayment with interest. Bonds have three main components:

- **Par value**—also called face value, usually $1,000 per bond
- **Coupon rate**—the interest rate you're paid twice a year until the bond matures
- **Maturity date**—the time at which you're paid the par value of the bond

If you like the idea of investing in bonds, you can buy them from the institution who issues them or through a mutual fund with bonds in its portfolio. They're not as risky as stock, which is why you'll hear people recommending against them for young investors, who can afford more risk.

Speaking of Risk

How much risk can you afford to take? That's a personal decision but the general rule of thumb is that the younger you are, the more risk you can take because you have more time to ride out the bumps and see your investment go up in value. Of the various classes of investments, stocks or mutual funds that contain stocks carry the highest risk and the highest potential return. Bonds and bond funds are next, followed by cash investments, which are the least risky.

The other reason young investors can afford to take more risks is that there's more time to recover if an investment goes south. For example, if you're using the money in your IRA to buy stocks and some take a turn for the worse, you have plenty of time to bounce back and see your money grow by the time you're 60.

Despite everything people say about taking risks when you're young, you should only do what makes you comfortable, short of keeping your money in a box under your bed.

All That Talk about Interest Rates

When you start paying attention to financial news, you notice a lot of people talking about interest rates—whether they're going up, down, a half a point, a quarter of a point—and you may wonder why. Interest rates affect the stock market, the bond market, bank accounts, and the prices of foreign currencies. Since these are all places you might invest your money, you need to know how interest-rate changes will affect your investments.

In short, if *interest rates go up, stock prices generally go down.* That's because people would rather put their money in banks with high interest rates than risk tying up their money in the stock or bond markets. An exception is when there's a bull market that *rallies* (stays high) even if interest rates and bond prices go up, something we've seen in the recent past.

Bond yields and interest rates, on the other hand, move in the same direction as each other. That's because bonds yield interest and can yield more of it when the Fed raises rates. The longer the bond's term, which can be up to 30 years, the more its price drops as interest rates rise.

Meanwhile, if interest rates go up, so do the rates you'll get in money market accounts and CDs. And on the international scene, if interest rates go down, the dollar falls against foreign currency.

It's a Mutual Thing

Ask anyone about investing and the first thing they'll tell you is that mutual funds are the investment taste of a generation. It seems that if you're part of the generation marketers were targeting when Snapple was invented, you're also a sucker for mutual funds. Does that mean they're right? Or does it just mean they'd rather not think long and hard and come up with some really good advice? It depends.

It's a Big, Big Batch

A mutual fund is kind of like a giant loaf of bread in the world of finance, and you get to buy a slice. It takes a lot of yeast, sugar, and flour to make such a big loaf, because we're talking BIG here, and you don't have the money to buy all the ingredients yourself. Similarly, you don't have money to go out and buy thousands of shares in thousands of companies. So a professional fund manager goes out and buys all those shares and calls them a mutual fund and sells you a little piece of the whole. A minimum investment is required, ranging from $100 to several thousand dollars.

The mutual fund is divided into shares at a certain price and your little piece is composed of a certain number of shares. You can always buy more shares or you can sell the ones you have. So when you hear all the garble about diversifying your investments, this is what they're talking about. Instead of owning a lot of one thing, like shares of one stock, you own a little bit of a lot of things.

The Ingredients

There are a lot of mutual funds out there. And the law of averages says that some are great, others stink, and some are just okay. They're only as good as the person managing them and the stocks, bonds, or other investments that comprise them. One nice thing about mutual funds is that you can look them up in the business section of most newspapers and chart their progress. There are several kinds of mutual funds from which you can choose.

Money Market Mutual Funds (Money Funds). These contain short-term investments like Treasury bills or CDs. If you invest in a money market mutual fund, you have liquidity, meaning you can get your money at any time. You'll earn a higher interest rate than a regular savings account offers, and they have low risk, and relatively low return. That's why money funds are good for the middle tier of your money picture. For the top tier of your money picture, you'll most likely want higher-risk, higher-return investments like stock and bond mutual funds and individual securities.

Stock Funds. This is where you'll get the highest return in exchange for the highest exposure to risk—less risk, however, than if you bought individual stock shares. Here's why. Say you choose a *stock mutual fund*, also called an equity fund. This protects you from the riskiness of buying individual stocks yourself because if a stock in the mutual fund portfolio takes a nosedive, there's the hope that other stocks in the portfolio have gone up to counterbalance it. The portfolio is spread out among so many investors and there are so many stocks in the portfolio that the impact of any one stock isn't felt so much.

This also means that if one stock goes flying through the roof, you may not see a great gain in your mutual fund value. This type of investing is not designed for a quick profit. You buy mutual funds when you want steady growth. And depending on what kinds of investments make up the fund, you can go for more risk and higher potential growth or less risk and slower growth.

Index Funds. Index funds are a particularly good choice for investors who don't want to spend a lot of time worrying about whether their mutual funds are performing better or worse than the market. That's because index funds are designed to match the market by matching the performance of a particular index, whether it's the Standard and Poor's 500 (S&P 500), the Wilshire 5000, or another index. The managers of index funds buy and sell stocks within those mutual funds in order to make them rise and fall along with the indices they are tracking. So rather than owning shares of every stock that makes up the S&P 500, you can buy shares in an S&P index fund and your investments will match the growth of the S&P. That may give you peace of mind at the end of the day when you know your investments are performing as well as the broader market.

What a Load

Start looking at mutual funds and you'll find that there's a lot of loaded talk. A load of what, you might wonder? In mutual-fund-speak, a load is like a commission that's paid to the people who sell you shares in it. You can have a front-load fund, where a percentage of your investment is taken out at the beginning; a back-load fund, where a percentage is taken at the end; or a no-load fund, where, you guessed it, there's no load. Why would anyone pay a load, you rightly inquire? The people selling front- and back-loaded funds will give you all sort of reasons, ranging from getting the commission over with now to paying the commission later with inflated dollars.

Loaded funds have historically performed about the same as their no-load siblings. There are enough good no-load funds out there to choose from that you should spend your time researching where you want to invest instead of feeding the mother load. The one charge you'll find that is different from a load is something called a *management fee*, typically about 1 percent per year of the total investment that pays for the costs of maintaining the fund. Ask about any fees up front.

Be wary of a broker/dealer who makes money each time you switch out of one fund and buy into another one. You could be told to swap one fund for another even though it won't affect the value of your account, just so the broker can earn a commission.

How to Tell a Good Fund from a Sinker

At first it seems like a great idea to call a bunch of mutual funds and ask for an annual report and a prospectus. You feel empowered. You've got this investing thing down. Answered all their questionnaires about your investing style. But how do you really know which fund is the best for you? Open any investing magazine and you'll see new funds springing up almost daily and always a new pick of the week. You don't want to be the one investor they write about who picked the one mutual fund that went down the toilet. So you need to do two things: Know yourself and know where to go for information.

Know Yourself. How can you determine which investments are right for you? Do some self-assessment to figure out which investments will make you the most comfortable and give your money the most room to grow:

- Can you commit to leaving your money invested for at least three years (the minimum for getting into mutual funds, stocks, and most bonds), or will you need access to it?
- Does the idea of the stock market going up and down and taking your money with it turn your stomach?
- Do you want your money to grow slowly and steadily with less risk, or do you want more aggressive growth accompanied by more risk?
- Do you want to actively watch and manage your investments or do you want to put your money somewhere and let someone else deal with it?

For Your Information. Start by calling Morningstar, (800)735-0700, or looking on its Web site, www.morningstar.com. Morningstar is a ratings service, like the *Zagat Guide* of mutual funds. It gives them stars for performance and rates the fund manager too.

The other thing you should consider when picking a mutual fund is your own gut instinct. If you're looking for a stock fund, look at the fund's biggest holdings and make sure you feel good about the companies. If you know a certain company to be an environmental enemy, you might not want to put your hard-earned dollars into a fund that buys a lot of shares of the beast.

Socially Responsible Investing

What happens if that great mutual fund your friend told you about turns out to invest in a company that just dumped gallons of toxic waste into the bay? The fund may have a great track record, but your conscience may not let you invest. Stick to your instincts. Investing isn't only about putting money away for later, it's about deciding who gets to use your money in the meantime. You may decide you don't want to invest in a company that's responsible for deforestation. You can call any fund and find out what its major holdings are before you invest.

Socially responsible investing doesn't only refer to environmentalism. You might want to invest in companies that contribute to charitable organizations or do pro-bono work. Determine your own criteria and get the facts. You also might want to check out the Trillium Asset Management Corporation's Web site for information on socially responsible investing: www.trilliuminvest.com.

How Do I Buy?

You can purchase mutual fund shares directly from the fund by calling its 800 number and asking for an application and a *prospectus*, a document that tells you how the fund invests and what fees it charges. You'll be asked whether you're investing funds from an IRA or regular funds. The applications are easy to fill out and your signed check completes the purchase.

If you want a certain amount of money to be automatically withdrawn from your checking or savings account and invested in mutual funds each month, contact the mutual fund for information on their procedures. Make sure there's always enough money in your account to cover the withdrawal.

To buy stocks, you'll probably want to use a discount brokerage until your account gets big enough that you want a full-service broker to take over and help you manage your investments. Here are the big discount brokerages that can direct you to an office near you:

- Charles Schwab, (800)648-5300
- Fidelity Broker Services, (800)544-7272
- Quick & Reilly, (800)793-8050

Cash Counts Too

When you talk investing, it doesn't only mean stocks, bonds, and mutual funds. There are many other investment vehicles out there, including things like gold coins, grain futures, and soy options. These are things for which you'll probably have little concern and no regard at this time in your investing life. But one investment you might still consider making is one in the form of cash: CDs, money market funds, and ordinary interest-earning savings accounts that were discussed in the last chapter.

If you can't leave your money invested for years and years because you'll need it sooner, say in six months for a car down payment, you can still earn something. It doesn't make sense to buy stocks or stock mutual funds if you're only going to keep them for a few months. This is because these investments could go down in that time instead of up. They only make sense if you can leave your money in long enough to weather the market's ebb and flow.

High Finance on the Web

These days, financial resources are so accessible on the World Wide Web that it's easy to get up-to-the-hour information rather than looking in the following day's newspaper or waiting for something to come in the mail. To get information about a specific company or mutual fund, log on to Yahoo, AltaVista, or another search engine and type in the company you want to find. Many of the online providers give stock market updates at a fifteen-minute delay or you can go through a search engine by looking up "latest free stock quotes" so you can track specific companies on your computer.

Invest in Yourself

All this investment talk is liable to make you feel as though you have to think like a trader, weather buying frenzies, and subscribe to other clichés. But only you know whether this is the right time for you to invest. If you have money sitting in a 401(k) or an IRA, you're not going to be able to touch it for a while, so you might as well try to make it grow. But if this isn't the time for investing, don't feel bad about putting your money toward your basic expenses.

This may be the time for you to go to graduate school or learn how to write computer programs. It may be the time to get certified to scuba dive or enroll in a foreign language course so you're more marketable in the job world. There are many options that will prove priceless to you in the long run. Consider these choices a valuable investment in yourself.

Putting money in stock may be the tried and true way to beat inflation. But putting stock in yourself can be the best investment you'll ever make.

19

YOUR TAXES

A Penny Earned Is Something the Government Wants

I remember the days when I actually looked forward to tax season because I could always expect a refund. And I used to believe in the tooth fairy too.

The first time I had any real income, I did everything wrong. I was in school and had one job on campus and a second at a restaurant. I didn't think much about my two-income status until tax season rolled around. The campus payroll department had been withholding taxes as though I had only one job. The restaurant had been doing the same.

When it came time to pay taxes, I found myself owing the government, big time. Need I say that I hadn't prepared for this eventuality? Not to mention that one of my roommates had suggested taking two exemptions so the government would take less out, the idea being that I'd invest it wisely in the interim and have plenty of money by the time I owed in April. Well, that hadn't happened either. And there I was . . . without a paddle.

I'm sure there are more ways you can go wrong when it comes to planning for April 15. You have a whole year, after all. A lot can happen. The purpose of this chapter is to give you the information you need, so nothing does go wrong.

Things to Keep in Mind All Year

How Many People Are You?

Here's where you get to calculate your exemptions. When you fill out a W-4 at work, you need to put something in the box that asks how many exemptions you want to take. The number you fill in will affect the amount of tax taken out of each paycheck.

For a single person filing alone, the general rule is that you get one exemption. So put a "1" in the box on your return. The only exception to this is if your parents claim you as a dependent on their taxes. They can only legally do this if you're a U.S. citizen under age 19 or a student under age 24 and you live with them when you're not in school. Your parents also have to be supplying more than half of your total support for the year. This may be the case the year you graduate. Following the year you graduate, however, you'll most likely claim yourself as one exemption and no longer be claimed as a dependent. If you're married and your spouse is your dependent, you can claim a second exemption.

How Many Jobs Do You Have?

If you've had more than one job during the past year, you could be in for an unpleasant surprise in April. The formulas used by the IRS to calculate how much you owe are not well designed for the multi-jobbed. At each job, the IRS instructs your employer to withhold taxes as though this is your only job. If you have two part-time jobs, where you earn $10,000 at each, you'll be taxed by each as though you only earned $10,000 all year, instead of $20,000 combined. So when tax time rolls around, the IRS will come in for the rest of what you owe. If you don't see this coming, chances are slim that you have the taxes you owe just sitting in a shoebox

> "When I was waiting tables, I thought my boss was taking taxes out of my paychecks to account for my tips. It turned out that I was supposed to be telling him how much to take out. When tax time came, I was in a deep hole."
>
> —Kyle, 24

by your bed. So if you have more than one job, be aware that you'll be paying come April.

You can try to compensate for this underwithholding by changing the exemptions that you claim when you file your W-4 with your employer. Ask that your exemptions be changed from "1" to "0" so you'll have more taken out of each paycheck. This will close the gap between what you pay and what you owe and may even entitle you to a refund. Just a reminder: Even if you have more than one job, you only file one tax return.

If you just graduated from college and only worked part of the year, your employer will still be withholding taxes as though you worked all year long. That means you'll be paying higher taxes than you should. Instead of just waiting around for your refund, you can compensate by asking for part-year withholding, which will calculate your taxes based on the number of months you worked.

Extra Income That's Taxable

If you earn income that doesn't appear on a bimonthly paycheck, you have two ways of dealing with it: You can instruct your employer to withhold taxes when you get paid, or you can pay the IRS yourself in April. If you wait until the end of the year to pay, keep the money somewhere, preferably in an interest-earning account, so you have it when it comes time to pay.

- *Tip income*. Money that you earn in the form of tips is supposed to be reported and taxed along with your regular pay. If you are a waiter, for example, the assumption is that you earn at least 8 percent of your sales in tips. The law requires your employer to withhold taxes from each paycheck to cover that 8 percent.

You're expected to pay taxes on the rest of what you take home in tips.

- *Stipend or fellowship income.* If you have this type of income from school, you need to report it on your tax return.
- *Lump-sum wages.* If you earned a bonus, commission, or other payment that you get in addition to your regular wages, it's taxable.
- *Interest income.* Any interest you earn on bank accounts, money market funds, or bonds is taxed as part of your income. You'll receive 1099 forms from each financial institution showing exactly how much you made in interest, so you won't have to calculate anything. Just fill in the interest income in the box on your tax form.
- *Investment income.* This includes dividend income from mutual funds or stock, plus any money you made from selling shares of either one. Like interest income, investment income shows up on 1099 forms that you'll get in the mail.

When It's Time to File

Deciding Which Forms You Need

Depending on where you live, you may or may not pay state taxes. If you live in a state like Florida or Nevada, consider yourself lucky because there are no state taxes. For the remainder of the American public, state taxes must be filed along with their federal counterparts on April 15. The form numbers are different in every state.

You have a choice over which federal tax form to use.

- **1040EZ.** To use this form, you need to be a single or joint filer with no dependents, that is, kids. You must have less than $400 in interest income and no itemized deductions. Your income must be less than $50,000. The 1040EZ is a one-page form on which you report the income shown on the W-2 or 1099 from your employer.

- **1040A.** To use this form, you must have less than $50,000 in income and no itemized deductions, except your IRA deduction. If you have interest or dividend income to declare, you'll use the 1040A form, with an attached schedule to show the additional income. The instructions in the tax booklets will take you through the process.
- **1040.** This is the form you'll use if you have $50,000 or more in income. You'll use it if you're self-employed or if you itemize your deductions. If you have capital gains to report, you must use the 1040 form. You'll also file one or more schedules with your return.

Preparing Your Tax Return

- **Step 1:** Go to the nearest post office or library and pick up the forms you need. You can also call the IRS directly, (800)TAX-FORM, and request forms, or print them out from the IRS Web

---

Getting Help from the IRS

The IRS offers free booklets to help you figure out the complexities of the tax system. Log on to the IRS Web site, www.irs.gov, to read any of these publications.

17	*Your Federal Income Tax*
334	*Tax Guide for Small Business*
910	*Guide to Free Tax Services*
501	*Exemptions, Standard Deduction, and Filing Information*
505	*Tax Withholding and Estimated Tax*
520	*Scholarships and Fellowships*
521	*Moving Expenses*
525	*Taxable and Nontaxable Income*
531	*Reporting Tip Income*
533	*Self-Employment Tax*
564	*Mutual Fund Distributions*
587	*Business Use of Your Home*
590	*Individual Retirement Arrangements (IRAs)*

---

site, www.irs.gov. When you get your form in the mail, check to make sure the address label has all correct information. If not, cross it out and fill it in yourself.

- **Step 2:** Collect the W-2 forms and 1099s you've received from your job, bank, mutual fund, or investment broker. If you haven't gotten them by mid-February, the IRS will send you copies if you call (800)829-3676.
- **Step 3:** Figure out your exemptions.
- **Step 4:** Fill out the forms. Unless your taxes are complicated, you can most likely do them yourself. (See the sections below for more complicated tax scenarios.) The IRS offers help through pre-recorded answers to popular questions at (800) TAX-1040. You should fill them out first in pencil, then go over them in pen once you're sure they're correct.
- **Step 5:** Check your forms over carefully, using a calculator. Even if someone else prepares your taxes for you, such as your own accountant or a gun for hire at H & R Block, make sure every item entered makes sense to you. Ultimately, you're responsible for the accuracy of your return, so it's smart to double-check. If you owe money, write a check. Then sign your return.
- **Step 6:** Make a copy, then mail your return. Use the preprinted envelope if one came with your return, or send your return to the IRS at the address in your tax booklet.

You can opt to file electronically, but you must go through an IRS-approved tax preparer to do so. Only use this method if you're expecting a refund—which you should get within 21 days—because high tech costs more than snail mail. Another option is to find out whether your employer offers you electronic filing.

The IRS also offers free filing by phone and will send you a package describing the service and eligibility requirements if you call (800)829-1040.

My tax-paying procedure has become somewhat of a tradition. Whenever I find myself owing money, I'm almost certain I must have made a mistake. Hasn't happened yet, but that's what I think.

So each time, I get a blank tax form and fill the whole thing out a second time, hoping for a different result. Then I briefly consider delinquency. I wonder what the worst thing is that the government could do to me. Then I realize what that might be and decide against tax evasion yet again.

I make a project of writing my check, moaning and groaning, and calling my parents to tell them how life isn't fair. I consider sending my return without any stamps, C.O.D., figuring the IRS isn't likely to send it back. I get a good chuckle out of this, then I decide I have better things to do with my time than attempt to bilk the IRS out of a dollar's worth of stamps. I return to human sensibility, stamp and seal the envelope, and drop it into the mailbox, no sooner than April 14.

When Your Taxes Get Complicated

Employee or Independent Contractor?

The distinction between being an independent contractor and an employee has been blurred in recent years. That's because employers have been finding it far more profitable to use independent contractors or freelancers when they need them instead of hiring a large staff. Employers save money because they don't pay any of their social security tax or offer them any benefits, like they would for regular employees. Some companies go so far as to hire a stable of full-time freelancers who work every day and are paid for the work they do but receive nothing in the way of employee benefits.

When you get paid as an independent contractor, you may be amazed and thrilled at how much money you're making. Then the reality sets in: no taxes have been taken out and you have to do all your health insurance purchasing and retirement saving yourself. Since your pay hasn't been taxed, you will have to pay later. Your first year as an independent contractor, you'll pay your taxes the following April 15. In subsequent years, the IRS will set you up on a quarterly payment plan, in which you estimate how much you'll owe at the end of the year and pay a fourth every quarter.

If you are an independent contractor, you'll receive 1099 forms by the end of January from anyone you worked for the previous year. Even if you don't receive a 1099, you're still responsible for reporting incomes earned on a freelance basis. Since your employer probably reported that the salary you were paid was a business expense, the IRS already knows about it. Everything gets cross-checked. So you don't want to risk owing back taxes, plus interest, when the IRS reminds you of your unreported income.

> *"I knew I was supposed to be setting aside some money from my freelance jobs to pay taxes, but I didn't know how much. Stupidly, I never asked an accountant. Then I figured out my taxes in April and realized I'd spent money I should have saved. Never again."*
>
> —Todd, 29

Taxes for the Self-Employed

If you're self-employed or have a part-time business, your taxes are likely to be more complicated because you'll owe self-employment taxes. You may also be taking business deductions. Self-employment taxes compute to about 15.3 percent of your income and the reason you pay them and other people don't is because you're considered both the employer and the employee. If you were employed by a company, your employer would pay half the cost of FICA, social security, and disability tax and the rest would come out of each paycheck. When you're self-employed, you're responsible for paying all these taxes yourself, in addition to your regular federal and state taxes. The good news is you can probably offset some of your income, that is, reduce the amount you'll pay tax on, by deducting expenses and writing them off.

This is where it gets complicated. What's considered a legitimate business expense? The computer you bought to use for work probably is, but then there's all this business about depreciating it over three years and stuff like that. The briefcase you bought for meetings might be deductible, but your dry-cleaning bill for work clothes probably isn't. Here's where you'll throw your hands up and go screaming toward the first available corporate job you can find just so you don't have to deal with it. But don't. If you find yourself swimming in profit-and-loss statements, acquisition of assets information, and travel expenses that were incurred for business purposes, it's probably time to see an accountant.

If you plan to have an accountant help you with your taxes, get on the ball sooner rather than later. Your accountant can advise you on which business expenses you'll be able to deduct, so you'll be able to document these expenses by saving bills, receipts, and canceled checks. For example, say you're a freelance movie reviewer, working for several local newspapers. None of them consider you their full-time employee so you have a handful of 1099 forms and no idea how to deduct business expenses. If you wait until the end of the year to first see an accountant, you may learn that you should have been saving movie stubs, video rental receipts, and the repair bill for your broken VCR.

How to Choose an Accountant

The most important thing you can do is find an accountant who deals with the kind of work you do. If you're a graphic designer, for example, you'll have different expenses than a business consultant. You might have to invest in a lot of expensive computer equipment that will have to be amortized, while the consultant might have a lot of travel expenses. Any accountant you choose should understand your business and your future plans.

You should also choose someone who will be able to grow with you. You don't want someone who is so busy with really big, high-rolling clients that you barely fit in the schedule. Keep in mind that if you choose an accountant your parents have used for years, he or she could be headed for retirement just when you're in your prime earning years. Your parents' accountant can be a good referral source, however, and can point you toward an accountant that suits your needs.

Taxes on Your Computer

An alternative to hiring a professional is to become one yourself. There are several programs that will make filing your taxes and keeping records much easier than the old pen-and-paper method. You don't even need a calculator. All are available on a CD-ROM or disk:

- Quicken—available for DOS, Windows, or Macintosh; www.quicken.com
- TaxCut—comes in versions for Windows and Macintosh; www.taxcut.com
- TurboTax—available for DOS, Windows, or Macintosh; www.turbotax.com

Keeping Records

Not that this is news at this point, but you should save everything. Even if you use a computer program and have entered everything, you still need hard copies of receipts, checkbook registers, and old bills. Organize them by year and keep them for three years. In the unlikely event you're audited, you won't have to reorganize everything.

Common Things Tax Filers Forget to Do
- *Check the address label that came with your return and make sure it's correct.*
- *Sign your return.*
- *Enclose your check with your tax form.*
- *Attach your W-2s, 1099s, and schedules.*
- *Make a copy of your return for your files.*
- *Finally, sit back, take a deep breath, and be glad you don't have to file for another year.*

Keep copies of old tax returns, along with any paperwork from your employer, such as W-2s, that you used to compute your taxes for seven years or longer—in case there's ever any question about whether you filed and what you paid. This way, if a question comes up later, you don't have to track down your boss from your freshman-year job at Dairy Queen to get a copy of an old W-2.

CONCLUSION

Y ou may be on information overload at this point and that's
pretty understandable. There's a lot to digest, and no one
said you had to be some instant Real-World wunderkind.
Just take a deep breath and let it all sink in. It's going to be great.
People who said youth was wasted on the young must not have
had a very good time when they were young. This is your time.

Do everything. Take risks. Laugh in the face of convention.
Remember what you've learned all these years in school and don't
let anyone ever tell you that having a college diploma is anything
you have to apologize for in the working world of "experience
required." Sure, experience counts, but that's what the rest of your
life is all about. Don't forget to leave work in time to see the sun-
set once in a while and buy yourself a nice dinner while you're at
it. The world is waiting for you. Good luck.

INDEX